Company Towns in the Americas

Company Towns
in the Americas

LANDSCAPE, POWER, AND
WORKING-CLASS COMMUNITIES

Edited by **OLIVER J. DINIUS**
and **ANGELA VERGARA**

THE UNIVERSITY OF GEORGIA PRESS
Athens & London

© 2011 by the University of Georgia Press
Athens, Georgia 30602
www.ugapress.org
All rights reserved
Designed by Walton Harris
Set in 10/13 Minion Pro

Printed digitally in the United States of America

Library of Congress Cataloging-in-Publication Data

Company towns in the Americas : landscape, power, and working-class
communities / edited by Oliver J. Dinius and Angela Vergara.
    p.   cm. — (Geographies of justice and social transformation)
Includes bibliographical references and index.
ISBN-13: 978-0-8203-3329-8 (hardcover : alk. paper)
ISBN-10: 0-8203-3329-8 (hardcover : alk. paper)
ISBN-13: 978-0-8203-3682-4 (pbk.   )
ISBN-10: 0-8203-3682-3 (pbk.   )
1. Company towns—America—History. 2. Industrialization—
America—History. 3. Social engineering—America—History.
I. Dinius, Oliver J. (Oliver Jürgen) II. Vergara, Angela, 1972–
HT121.C66 2011
307.76'7097—dc22   2010020411

British Library Cataloging-in-Publication Data available

CONTENTS

ILLUSTRATIONS

FOREWORD

MARSHALL C. EAKIN

Interdisciplinary, collaborative, transnational — for some time now scholars from across the academy have called for work that takes these concepts seriously. *Company Towns in the Americas* is a rare collective work that heeds this call and provides the reader with a group of truly collaborative, transnational, interdisciplinary studies. Equally important, the authors and editors have taken seriously the call for a new "American" studies, one that seeks to investigate all of the Americas — from the Arctic to Tierra del Fuego — in a comparative framework. With studies that range from Argentina to Canada across the length of the twentieth century this book brings together the experiences of the inhabitants of towns dominated by the production of textiles, copper, steel, rubber, machinery, armaments, and the largest port in South America. It is work of scholars in the disciplines of history, geography, architecture, and economics. What unites all of these themes and places is the advance of industrial capitalism in the twentieth century into the farthest reaches of all of the Americas.

One of the contributions of this work is to illustrate the uneven spread of industrial capitalism across the region — both temporally and spatially. The dominant narrative of the rise of industrial capitalism in the Americas has emphasized the spread of textiles in New England, then the Second Industrial Revolution across the Northeast and Midwest of the United States in the late nineteenth century followed by its expansion across the North American continent in the first half of the twentieth century. This narrative brings Latin America into the picture in the late nineteenth century with the emergence of industry around a few major centers, in particular in Mexico (Mexico City and then Monterrey), Brazil (Rio de Janeiro and then São Paulo), and Argentina (Buenos Aires). These three nations remained the economic and industrial leaders of Latin America through most of the twentieth century, and the focus of most studies of industrialization in the region has been these major cities — with the addition of secondary centers such as Medellín (Colombia), Córdoba (Argentina), and Santiago (Chile) by the mid-twentieth century. One of the virtues of this book is to decenter this story of industrialization and shift the focus from the large metropolitan, industrial centers to highly industrialized towns often far removed from the major urban centers of North and South America.

What these company towns clearly demonstrate is the dreams of social engineering that prevailed among the capitalists and their managers regardless of the location of their enterprise — be it the Amazonian jungle, the Chilean desert, or an old coffee plantation in Brazil. These dreams, what Andrew Herod in his essays refers to as "deliberative efforts to shape the built environment in particular ways," rarely go according to plan, as he observes. In each of the cases in this volume, the so-called logic of capitalism was to create powerful symbols of modernity that would both impress the outside world and "civilize" the locals — in most cases, rural peoples. In these "spaces of transnational interaction," industrial capitalism not only transformed peoples and landscapes but also had to adapt to local circumstances. In some cases, such as Henry Ford's rubber plantations in the eastern Amazon, the capitalists failed — miserably. In others, here I am thinking of Volta Redonda, capitalism completely transformed what was once a rural community, turning it into one of the most intensely industrial, working-class communities in the Americas. One of the great strengths of this volume is that it reveals a range of successes, failures, transformations, and adaptations of industrial capitalism in a variety of "American" towns.

The transnational framework of this book allows us to see these towns, often located far from the core of the nation's economic heartland, as deeply entwined in the international capitalist system. Rubber from the Amazon (had the plantations been successful) and copper from the Atacama Desert were crucial inputs to the modern industrial economy of the twentieth century. Textiles from the Orizaba Valley (Mexico), steel from Volta Redonda (Brazil), machinery from Firmat (Argentina), and armaments from Sunflower Village (Kansas) all contributed to the building of national economic strength with international consequences. These case studies highlight not only the enormous reach of industrial capitalism in the twentieth century but also the critical connections and interactions between the global and the local.

The transnational approach also allows us to see "U.S." multinational corporations in new ways. So often the narrative of capitalism in twentieth-century Latin America has been to focus on these companies as agents of the United States extracting wealth from Latin America. Multinationals like Anaconda take on a different look when one sees their role in mining towns in Canada, the United States, and Chile in transnational focus. The transnational dimension of industrial capitalism refocuses the story for all three sites, in both the powerful economies of North America and the less powerful in South America.

Our views on capitalism, towns, workers, gender, and class have to be rethought when we see them in this larger framework.

This volume also reminds us of the importance of studying gender, workers, race, and class across national boundaries, cultures, and societies throughout the Americas. As we work in our own small corners of the American continents we too easily lose sight of the larger national scene, and the even broader international context. Although it has been common for at least a generation to argue that categories such as race, gender, and class are socially constructed, the tendency is still to study these constructions within the confines of geographically and culturally defined regions — Europe, the United States, Latin America. The authors of the essays in this volume have consciously constructed a collection of essays — and they have done this collaboratively over a period of years — that begins to place case studies across the Americas within a transnational context that is both sensitive to local conditions and aware of the larger context of an industrial capitalism that recognizes no boundaries or borders. We should be thankful to Oliver Dinius and Angela Vergara for the years of labor they have put into conceptualizing and editing this volume and their fellow authors for taking up the difficult but important task of creating an interdisciplinary, collaborative, transnational analysis of company towns in the Americas.

ACKNOWLEDGMENTS

In the five years that this book has been in the making, we have received the support and encouragement of many colleagues and institutions. It all began with a panel at the annual conference of the American Historical Association in January 2005, when Marshall Eakin, the discussant, suggested that we consider putting together an edited volume on company towns in the Americas. We are deeply grateful for his support of the project since its inception and very happy that he agreed to write the foreword to this book.

The Croft Institute for International Studies at the University of Mississippi deserves our gratitude for its decision to fund a workshop, in early 2007, that united the contributors to this volume in Oxford (Mississippi) for stimulating discussions on how to think about company towns from a comparative and transnational perspective. The workshop would not have been such a success without the full support of Michael Metcalf, then director of the Croft Institute, the staff of the institute, and the members of the history department at the University of Mississippi (Kees Gispen, Susan Grayzel, Joshua Howard, and Douglass Sullivan-González) who generously agreed to serve as discussants of the workshop papers. The Croft Institute, under its current director Kees Gispen, also subsidized the production of a map for the introduction to the volume.

An invitation by the University of Toronto's Sawyer Mellon Seminar on "Globalizing the Americas" in March 2007 provided us with a precious opportunity to present the results of the workshop and to discuss the transnational dimension of the project. We could not imagine a better host than Rick Halpern for that workshop. We are grateful to all the participants of the Sawyer seminar session on company towns, and in particular the discussants of our papers, for their useful suggestions.

Special thanks go to our editor at the University of Georgia Press, Derek Krissoff, who steered the project through the review process with enthusiasm and efficiency and has been most responsive to all our questions and concerns. Jon Davies, the staff editor, has made the production process refreshingly transparent and ensured that last-minute issues with illustrations were resolved to our satisfaction. Our copy editor, Jane Curran, did more than just her job of making the manuscript stylistically consistent and more readable. Her acute observations on the content of the introduction helped us to avoid several potentially embarrassing mistakes.

Andy Herod deserves our gratitude for bringing the project to the attention of the University of Georgia Press, showing us historians the importance of geography for understanding company towns, and helping us recruit Christopher Post as contributor.

We would also like to thank the two anonymous reviewers, whose suggestions made the book more focused and thus stronger.

The final thanks go to all our contributors, who stayed with the project through all those years with patience and commitment.

Company Towns in the Americas

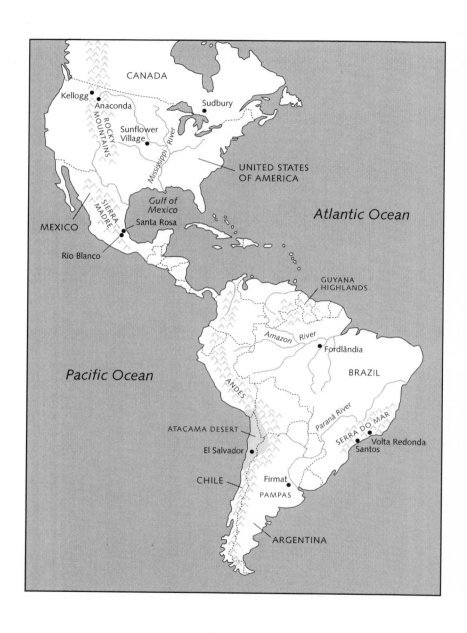

COMPANY TOWNS IN THE AMERICAS

An Introduction

OLIVER J. DINIUS and ANGELA VERGARA

The company town, a planned community owned or controlled by a single company, has symbolized the power of industrial capitalism to exploit natural resources and transform society both in its vast ambition and its remarkable futility. It has represented the ambitions of industrialists and social reformers to transform working-class culture and impose work habits that could increase labor productivity and diminish social conflict. It has embodied the vision of architects and urban planners for new spaces of human habitation that promised — but not necessarily accomplished — improvements in living conditions for working families in material, social, and spiritual terms. Company towns have symbolized the controlling presence of industrial companies, but they have also been the site of working people's struggles to improve the conditions of work and build communities on their own terms. The essays in this volume examine the economic, political, social, and cultural history of company towns in Argentina, Brazil, Canada, Chile, Mexico, and the United States to illustrate the impact — often uneven and contradictory — of processes of industrial modernization on working people throughout the Americas.[1]

The title of this volume unites two concepts, "company towns" and "the Americas," whose definitions and analytical use are still matters of scholarly debate. This volume does not resolve those debates, but it clarifies the concept of "company town" by exploring a spectrum of cases, and it shows by example how a focus on the Americas enriches our understanding of industrial modernity at both the micro and macro level. The introduction prepares the ground by providing a brief history of the company town with particular attention to its importance for the industrial development of the Americas. Moreover, the introduction explores past uses of the term "company town" and discusses similar analytical concepts used in the scholarly literature. The review of the scholarly literature focuses heavily on the historiography of labor in the Americas, which has been the main line of investigation on company towns and the people who inhabit them. The individual contributions that compose this volume strongly reflect that scholarly tradition, as is evident in the last part of this introduction, which lays out the structure of the book. The brief presentations of the chapters identify themes that have dominated the debate of company towns such as, to name a few examples, the role of company stores, the importance of control over space, an emerging "sense of place" among inhabitants, and the transformation into union towns.

COMPANY TOWNS AND THE AMERICAS

Company towns have been an integral part of the rise of industrial capitalism since the early nineteenth century.[2] New technology, sources of energy, and the expansion of markets made possible the establishment of large factories and required the extraction of natural resources on a large scale. While employers preferred to locate their factories near existing population centers, they often had to create the infrastructure to be able to exploit natural resources or manufacture industrial goods in places that lacked extensive urban development. To recruit and establish the material conditions for the retention of a workforce in isolated areas, they built accommodations and provided basic services such as health care, education, and recreational facilities for workers and their families. Company towns thus owed their existence to the same economic rationale that drove all investment by industrial capitalists: production and profit. Social ideas also played an important role. Company owners hired architects and engineers to design model towns and established offices to assist the residents in their daily lives in order to exercise a degree of control over local society. They hoped to insulate workers from class and political conflicts, increasing productivity, and achieving social harmony. While social ideology often shaped the town's design and internal organization, the company's administrative practice always had to make concessions to the town's unique physical, political, and cultural environment.[3]

The first experiments with industrial company towns and associated welfare programs took place in the late eighteenth and early nineteenth centuries in Western Europe. Robert Owen introduced social reforms inspired by his utopian socialism in the Scottish textile town of New Lanark. In France, the brothers Eugène and Adolphe Schneider tried to preempt labor strife at the Le Creusot iron works by expanding company housing and social services. In the United States, companies experimented with model industrial towns throughout the nineteenth century.[4] The New England textile machinery company Draper Manufacturing developed Hopedale (Massachusetts) from a rural commune into an industrial town with very low labor turnover. Railroad car magnate George Pullman had a company town built just south of Chicago with all modern amenities, although rigid paternalist management eventually became the town's undoing. In 1894, some three thousand Pullman workers went on strike to protest wage reduction, inspiring a wave of strikes and radical labor protests throughout the country. The social unrest led to an intense debate in the United States about the shortcomings of company towns and triggered the "new company town" movement.

Influenced by the social ideas of the Progressive Era, architects and social reformers questioned the paternalistic role of the company. The alternative was the "new company town" (or "modern industrial town") that came to dominate the industrial landscape throughout the first half of the twentieth century. It resembled the garden city more than the geometrical camp, offered a wide range of social programs, and provided support for workers' home ownership. In places such as Fairfield (Alabama), Torrance (California), and Goodyear Heights (Ohio), companies had programs to sell both lots and houses to their employees.[5] Welfare capitalism replaced Pullman paternalism, and the company's welfare department took the place of the factory owner's often arbitrary acts of generosity. Companies assumed responsibility for providing a wide range of urban services and offered social assistance programs to improve the life of the workers and their families. In the 1920s, Henry Ford paid his autoworkers benefits that included support to pay for doctor's bills, housing, and even furniture. He inspired industrialists in the United States and all over the world, and many applied the methods of what came to be called Fordism. Like Ford, they believed that an investment in the workers' quality of life would increase productivity and improve labor relations. It was still a form of labor control, but a less arbitrary one than the old paternalism.[6]

Company towns remained an integral part of the advance of industrial capitalism in the Americas throughout the twentieth century. The transformation experienced by the United States during the New Deal and World War II created the conditions for the creation of federally owned company towns such as Sunflower Village (Kansas), Norris (Tennessee), and Boulder City (Nevada). As the frontiers of settlement and industrial exploitation moved west throughout the twentieth century, private companies continued to build company towns and adapted to new economic and social demands.[7] In 1953, Magma Copper Company built San Manuel in Arizona, and Anaconda inaugurated a new mine and a town in Yerington, Nevada; both towns had a curved layout, modern infrastructure, and extensive welfare benefits. New forms of urbanization in the Sun Belt and the western part of the country included variations of the company town such as Walt Disney in Anaheim and Stanford Industrial Park, both in California.[8]

In Canada, the second phase of industrialization based on the large-scale extraction and processing of natural resources began around 1900, and company towns were an integral part of this expansion. Resource towns sprung up on the eastern, northern, and western frontiers as staple industries such as cod fishing, mining, and logging became a driving force in Canada's economic and social development. Nearly half of Canada's resource towns still in existence by 1971 had been built after World War II.[9] Schefferville in northern Québec was one such mining town, created by the Iron Ore Company of Canada in the 1950s. It became home to as many as four thousand people before the mine closed in the early 1980s.[10] A similarly emblematic case was the uranium camp of Elliott Lake in northern Ontario, originally established in 1955, which went through several boom and bust cycles before the mines finally closed in the 1980s.[11] The recent boom in Alberta oil sands suggests that Canada might not have seen the last of resource towns, as companies search for the best strategy to exploit resources and deploy workers on the frontier.

In Latin America, the first wave of industrialization only began in the late nineteenth century and remained limited to small pockets of the subcontinent until well into the twentieth century. Textile companies and light industries built worker housing, even entire neighborhoods, in cities such as São Paulo (Brazil), Medellín (Colombia), and Santiago (Chile). Some cities depended on one industry or one economic activity. In Berisso (Argentina), for example, meatpacking companies dominated the economic life of the city and provided urban services to its residents.[12] Company towns played an important role in the advance of industry in Latin America, especially to exploit mineral resources in remote and inhospitable places such as the Atacama Desert and the Lake of Maracaibo, where copper mining and oil companies, respectively, built camps to house their workers. Beginning in the 1940s, under a policy known as import substituting industrialization, Latin American states promoted and often financed the establishment of heavy industrial complexes including steel mills, copper refineries, and petroleum complexes. Company towns became an integral part of this new industrialization effort.

Company towns played a similar role — if at different times — in the economic and social history of all parts of the Americas. They pushed the frontier of industrial capitalism into new areas. Mining, logging, and railroad towns, in particular, became outposts of industrial modernity connecting remote and sparsely settled areas to urban centers and strengthening their integration into the nation-state. Not unlike trading posts or military forts in earlier stages of the colonization of the Americas, they brought more land, more natural resources, and more people (i.e., workers and consumers) under the control of the European colonizers and their descendants. In his observations on "The Nature of the Company Town," the British geographer J. Douglas Porteous noted that it generally "throve in areas of white colonial settlement" and could therefore "perhaps be fitted into [Frederick Jackson] Turner's frontier model."[13] Conceiving of company towns in terms of their place on the frontier embeds them in the larger narrative of European colonization in the Americas and emphasizes the spatial dimension of industrial development.

Company towns became powerful symbols of industrial modernity. They housed workers for large-scale mines, integrated steel mills, aluminum smelters, and arms manufacturers, all industries that represented the new industrial age because they made the mass production of capital goods and consumer durables possible. Socially, the company town symbolized the harsh realities of working and living under industrial capitalism, even if the residents sometimes enjoyed better conditions of work and life than the urban proletariat. Workers in company towns, often migrants from a rural background, learned what it meant to work for wages, follow a strict work discipline, and be subject to far-reaching capitalist control symbolized by the company store. In fact, companies saw it as their mission to prepare workers for the modern industrial world. This mission was often shaped and reinforced by the racialized perceptions of Latin Americans then so common in North America. The Panama Canal Company, for example, provided its workers with housing and basic urban service and explicitly conceived of its company town in the Canal Zone as a mechanism to "civilize" the land and the local population.[14]

Company towns became an important element of inter-American relations in the twentieth century and reinforced their neocolonial character. The United States shared with Latin America a history of colonial rule and of struggles for independence from European powers in the late eighteenth and early nineteenth centuries, but the historical trajectories diverged in the nineteenth century. The United States became an industrial power while Latin American economies fell behind.[15] By the 1920s, most of Latin America (with Argentina as a notable exception) saw more foreign investment in manufacturing, mining, and export agriculture from the United States than from any other country. U.S. capital financed company towns in Latin America that became places of cultural encounter as managers transferred their urban visions and social ideologies from the North to the South.[16] In Venezuela in the 1920s, oil companies built camps for their employees to remove them from the gambling and prostitution that characterized life in existing towns and to foster a stable community.[17] The unequal economic and political relationship between the United States and Latin America and the association of U.S. corporate power with abusive practices added a strong nationalist and anti-imperialist tone to the labor conflicts in Latin American company towns.[18]

The study of twentieth-century company towns in the Americas opens a window into both the comparative and transnational histories of labor under industrial capitalism. As comparative history, this volume unites histories of working communities from Latin America and the United States and Canada. The cases highlight the similarities among company towns in different countries, but they also reiterate the significance of national economic, political, and cultural contexts. The volume offers a transnational perspective on the history of the Americas by showing how workers' experiences and struggles in company towns transcended national boundaries and how employers' ideologies were subject to local influences as they spread across the region. Sandhya Shukla and Heidi Tinsman stress that recent work on the history of the Americas has taught us to pay attention to the "history of transnational interactions — spaces of dialogue, linkages, conflicts, domination, and resistance — that takes place across, sometimes outside, the confines of national borders and sensibilities."[19] Company towns were such spaces of transnational interaction.

THE "COMPANY TOWN": DEFINITIONS AND SCHOLARSHIP

Scholars have struggled to offer a concise definition of "company town" because the term encompasses a spectrum of settlement types with important differences in location, industrial base, administrative structure, and character as a social space. Mining and logging camps shared some economic, administrative, and social characteristics with a model town such as Pullman, but their geographical isolation, the sense of transience, and the male-dominated culture of such camps fostered very different communities. For industries near an existing urban center, companies often built worker neighborhoods and offered urban services but never attempted to control all aspects of daily life. In some cases, some companies never invested in housing or infrastructure but still came to control a town because of their dominance as employer and their political clout. Manufacturing towns and resource towns developed very differently: manufacturing companies commonly knew their labor requirements and could design a company town to meet those needs, while resource-extracting companies went through an exploratory phase to test the potential of the location and establish market access. Simple mining camps only became modern mining towns as the result of a redesign once the company knew that it could generate profits in the long run.[20]

The now seventy-year-old *Encyclopedia of Social Sciences* still serves as a useful starting point for a working definition for "company town": "a community inhabited solely or chiefly by the employees of a single company or a group of companies which also owns a substantial part of the real estate and houses."[21] The definition emphasizes the company's status as dominant property owner and the town's dependence on a single industry. Other conventional definitions highlight the town's isolation, residential segregation, and company control over urban services, education, and leisure activities. Historically, company towns often met several of these criteria, but only a few model towns met all of them. This volume therefore works with a broader definition of company town that includes company-administered neighborhoods within cities as well as towns dominated by a single industry but not necessarily owned by one company. Key is the combination of a single dominant industry with extensive company control over the daily life of the town. The examples in this volume illustrate that an overly rigid definition cannot capture the historical fluidity: a model company town could over time become a company-dominated town, but that did not necessarily change the social dynamics of daily life. More technical terms such as "resource town," "single-industry town," or "single-enterprise town" do not offer a satisfying substitute; they highlight the economic status but do not evoke the power relations in the same way as the term "company town."

The existing scholarship on company towns reflects both differences in the historical trajectories of industrialization and intellectual priorities of academic communities across the Americas. In Canada and the United States, where model company towns played an important role for industrial development, they have received sustained scholarly attention. In Latin America, on the other hand, classic company towns played a lesser role and did not generate the same scholarly interest. However, Latin American scholars have studied company towns in the broader sense, as we define them in this volume, and have analyzed their place in the social and economic development of the respective countries. Regrettably, there has been little dialogue between scholars across the region in the past, not least because of language barriers and diverging scholarly agendas. This volume brings together contributions by scholars from different parts of the Americas to stimulate debates about the historical significance of company towns for the entire region, transcending conventional geographic dividing lines (North versus South America) as well as linguistic boundaries between English- and French-speaking North America, on the one hand, and the Spanish- and Portuguese-speaking countries of the Americas on the other.

The literature on twentieth-century company towns is especially rich for Canada, where — in the words of sociologist Rex Lucas — "communities of single industry are twentieth-century products of an age of industry and technology."[22] Canadian government officials and urban planners paid close attention to company towns because they produced a large share of the nation's wealth and were home to a significant share of its population. Starting in the 1910s, Canadian engineering and urban planning journals published articles on the building of "new towns," "company towns," and "modern industrial towns."[23] National and provincial governments regularly commissioned studies on various aspects of life in company towns.[24] Social scientists have long recognized company towns as a core element of the country's modern history. The historical geographer Harold Innes identified "staples" industries such as cod fishing and logging as a driving force in Canada's economic and social development. He argued that they made a crucial contribution to the country's unity and should be regarded as an integral part of Canadian identity.[25] Innis's pioneering work inspired several generations of scholars to refine and critique the "staples" paradigm in their analyses of the resource frontier and its significance for the country's political economy.[26]

Rex Lucas's 1971 study *Minetown, Milltown, Railtown: Life in Canadian Communities of Single Industry* represents the most ambitious attempt yet to create a framework for the sociological study of company towns. Working in the tradition of community studies, Lucas developed criteria to identify company towns and provided a sweeping survey of their economic, social, cultural, and even psychological dynamics. His definition of the "community of single industry" encompassed towns of less than thirty thousand inhabitants where "at least 75% of the working population serve[d] the single industry and its supporting institutional services." At the time, 636 Canadian towns home to more than nine hundred thousand people fulfilled the criteria. Lucas used census data, field visits, and extensive interviewing to trace the company towns' stages of development, analyze their organization of work, provide a panorama of day-to-day community life, and discuss social conflict and social control.[27] But as Lorne Tapperman notes in his introduction to the book's 2008 anniversary edition, Lucas's main contribution was to raise new questions and delineate a future research agenda rather than to offer a concise model for the sociological analysis of company towns.[28]

Lucas observed an important difference in the attitude toward company towns in Canada and the United States. Much of the Canadian scholarship had a pragmatic goal: to analyze the challenges created by fluctuating demand for the "staple" and by the eventual exhaustion of the resource in order to formulate policies to alleviate the stress on the community. This is most apparent in studies of company towns' "wind-down phase" that commonly include an analysis of strategies to revive the local economy.[29] Academic work on company towns in the United States, on the other hand, often displayed a nostalgic touch. Lucas noted that many U.S. scholars portrayed the arrival of industry as a disruption of an ideal Jeffersonian community, ending the people's control over their own affairs.[30] In essence, company towns served as villains in an anti-corporate narrative that lamented the end of a (largely imagined) society of independent producers. An edited volume on the global expansion of multinational corporations illustrates the point nicely. Entitled *The World as Company Town*, it offers no discussion of the "company town" as a specific urban form or social space; the term merely serves to evoke the notion of excessive corporate control.[31]

Labor scholars in the United States have been studying company towns since the late 1970s as part of broader debates about the rise of industrial communities, the resistance of industrial workers, and the contradictions of paternalism and welfare measures. Labor historians and urban historians examined emblematic cases of industrial towns (often textile towns) and mining camps in the second half of the nineteenth century and concluded that company-sponsored welfare programs played an important role in transforming the United States into an industrial society.[32] On the matter of worker resistance, historians argued that company towns fostered labor acquiescence while others insisted that it triggered radical protests.[33] Since the 1980s, U.S. labor historians have moved to incorporate the study of race and gender as important factors that shaped both managerial approaches and workers' experiences in company towns. Historians such as Mary Murphy and Laurie Mercier have demonstrated how special programs for women reinforced traditional gender roles, strengthened the family, and helped assimilate recent immigrants.[34] The scholarship on company towns in the United States has covered a wide range of experiences, and historians such as Margaret Crawford and Linda Carlson have made efforts to create a framework for the analysis of U.S. company towns.[35]

In Latin America, the study of company towns has benefited from the dialogue across disciplinary and country boundaries. In the context of broader debates about the region's political and social history, scholars have studied classic company towns, company-financed working-class neighborhoods, and single-industry towns. In the 1960s and 1970s, social scientists analyzed the experiences of workers in such towns as part of projects on industrialization and class conflict. Dependency scholars, who focused on the unequal trade relationship between an industrialized core and an underdeveloped periphery, saw company towns as an extreme case of an enclave: owned by foreign capital, oriented to the external market, and with few linkages to the rest of the national economy. Foreign capital, they argued, maintained isolated mining camps and plantation towns to exploit natural resources and the native labor force, leading to conflictive labor relations and nationalist working-class political culture.[36] In the late 1960s, scholars led by Argentinean sociologist Torcuato di Tella and French sociologist Alain Touraine conducted a series of studies on single-industry towns to explain the emergence of an industrial culture in Latin America. They showed that in places such as the steel town of Huachipato (Chile), company welfare policies shaped the union movement and its demands.[37] The rise of a new labor history in the 1980s inspired scholars to examine company towns as an integral part of the experience of working people. Recent studies have also focused on the urban structure of company towns and their distinctive system of social relations as shaped by gender, race, and political relations.

The national historiographies on company towns reflect their prevalent form in their respective countries. In Argentina and Brazil, manufacturing (textile, metalworking) and processing (meatpacking) industries, usually located in or near existing urban centers, established company towns.[38] For the Andean countries of Bolivia, Chile, and Peru, the scholarship has focused on mining camps, located in isolated areas and commonly owned by foreign companies. The focus has been on how company towns and their labor regimes enhanced exploitation and created an industrial proletariat.[39] In Mexico, company towns mattered since the late nineteenth and early twentieth centuries, in particular for the expansion of the foreign-owned mining and oil industries. Strikes against the paternalistic agenda of the mining companies — most famously at the Cananea copper mine in 1907 — became important events for the growth of the national labor movement.[40] During Mexico's rapid industrialization in the 1950s and 1960s, the government supported the creation of industrial zones such as Ciudad Sahagún in the state of Hidalgo, which required the construction of worker housing and created a new industrial town with an urban culture.[41]

Scholars studying company towns across the Americas have illustrated the impact their physical, institutional, and cultural characteristics had on the workers and their families. They acknowledge, on the one hand, that company towns led to a dependent population because of the controlling role capital played as both employer and provider of housing, education, health care, transportation, and recreational facilities. On the other hand, recent studies have highlighted the ability of working-class communities to adapt to company control, contest it, and transform managerial strategies, their daily lives in these company towns, and in some cases even their nations' histories. Microhistories of such company towns have revealed a variety of communities whose distinctive cultures incorporated local customs, the influence of migrant workers, the companies' social ideologies, and the impact of transnational social and economic forces. The essays in this volume reflect the variety of company towns with respect to their geographic location, their industrial base, their specific urban form, their place in transnational commodity chains, and — most important — their communities' responses to an omnipresent company.

STRUCTURE OF THE BOOK

The volume explores the history and geography of industrial company towns in the Americas through a theoretical essay and eight historical case studies. Labor geographer Andrew Herod focuses on the relationship between spatial engineering and social engineering as manifest in the concept of the "sociospatial dialectic." He argues that the physicality of landscapes reflects the social interests of those who construct them and that the production of the landscape shapes the ways in which social relations subsequently unfold. The spatial constitutes the social as much as the social constitutes the spatial. In company towns, Herod observes, the goal of employers is to control workers' social and political activities by controlling the physicality of the built environment. Their strategies include developing "model" industrial relations and physically isolating workers to limit their exposure to "corrupting" influences. The chapter provides brief examples of deliberate spatial engineering for the purposes of social engineering to illustrate the theoretical arguments and concludes with broader theoretical points about the spatiality of capitalism and the labor process.

The remaining chapters provide historical analyses of specific company towns in different parts of the Americas: two cases focus on the United States, three on Brazil, and one each on Argentina, Chile, and Mexico. The case studies cover a broad spectrum of industries: textiles, copper mining, steel, a port, machine manufacturing, and armaments production. The essays all address a set of overarching questions: How did the management structure and conceptualize the company town as a space in order to create a stable and productive labor force? What social ideologies guided the management, how did that translate into welfare policies, and to what extent did such ideologies inform the day-to-day administration of the town? How did workers and their families contest managerial policies by building strong communities and organizing unions that challenged the preeminence of the company? How did the global forces of industrial capitalism shape and reshape these geographically isolated company towns? Each author addresses several or all of these questions, reconstructing the economic, social, and political dynamics that made the history of the respective company town(s) unique.

Aurora Gómez-Galvarriato studies the formation and early development of Santa Rosa and Río Blanco, two textile towns built at the end of the nineteenth century in the Orizaba valley (Veracruz, Mexico). She focuses on the issues of company housing, education, and the company store, analyzing how they shaped the interactions of the three central actors: textile companies, the local working communities, and the national state. Gómez demonstrates that between the early 1900s and the early 1930s, first the workers and then the national state gained ever greater influence over these towns at the expense of company control. What began as company towns with the usual mechanisms of social control ultimately became union towns, places where workers and their families gained the power to have a community life beyond the purview of the company. Gómez highlights the changing role of the state (national and local), which went from a feeble presence in 1900 to an increasingly important role after the mid-1920s.

Fernando Teixeira da Silva's chapter on the port city of Santos (Brazil) provides at once a counterpoint and a parallel to Gómez's story. Santos was never a classic company town, but rather a city dominated by one company. The Santos Docks Company operated Latin America's largest port, which put it in a position to shape the urban landscape, to control the local labor market, and to exercise an extraordinary degree of political clout. Silva examines the changing relationship between the Santos Docks Company and its workers from the end of the nineteenth century to the early 1960s with a focus on the ways the company inserted itself in the larger urban space and the workers' responses to its strong presence. Seasonal work, the predominance of casual labor, and a predominantly male workforce made families much less important than in most company towns, but the workers formed strong bonds of solidarity that allowed them to contest (and on occasion evade) the company's control over their lives. Because the port was economically strategic for all of Brazil as much as for the city, Silva argues, the worker mobilizations reverberated not only locally but also in the national labor movement.

Elizabeth Esch examines how racial thought shaped the planning of two plantation camps in the Brazilian Amazon: Fordlândia and Belterra. She argues that they exemplified the ways in which U.S. corporations attempted to transplant production and managerial ideas to Latin America. To achieve control over both wild nature and human beings, Ford managers drew on their experience in the United States as they attempted to create two model company towns that would offer housing, social services, and schools to the workers and their families. But their project was driven by greater ambition than simply recruiting and retaining a labor force for a remote plantation: they wanted to civilize their workers and teach them industrial work habits. What informed this civilizing mission were ideas about modern management, but also a deeply rooted *racialized* view of the world that imposed strict hierarchies based on U.S. experience on a labor force in a country with a history of much greater racial mixing: Brazil.

Christopher W. Post's essay discusses the unusual case of Sunflower Village (Kansas), a government-built community operated by the U.S. Federal Public Housing Administration. From 1943 to 1959, it housed the workers of the nearby ammunitions plant, Sunflower Ordnance Works. Post uses the case study to illuminate the emergence of a "sense of place" among the inhabitants. He illustrates how the federal government tried to use urban planning, in the tradition of the garden city movement, and a variety of social services and leisure programs to get the workers "acclimated." He argues that Sunflower Village had a unique urban landscape for the United States, which shaped the memories of the residents and contributed to the formation of a strong "sense of place." He notes that the formation of such a strong community with a sense of attachment to the place contradicts assumptions about company towns as "hard places to live." Post traces in detail how residents developed a "sense of place" and what that means in light of the short life cycle of federal company towns such as Sunflower.

Oliver Dinius analyzes the case of Volta Redonda (Brazil), a classic company town built in the early 1940s. The state-owned National Steel Company, the centerpiece of Brazil's industrialization drive, wanted Volta Redonda to become a model for industrial modernity with respect to the standard of living and social relations. The company offered far-reaching social assistance programs under a paternalism based in the principles of social Catholicism, but Dinius's analysis shows that the company fell short of its ambitious goals as it had to adapt to financial constraints and demands by a strong union. By the late 1950s, company management increasingly saw the responsibilities for the company town as a burden and took steps to reduce its social assistance programs in order to contain costs. In an ironic twist, the metalworkers union stepped up to defend the social assistance programs and to demand their extension to all of Volta Redonda, including areas outside the original company town that had been settled as the city's population expanded in the 1950s. The union in effect wanted the material benefits of the company town but without the company's social control, which serves to illustrate the ambiguous relationship that workers had with this urban form.

Laurie Mercier's essay highlights a dimension that is often overlooked in the study of male-dominated industries: gender. She focuses on the role of women as agents of change in mining camps along the U.S.-Canadian border and explores how contested ideas about gender and anticommunism influenced union politics in more significant ways than tangible political borders. Mercier focuses on a controversy about women auxiliaries in the International Union of Mine, Mill and Smelter Workers, which strained the relations between women workers and male-dominated unions and thus serves to illustrate how gender ideologies in the context of the Cold War weakened the labor movement. The analysis also demonstrates, however, that capitalist models for company towns and labor control as well as workers' ideas about gender, unionization, and labor politics crossed borders freely. These mining towns, in all their physical isolation, were sites for the circulation of transnational ideas and sites of action for international unions, and Mercier's essay brings into focus how those were shaped by gendered social relations.

Eugenio Garcés Feliú and Angela Vergara examine the history and architecture of the mining town of El Salvador in northern Chile, built by the U.S.-based Anaconda Copper Company in the late 1950s. Their analysis focuses on the transformation of ideas about company towns in the mid-twentieth century. They interpret the construction of El Salvador as a manifestation of changes in managerial ideologies as the company aimed to modernize its practices with respect to production as well as labor relations. El Salvador fascinated national and international observers because its design incorporated the newest ideas about industrial management and urban planning, but in the end it was still a company town with all the benefits and drawbacks that urban form entailed. Moreover, it was a company town attached to a foreign-owned mine and as such was still the target of the same nationalist critiques that export-oriented industries had faced since the late nineteenth century. The modern urban design could not make those fundamental contradictions disappear.

Silvia Simonassi investigates the history of factory communities in the southern part of the Argentine province of Santa Fe. In the second half of the twentieth century, several important steel mills and metal factories opened in this otherwise agricultural region of the Pampa. Simonassi looks at the history of an agricultural-machine plant, the Vassalli Metallurgical Factory, located in the small city of Firmat and traces how paternalistic social relations dominated the development of social relations inside the factory and in the town. Although Vassalli never provided housing for its employees nor assumed any responsibility for urban services, as would have been the case in a classic company town, Simonassi observes that the establishment of the factory gave the owner, Roque Vassalli, extensive influence over the town. Unlike in the case of El Salvador, discussed by Garcés and Vergara, Vassalli did not set out to remake the town according to an urban or social vision, but in effect Firmat became a company-dominated town with social and economic relations not so different from a "classic" company town.

The case studies in this volume suggest that it is useful to think of company towns as a spectrum of urban forms dominated by one company, but not necessarily to limit attention to towns that display all the characteristics that scholars have come to associate with the term "company town." The chapters on towns with company-owned housing, company-managed urban services, and company-sponsored leisure activities show how these arrangements shaped the community and its social relations, but the comparison with towns where the company had less institutionalized power suggests that capitalists could exercise extensive control regardless of the specific property relations and the structure of local government. Conversely, the cases illustrate that even in "classic" company towns, designed to produce particular social relations that corresponded to a managerial ideology, workers formed bonds of community that empowered them to contest company policies and reshape them in ways that suited their interests. Depending on the local, regional, and national context, such as the existence of a strong union and the forceful intervention of a welfare state, those processes of transformation took very different paths and resulted in changes ranging from the moderate to the radical.

Even as workers developed local communities and reshaped the towns in which they lived, they never did so entirely under conditions of their own choosing. Company towns owed their existence to national and global economic forces. They helped integrate the Americas into the global economy, and they reshaped national geographies of industrial labor, motivating people in search of work to migrate to remote locations and create new strongholds of labor power away from earlier industrial centers. As much as the workers were able to transform company towns throughout the twentieth century, they could not escape the larger forces of industrial capitalism. Beginning in the 1970s, changes in global capitalism associated with de-industrialization and de-regulation called into question the economic rationale and the social utility of company towns. Cheaper transportation has made it possible for companies to house workers in nearby cities and bus or fly them to work, thus avoiding investment in an isolated camp or town. Workers in Chilean mines or Canadian oil fields, for example, commute back to their hometowns for their off days after they have spent four to six days working. At the beginning of the twenty-first century, the company town of old lives on only in people's memories.

The volume concludes with a selected bibliography on company towns in the Americas. This is not a conventional bibliography listing all the works the reader would encounter in the notes, but rather a reference tool to serve as a guide to publications that focus on the company town as an economic, urban, political, social, and cultural phenomenon. It includes many books whose titles indicate a focus other than the company town, but they all address — often in several chapters — the issues that lie at the core of this volume. For the full bibliography of the primary and secondary sources cited by the individual contributors to the volume, the reader will need to consult the notes of the respective chapters. We opted for a thematic bibliography that can serve as a reference tool and a guide to further reading in the hope that it will stimulate future work on company towns, and in particular systematic comparative as well as transnational studies on the Americas. While the model company town as an urban form might have passed into history, there still is much to study and learn about the spectrum of company towns that played such an important role for industrial capitalism in the Americas throughout the twentieth century.

NOTES

1. This answers a call by Frederick Cooper, who urged social historians of labor to consider capitalism not merely as an abstract force but rather in all its contingent and contested manifestations. Otherwise, he argued, they could not possibly make sense of the struggles of the working class. Frederick Cooper, "Farewell to the Category-Producing Class?" *International Labor and Working-Class History*, no. 57 (April 2000): 60–68.

2. John S. Garner, ed., *The Company Town: Architecture and Society in the Early Industrial Age* (New York: Oxford University Press, 1992); and a special journal issue on company towns edited by Federico Bussi, *Rassegna*, no. 70 (1997).

3. For a historical study of failed social engineering projects, see James C. Scott, *Seeing like a State: How Certain Schemes to Improve the Human Condition Have Failed* (New Haven: Yale University Press, 1998).

4. For "classic" nineteenth-century cases in the United States, see John S. Garner,

The Model Company Town: Urban Design through Private Enterprise in Nineteenth-Century New England (Amherst: University of Massachusetts Press, 1984); Carl S. Smith, *Urban Disorder and the Shape of Belief: The Great Chicago Fire, the Haymarket Bomb, and the Model Town of Pullman* (Chicago: University of Chicago Press, 2007); Daniel J. Walkowitz, *Worker City, Company Town: Iron and Cotton Worker Protest in Troy and Cohoes, New York, 1855–1884* (Urbana: University of Illinois Press, 1978).

5. Margaret Crawford, *Building the Workingman's Paradise: The Design of American Company Towns* (New York: Verso, 1995); Crawford, "John Nolen, the Design of the Company Town," *Rassegna*, no. 70 (1997): 46–53; Crawford, "The 'New' Company Town," *Perspecta*, no. 30 (1999): 48–57; Gwendolyn Wright, *Building the Dream: A Social History of Housing in America* (Cambridge, Mass.: MIT Press, 1998).

6. On Fordism see Stephen Meyer III, *The Five Dollar Day: Labor Management and Social Control in the Ford Motor Company, 1908–1921* (Albany: State University of New York Press, 1981), and for industrial welfare in Latin America see Barbara Weinstein, *For Social Peace in Brazil: Industrialists and the Remaking of the Working Class in São Paulo, 1920–1964* (Chapel Hill: University of North Carolina Press, 1996).

7. Linda Carlson, *Company Towns of the Pacific Northwest* (Seattle: University of Washington Press, 2003).

8. John M. Findlay, *Magic Lands: Western Cityscapes and American Culture after 1940* (Berkeley: University of California Press, 1992).

9. L. D. McCann, "The Changing Internal Structure of Canadian Resource Towns," *Plan Canada* 18, no. 1 (1978): 46–59.

10. Graham Humphreys, "Schefferville, Québec: A New Pioneering Town," *Geographical Review* 48, no. 2 (April 1958): 151–66; John H. Bradbury and Isabelle St. Martin, "Winding Down in a Québec Mining Town: A Case Study of Schefferville," *Canadian Geographer* 27, no. 2 (1983): 128–44.

11. Anne-Marie Mawhiney and Jane Pitblado, *Boom Town Blues: Elliot Lake: Collapse and Revival in a Single-Industry Community* (Toronto: Dundurn Press, 1999).

12. Mirta Zaida Lobato, *Trabajo, protesta, y política en una comunidad obrera, Berisso (1904–1970)* (Buenos Aires: Prometeo Libros, 2001).

13. J. Douglas Porteous, "The Nature of the Company Town," *Transactions of the Institute of British Geographers*, no. 51 (November 1970): 127–42.

14. Julie Greene, *The Canal Builders: Making America's Empire at the Panama Canal* (New York: Penguin Press, 2009).

15. See Stephen Haber, *How Latin America Fell Behind: Essays on the Economic Histories of Brazil and Mexico, 1800–1914* (Stanford: Stanford University Press, 1997); John H. Coatsworth, "Notes on the Comparative Economic History of Latin America and the United States," in *Nord und Süd in Amerika: Gegensätze, Gemeinsamkeiten, Europäischer Hintergrund*, ed. Wolfgang Reinhard and Peter Waldmann (Berlin: Rombach Verlag, 1993), 595–612.

16. Thomas F. O'Brien, *The Revolutionary Mission: American Enterprise in Latin America, 1900–1945* (New York: Cambridge University Press, 1996); Aviva Chomski, *West*

Indian Workers and the United Fruit Company in Costa Rica, 1870–1940 (Baton Rouge: Louisiana State University Press, 1996); Felipe Préstamo, "The Architecture of American Sugar Mills: The United Fruit Company," *Journal of Decorative and Propaganda Arts*, no. 22 (1996): 63–80.

17. Miguel Tinker-Salas, *The Enduring Legacy: Oil, Culture, and Society in Venezuela* (Durham, N.C.: Duke University Press, 2009).

18. Charles W. Bergquist, *Labor in Latin America: Comparative Essays on Chile, Argentina, Venezuela, and Colombia* (Stanford: Stanford University Press, 1986).

19. Sandhya Shukla and Heidi Tinsman, "Editors' Introduction," *Radical History Review*, no. 89 (2004): 1–10. See also Aviva Chomsky, *Linked Labor Histories: New England, Colombia, and the Making of a Global Working Class* (Durham, N.C.: Duke University Press, 2008); Sandhya Shukla and Heidi Tinsman, eds., *Imagining Our Americas: Toward a Transnational Frame* (Durham, N.C.: Duke University Press, 2007); Micol Seigel, "Beyond Compare: Comparative Method after the Transnational Turn," *Radical History Review*, no. 91 (Winter 2005): 62–90.

20. Crawford, *Building the Workingman's Paradise*, 129–51.

21. Horace B. Davis, "Company Towns," in *Encyclopedia of the Social Sciences*, vol. 4 (New York: Macmillan, 1931), 119.

22. Rex A. Lucas, *Minetown, Milltown, Railtown: Life in Canadian Communities of Single Industry* (Toronto: University of Toronto Press, 1971), 20.

23. See, for example, "Planning and Building New Towns in Canada: Kipawa," *Conservation of Life* (Commission of Conservation, Canada) 5, no. 1 (1919): 10–16; J. A. Walker, "Planning of Company Towns in Canada," *Canadian Engineer* 53, no. 3 (1927): 147–52; "Planning and Building a Modern Industrial Town in Northern Québec," *Journal of the Town Planning Institute* 7, no. 1 (1928): 10–12 and 14–15; S. D. Lash, "Recent New Towns in Canada," *Engineering Journal* 41, no. 3 (1958): 46–58; McCann, "Changing Internal Structure." See also Robert S. Robson, "The Politics of Resource Town Development: Ontario's Resource Communities, 1883–1970" (PhD diss., University of Guelph, 1986).

24. See, for example, Institute of Local Government, Queen's University, *Single-Enterprise Communities in Canada: A Report to the Central Mortgage Commission* (Kingston, Ont.: Queen's Printer, 1953); Melissa Clark-Jones, *The Logic and Survival of Single-Industry Towns* (Lennoxville, Qué.: Eastern Townships Research Center, 1997).

25. Harold Innis, "Settlement and the Mining Frontier," in *Settlement and the Forest Frontier in Eastern Canada*, ed. Arthur R. M. Lower (Toronto: Macmillan of Canada, 1936), 170–407.

26. Melissa Clark-Jones, *A Staple State: Canadian Industrial Resources in Cold War* (Toronto: University of Toronto Press, 1987); Louise Dignard, "Reconsidering Staple Insights: Canadian Forestry and Mining Towns" (PhD diss., Carleton University, 2004).

27. Lucas, *Minetown, Milltown, Railtown*, 17.

28. Lorne Tepperman, introduction to Lucas, *Minetown, Milltown, Railtown*, anniversary ed. (Don Mills, Ont.: Oxford University Press, 2008).

29. Robert Keyes, "Mine Closures in Canada: Problems, Prospects, and Policies," in *Coping with Closure: An International Comparison of Mine Town Experiences* ed. Cecily Neil, Makku Tykkläinen, and John Bradbury (London: Routledge, 1992), 27–43.

30. Lucas, *Minetown, Milltown, Railtown*, 1971 ed., 18.

31. Ahamed Idris-Soven, Elizabeth Idris-Soven, and Mary K. Vaughan, eds., *The World as Company Town: Multinational Corporations and Social Change* (The Hague: Mouton, 1978).

32. The classic study on the industrial company town is Walkowitz, *Worker City, Company Town*. On mining and smelting towns in the United States see David M. Emmons, *The Butte Irish: Class and Ethnicity in an American Mining Town, 1875–1925* (Urbana: University of Illinois Press, 1989); John Gaventa, *Power and Powerlessness: Quiescence and Rebellion in an Appalachian Valley* (Urbana: University of Illinois Press, 1982); Laurie Mercier, *Anaconda: Labor, Community, and Culture in Montana's Smelter City* (Urbana: University of Illinois Press, 2001); Mary Murphy, *Mining Cultures: Men, Women, and Leisure in Butte, 1914–41* (Urbana: University of Illinois Press, 1997); Mónica Perales, "Smeltertown: A Biography of a Mexican-American Community, 1880–1973" (PhD diss., Stanford University, 2004).

33. For a debate on U.S. labor history see David Montgomery, "Trends in Working Class History," *Labour/Le Travail* 19 (1987): 13–22; Leon Fink, "American Labor History," in *The New American History*, ed. Eric Foner (Philadelphia: Temple University Press, 1990), 233–50.

34. On gender relations in U.S. company towns see Janet L. Finn, *Tracing the Veins of Copper: Culture and Community from Butte to Chuquicamata* (Berkeley: University of California Press, 1998); Mercier, *Anaconda*; Murphy, *Mining Cultures*. On race and ethnicity see Emmons, *Butte Irish*; Perales, "Smeltertown."

35. Carlson, *Company Towns of the Pacific Northwest*; Crawford, *Building the Workingman's Paradise*.

36. Manuel A. Fernández, "El enclave salitrero y la economía chilena, 1880–1914," *Nueva Historia* 1, no. 3 (1981): 2–42; Manuel Barrera, *El conflicto obrero en el enclave cuprífero* (Santiago: Instituto de Economía y Planificación, Universidad de Chile, Facultad de Economía Política, 1973).

37. Torcuato Di Tella et al., *Sindicato y comunidad: dos tipos de estructura sindical latinoamericana* (Buenos Aires: Editorial del Instituto, 1967).

38. Eva Alterman Blay, *Eu nao tenho onde morar: vilas operárias na cidade de São Paulo* (São Paulo: Livraria Nobel, 1985); José Sérgio Leite Lopes, *A tecelagem dos conflitos de classe na "cidade das chaminés"* (São Paulo: Editora Marco Zero, 1988); Rosélia Piquet, *Cidade-empresa: presença na paisagem urbana brasileira* (Rio de Janeiro: Jorge Zahar Editora, 1998).

39. Finn, *Tracing the Veins of Copper*; Thomas M. Klubock, *Contested Communities:*

Class, Gender, and Politics in El Teniente's Copper Mine, 1904–1951 (Durham, N.C.: Duke University Press, 1998).

40. Nicolás Cárdenas, *Empresas y trabajadores en la gran minería mexicana, 1900–1929* (Mexico City: Instituto Nacional de Estudios Históricos de la Revolución Mexicana, 1998); Myrna Santiago, *The Ecology of Oil* (New York: Cambridge University Press, 2006); Juan Luis Sariego, *Enclaves y minerales en el norte de México: historia social de los mineros de Cananea y Nueva Rosita, 1900–1970* (Mexico City: CIESAS, 1988); Juan Luis Sariego, "Los mineros de la Real del Monte: un proletariado en formación y transición," *Revista Mexicana de Sociología* 42, no. 4 (1980): 1379–404.

41. Victoria Novelo and Augusto Arteaga, *La industria en los Magueyales: trabajo y sindicato en Ciudad Sahagún* (Mexico City: Editorial Nueva Imagen, 1979).

CHAPTER ONE

Social Engineering through Spatial Engineering

Company Towns and the Geographical Imagination

ANDREW HEROD

Space is fundamental in any exercise of power.
 —MICHEL FOUCAULT, *"Space, Knowledge, and Power"*

We shape our buildings, and afterwards our buildings shape us.
 —WINSTON CHURCHILL, *October 28, 1943*

Company towns are the product of their designers' hope that shaping the built environment in particular ways will allow them to further their political, economic, and cultural goals, whether these be exerting greater control over their labor force, ensuring the development of particular types of industrial relations, or, perhaps more altruistically, providing their workers with better housing than they might otherwise be able to secure. Company towns are, then, an attempt to put "social thought in three dimensions," as Robert Fishman has termed it.[1] They are a concrete example of what I am here calling "spatial engineering" — the deliberate manipulation of the landscape — for purposes of social engineering.

The concept of spatial engineering is important because it provides an entrée into theorizing more broadly how the landscapes within which workers find themselves are socially produced, how these landscapes mold workers' economic and political praxis, and how, in turn, their praxis recursively fashions the economic and cultural landscape. This approach to thinking about how workers' praxis shapes, and is shaped by, spatial context has been termed "labor geography."[2] At its core, labor geography argues that landscapes are not simply geographical stages upon which social life unfolds. Rather, they are both reflective of, and constitutive of, such life. Hence, although at a very basic level social actors' geographical location affects the types of interactions in which they are likely to engage and the life experiences they are liable to enjoy or endure, at a more fundamental level landscapes can be subject to significant political contestation. For instance, unions and employers may struggle over where work is to be located, with the outcome of such struggle determining whether a particular region remains a landscape of employment or becomes one of unemployment. Likewise, powerful rural landlords may work to stop the construction of roads into their regions because the lack of roads keeps them isolated and so limits local workers' ability to leave for greener pastures. The landscape's physical form, then, is the outcome of conflicts between different social actors, some of whom have more power to impose their vision on it than do others.

Given the important connections hinted at above concerning how the landscape can be proactively structured in the hope of constituting the social relations of life in particular ways, in this chapter I do three things. First, I provide a theoretical framework for situating the phenomenon of company towns, outlining especially how the landscape's purposeful construction can be a central element in political conflict. In particular, I explore the relationship between spatial engineering and social engineering as manifested through the concepts of what geographers call the "socio-spatial dialectic" and "spatial praxis," concepts that refer to the idea that the physicality of landscapes is a reflection of the social interests of those who construct them but also that how landscapes are made shapes how social relations subsequently unfold. The social and the spatial, in other words, are mutually constituted and constituting, and social actors shape the landscape but must also negotiate it, with all the consequences this has for their social behavior. Second, I present a brief empirical overview of several cases of intentional spatial engineering for the purposes of social engineering, cases that illustrate the theoretical arguments about the socio-spatial dialectic and spatial praxis and place company towns within a broader spectrum of spatial engineering that stretches from designing the layout of specific workplaces to that of entire landscapes. Finally, I draw out some broader theoretical points about the geography of capitalism and the labor process.

ON SPATIAL PRAXIS

It has long been recognized that the physical form of the built environment reflects particular social values but can also be manipulated to pursue social or political objectives. For example, the ancient Greeks visualized the city as an areal representation of the cosmos, with the city's *agora* serving symbolically as the world's focal point out from which the rest of the landscape flowed in concentric fashion.[3] Likewise, Roman city planners imposed a visual and functional order on the built environment through grid systems and building codes, with such urban order being allegorical for the order they wished to see imposed throughout their vast empire. For their part, nineteenth-century social reformers like Patrick Geddes and John Ruskin argued that social processes and spatial form are related, such that changing the landscape's spatial form should make it possible to change a society's social structure.[4] However, within the past two decades the social sciences have seen a broader theorization of how struggles over the built environment's physical form — and over the wider geography of capitalism — are central elements in political and social conflict. Much of the impulse for such theorization came out of a desire by various leftist writers — particularly within geography, but also other social sciences — to think about how to conceptualize the processes whereby more liberatory landscapes could be constructed as part of a general politics of social emancipation. Taking to heart French social theorist Henri Lefebvre's admonition that "every society produces a space, its own space," and that, consequently, "new social relationships call for a new space, and vice versa," they sought to understand the connection between the social relations of capitalism and its spatial structures, in the hope that they could challenge both.[5] Three distinct iterations of thinking about the relationship between the social and the spatial can be identified.[6]

Initially, in the 1970s Marxist geographers began to ponder how the social relations of capitalism produced particular types of landscape.[7] Why, they asked, do we find areas of poverty in a landscape of plenty, why do cities in capitalist societies look so different from those in noncapitalist ones, and how do we explain spatial patterns of environmental degradation? To answer such questions, these authors began to investigate the social relations of capitalist accumulation, suggesting that their operation was the principal driving force shaping the economic geography of capitalism. However, these early endeavors tended to view the economic landscape and the geography of capitalism as simply a reflection of capitalism's social relations. In response, a number of scholars began to think in more dialectical terms about the relationship between the social relations of capitalist production and the spatial structures thereof, suggesting that there existed what Edward Soja has called a "socio-spatial dialectic."[8] This second iteration recognized that the landscapes laid out under capitalism reflect the extant conditions and requirements of capitalist accumulation, but that they also play a constitutive role in how those conditions come about. For instance, David Harvey argued that for accumulation to take place capitalists have to arrange the landscape in certain ways, ensuring that raw materials and workers are brought together in particular places at particular times. Capitalists, in other words, must develop certain "spatial fixes" of their investments, with the result being that capital seeks to represent itself in the form of a physical landscape "created in its own image."[9] However, he also maintained that, once established, such spatial fixes shape subsequent flows of capital, goods, people, and information across the landscape, at least until changing accumulation demands require new fixes be established.

For her part, Doreen Massey outlined how the social division of labor generates particular spatial divisions of labor, with various economic activities (manufacturing versus research and development versus office functions) often conducted in different places, depending on their requirements. Significantly, though, she also argued that such spatial divisions of labor can affect subsequent geographies of investment and social divisions of labor. Hence, deindustrialization in the 1960s of the industrial regions upon which Britain's nineteenth-century economic strength had been built provided lots of unemployment and thus a ready workforce for light manufacturers looking for new locations in which to locate in the 1970s and 1980s.[10] The structure of the economic landscape, Massey argued, was therefore "not just an outcome" of how social relations unfolded but was also "part of the explanation."[11] As she put it: "The geography of a society makes a difference to the way it works."[12] Hence, she maintained, "[i]t is not just that the spatial is socially constructed; the social is spatially constructed too."[13] What these authors in their different ways were seeking to argue, then, was that capitalism (and all social systems, for that matter) has a certain spatial structure to it — it relies on capitalists' ability to construct a particular set of spatial arrangements if they are to generate and realize profits.

However, as much as these approaches linked capitalism's geography much more closely with how capitalism is organized socially, laying out a theoretical framework for understanding how social relations shape spatial structures and vice versa, they did appear to be rather capital-centric explanations of how the built environment is configured. In contrast, a number of authors argued that a fuller understanding of how capitalism functions requires exploring not just how capitalists are geographically embedded in particular places but so, too, how workers are, since this will shape their ability to act politically or economically.[14] Consequently, workers also have a vested interest in ensuring that the economic landscape and geography of capitalism are structured in particular ways. For instance, workers who are less spatially mobile because they have mortgages for houses they are unable to sell may be more willing to engage in local boosterist coalitions to attract circulating investment or to engage in wage cuts than are those who are freer to move on to greener pastures. Central to these arguments, then, has been the contention that not only is there a socio-spatial dialectic at work but also, because of the different sets of interests that exist between and also among workers and capitalists, that the form of the economic landscape and the broader geography of capitalism are subject to active contestation as different groups of workers and capitalists attempt to impose their spatial vision on the landscape.[15] This recognition that different social actors may have quite diverse spatial visions and varied capacities to implement them shifted the theoretical focus of analysis from understanding how things exist *in* space to the production *of* space.

The idea that the production of space is central to how capitalism and other social systems operate and that spatial praxis is a fundamental element in political and economic struggles leads to a much deeper consideration of the nature of space and how social actors actively seek to shape its production. One of the key theoreticians in this regard was Henri Lefebvre. Specifically, Lefebvre developed a triadic way of understanding space, distinguishing between the following:

Spatial practice, which "embraces production and reproduction, and the particular locations and spatial sets characteristic of each social formation" and is the means whereby the material spaces of any social system are made and the mechanism by which people make use of, and transform, such spaces;

Representations of space, which "are tied to the relations of production and to the 'order' which those relations impose, and hence to knowledge, to signs, [and] to codes"; and

Spaces of representation, which embody "complex symbolisms" linked to everyday life, overlay physical space, and make symbolic use of what it contains, such that they are "directly *lived* through . . . associated images and symbols."[16]

Lefebvre argued that *spatial practice* is that social activity which "secretes" a society's space.[17] *Representations of space*, on the other hand, are the formalized portrayals of space presented by urban planners, scientists, architects, engineers, artists, and so forth via a system of verbal and nonverbal signs and images — maps, models, plans, paintings, and so on — through which they guide how the built environment is materially constructed and conceptualized, such that historical transformations in ideology can be delineated through examining how plans for particular spaces change over time.[18] *Spaces of representation*, meanwhile, are the physical places in which everyday life is lived and wherein symbolic meanings are enacted in spatial form and are drawn from the built environment, as through murals, advertising billboards, vernacular architecture, and so forth. These three elements in the triad correspond with what Lefebvre called "perceived space" (*l'espace perçu*), "conceived space" (*l'espace conçu*), and "lived space" (*l'espace vécu*), with all spaces exhibiting simultaneously these three elements.[19] However, while these three types of space together constitute a unity, they do not necessarily constitute a coherence, for each is deeply contradictory. Hence, as Stuart Elden puts it: "This Lefebvrian schema sees a unity . . . between physical, mental and social space. The first of these [*l'espace perçu*] takes space as physical form, *real* space, space that is generated and used. The second [*l'espace conçu*] is the space of *savoir* (knowledge) and logic, of maps, mathematics, of space as the instrumental space of social engineers and urban planners, of navigators and explorers . . . [s]pace as a mental construct, *imagined* space. The third [*l'espace vécu*] sees space as produced and modified over time and through its use, spaces invested with symbolism and meaning, the space of *connaissance* (less formal or more local forms of knowledge), space as *real-and-imagined*."[20]

For Lefebvre, then, the spatiality of capitalism is constituted through this triad. Hence, capitalists and capitalism cannot survive without creating the appropriate material geographies that allow the extraction and realization of surplus value. Based on this, the ability to configure and reconfigure space is evidently essential to making the system work, both at the scale of planetary capitalism and at a more local scale — capitalists must make sure, for instance, that workers live close enough to work that they can put in a full day's labor, a fact that in some cases may require them to provide worker housing if the local housing market is not sufficiently developed that workers can themselves buy or rent homes close to their work. At the same time, though, the material spaces that are so produced are also reflections of how the spaces of the social system have either been consciously designed through maps, urban plans, and so forth or have come about in a more organic, less formalistic way as the outcome of different social actors' geographical visions for how the built environment should look. Whether the product of conscious planning or not, these spaces are also all imbued with symbolic meaning.

Such considerations led Lefebvre to ponder the relationship between fundamental social change and the transformation of a society's spatiality and to ask the question "can you have one without the other?" Hence, he maintained, a social "revolution that does not produce a new space has not realized its full potential; indeed it has failed in that it has not changed life itself, but has merely changed ideological superstructures, institutions or political apparatuses." Rather, for a social transformation to be "truly revolutionary in character, [it] must manifest a creative capacity in its effects on daily life, on language *and on space*."[21] This means that class struggle is fundamentally spatial.

Whereas Lefebvre was interested in the relationship between the production of space and the survival of capitalism, Michel Foucault explored how space reflects power relations but is also a medium through which power flows. Foucault investigated the relationship between space and power in a number of ways that have relevance for thinking about company towns. For instance, he was particularly fascinated by the panopticon, a prison building designed by English utilitarian philosopher and social reformer Jeremy Bentham. Specifically, Bentham's layout for the building was such that a jailer could observe prisoners without the latter knowing when they were being observed. Consequently, Bentham hoped, prisoners would discipline themselves by being on their best behavior at all times. Foucault, though, took the panopticon to be broadly emblematic of a new way of controlling the body that emerged with the Industrial Revolution, one that makes workers sufficiently docile to work in regimented environments like factories. Hence, he argued, the prison and other institutions of the industrial age (factories, schools) are usually designed so that their physical layout shapes the behavior of those contained within them, with the key being to develop sufficient "supervisory architecture" and "disciplinary space" to bring about conformity. The panopticon is thus supposed to "induce in the inmate a state of conscious and permanent visibility that assures the automatic functioning of power," such that "this architectural apparatus should be a machine for creating and sustaining a power relation independent of the person who exercises it." In short, it should establish a spatial system of surveillance in which those observed are "caught up in a power situation of which they are themselves the bearers."[22]

Foucault argued that "discipline proceeds from the distribution of individuals in space" and that disciplining workers' and others' bodies rests, at least in part, on the ability of those seeking control to be able to enclose or partition spaces. Hence, he maintained, discipline "sometimes requires [spatial] *enclosure*, the specification of a place heterogeneous to all others and closed in upon itself," for this allows those in charge to regulate spaces more easily by controlling what and who enters and exits them.[23] Equally, enclosure can elicit greater self-discipline from workers, who recognize that they are now in a work (as opposed to a nonwork) space and that different types of behavior are expected from them than are tolerated outside the workplace — crossing the boundary that encircles the workplace, in other words, reinforces in them expectations about "appropriate" workplace behavior to a greater degree than when the distinction between work space and nonwork space is less physically marked.

Enclosure, then, can be used as part of a spatial technology of control. However, it is usually not sufficient on its own. Thus, Foucault also saw spatial "partitioning" as a central element in developing a geography of bodily discipline. Through such partitioning — as when workers are seated in individual cubicles or offices, for instance — individuals are separated from one another within enclosed spaces so as to reduce the possibilities that collective consciousness might develop. The ultimate goal in all this is to "break up collective dispositions [and] eliminate . . . the uncontrolled disappearance of individuals [i.e., individuals' ability to make themselves invisible to those monitoring them], their diffuse circulation, their unusable and dangerous coagulation [and] to establish presences and absences, to know where and how to locate individuals, to set up useful communications, to interrupt others, to be able at each moment to supervise the conduct of each individual, to assess it, to judge it, to calculate its qualities or merits."[24] Within these spaces, control of individuals can be maintained both by the physical arrangement of the built environment and through the establishment of timetables and the manipulation of objects (like machines in factories) that require that the body be posed in certain ways. As such, the spatiality of the built environment and how this spatiality is used to inculcate particular ideas and ways of being within the heads of those who occupy it are connected to what Foucault calls "governmentality" — the notion that governments (though in the case of company towns we could substitute company managers) try to produce citizens/workers best suited to the government's/company's wants and desires.[25]

To summarize, then, social actors are spatially embedded, but such actors have varying capacities to cross space and to shape the geography of capitalism. This fact can influence their outlook and political praxis. Through their social actions workers, capitalists, and others thus struggle to produce the landscape and broader geography of capitalism in particular ways, which has an impact upon how the social relations within which they live and struggle unfold.

Spatial structures thus not only are the outcome of power relations but can also facilitate the exercise of power. There are, however, two important final issues to consider when thinking about spatial praxis and how the built environment may be manipulated for social engineering purposes.

First, it is essential to remember that social actors are not completely free to engage in such praxis just as they please. To paraphrase Marx, people make their own geographies but not under the conditions of their own choosing.[26] Rather, individuals' abilities to manipulate the landscape and broader geography of capitalism are clearly shaped by the social relations within which they find themselves, such that they do not have complete free will. At the same time, though, those very social relations are shaped by the spatial structures that social actors confront. Second, in addition to this synchronous socio-spatial dialectic there is also a diachronic dialectic at work. Specifically, the spatialities of the present are always in dialogue with those of the past, for landscapes have a certain "path dependence" to them. Thus, because built environments reflect accumulation conditions at the time they were initially constructed, they have the effect of ossifying in the landscape the social relations extant at the time of their creation. The result is that the spatial structures that facilitated the accumulation process at one historical moment may increasingly come to limit it later on and may have to be swept away to provide spaces for new spatial fixes. Hence, as David Harvey has put it, whereas "capital builds a physical landscape appropriate to its own condition at a particular moment in time," it may "have to destroy it, usually in the course of a crisis, at a subsequent point in time."[27] The landscapes of the past, then, have a degree of hold on those of the present, shaping how they are made, even as the making of these new landscapes gradually erases those of the past.[28]

PLACING COMPANY TOWNS

Having outlined in general terms some of the arguments about spatial praxis and how the landscape and wider geography of capitalism are contested social products, I now want to situate the phenomenon of company towns within a broader spectrum of efforts to shape spatial relations so as to mold social practices and identities, a spectrum that stretches on a geographical scale from the layout of single workplaces to that of entire landscapes. Locating company towns in the context of this broader range of spatial engineering is helpful, I would aver, because it sees them as different expressions of broader efforts to pursue social goals through conscious design of the built environment, rather than as unique objects of analysis.

At the smallest end of the geographical scale, then, are individual workspaces, the design of which has often been seen as an important element in managers' ability to control workers. Hence, whereas a factory's layout is primarily planned to ensure that production can occur (in other words, various machines' requirements for proximity principally shape the shop floor's physical arrangement), considerations of labor control have also often played a role. For example, at the beginning of the twentieth century factory toilet areas were often designed so that there were no doors on the front of cubicles nor walls dividing rows of sinks placed back to back, thereby making it easier for managers to detect loitering workers. Equally, factory designers would generally seek to limit the number of unobservable places on the shop floor, places where workers could avoid work or plan nefarious activities. Shop floors were also frequently designed with a single entrance, which made it easier for managers to monitor workers' movements onto and off the shop floor, even if it raised questions about safety in the event of fire. Similarly, early twentieth-century factory designers warned against placing service areas in places that were too out-of-the-way, lest this facilitate workers' idling when they should have been hurrying back to the shop floor.[29]

Such ideas were implemented in numerous other types of workplaces. Hence, nineteenth- and twentieth-century hospital ward design not only reflected theories of disease transmission but also the "need" for supervisors to monitor growing numbers of nurses.[30] Likewise, the nature of office work was transformed in the late nineteenth century not just by the growth of large and increasingly diverse corporations that required the generation of reams of paperwork to operate, but also by the desire to control the legions of new office workers who handled this paperwork. This resulted in the creation of large, open floor spaces, with desks frequently arranged orthogonally and all facing in the same direction toward a supervisor, who was generally seated in a separate but windowed office at one end to keep an eye on the office workers.[31] Importantly, such ideas gradually spread to Europe and elsewhere through magazines, books, and trade shows, even as they were adapted to European cultural and other norms.[32]

As opinions about worker management changed, however, so did office layouts. In the 1960s the *Bürolandschaft* model, wherein managers were no longer separated in executive suites, was developed in West Germany and became popular elsewhere. This was followed by other models, including the "action office" (a modular organizational form with low dividers and flexible work surfaces), the "cube farm" (a more extreme version of the action model), the "virtual office" (in which office workers simply sat at whatever desk was free), and the "networking" model (wherein the office layout consists of movable, semi-enclosed pods and connected desks, with the pods arranged so as to separate work areas without the need for traditional dividers).[33] Given how the built environment reflects extant social relations, such changes in offices' physical layout can be used to date broader shifts in management discourses about control and surveillance — the implementation of the *Bürolandschaft* model, for instance, represented the replacement of a Taylorist vision of worker management (in which it was believed that workers had to be closely monitored to ensure they worked hard) with one derived from organization theory, wherein it was felt that social networks within groups should be fostered so as to facilitate the flow of communication within the organization, thereby encouraging workers to be more efficient.[34]

To move up the size scale from the individual workplace, entire buildings also are often spatially engineered for purposes of deliberative social control. Many factories, for instance, have been designed to facilitate panopticonic gazes across their entire domain, not just specific shop floors. Thus, all other production considerations being equal, the rectangle became a favored shape in the late nineteenth and early twentieth centuries while buildings in the form of giant Es, Ls, or Ts — with their awkward corners around which workers could hide — were less favored. Such practices reflected Taylorist scientific management principles and were deeply intertwined with modernist ideas that glorified the machine and rationality.[35] Hence, as industrial engineers planned new buildings and layouts, "one dominant image guided them — the factory as machine," an image that embodied rationality, predictability, controllability, and nonidiosyncrasy and in which "the workers would have to work in a systematic way, giving up their old idiosyncratic habits that so bothered engineers and managers."[36]

Myriad office buildings were likewise constructed to assist management's control of workers. Whereas offices had formerly often been located in factory annexes or small, residential-like buildings, office work's growth in the late nineteenth century meant that managing hundreds, if not thousands, of workers in numerous small outbuildings proved increasingly challenging.[37] Consequently, facilitated by technological advances like elevators, office buildings increasingly came to grow in size and to take on the function and form of vertical "white-collar factories," with their occupants spatially disciplined in similar ways to their blue-collar cousins. Moreover, buildings' architecture was used to project a sense of awe in the public generally and in those who worked in them specifically, with corporate skyscrapers becoming, for many, the modern versions of medieval cathedrals. In this regard, Umberto Eco has suggested that buildings present a kind of typological code through which they communicate to the broader world their function — tall buildings with lots of reflective glass can be intended to express corporate power, for instance.[38] However, again there has been geographical variation in this — European skyscrapers, for example, historically have tended to be not as tall as those in the United States, the result of different building codes, business cultures, and, perhaps, a greater suspicion of corporate power.[39]

Various schemes for shaping social relations through spatial engineering have also been implemented on the domestic front. For instance, numerous nineteenth-century utopians, especially feminists, argued that homes should be redesigned without kitchens as a way to force the socialization of domestic work — food would be cooked at large communal kitchens and then either delivered to private residences or eaten collectively at such facilities. Such a redesign, they believed, would liberate women from the drudgery of private domestic chores that disproportionately fell on their shoulders.[40] Significantly, though, while plans such as these were being devised as a way to transform extant social relations in the domestic sphere, others were being drawn up to reinforce them. Hence, some designs for Victorian upper- and middle-class homes emphasized that houses should be built so as to separate servants from their employers, with the classes' various spaces in the home zoned to facilitate the employer's surveillance of servants but also to limit the social awkwardness of the two classes coming into accidental contact in situations less formal than those of an employer instructing a servant on work-related matters.[41] At about the same time, though, alternate ideas also coursed through the architectural and political communities as people like Catharine Beecher and Harriet Beecher Stowe hoped to see what they believed were biblical precepts reflected in the layout of homes. Thus, rather than reinforcing extant class relations through the home's physical construction, they argued that the isolated, single-family suburban house represented the ideal domestic form, a Christian "commonwealth" with the housewife as the "minister of home" and in which women would do their own housework — a development that, they suggested, would provide for greater self-assertion by middle- and upper-class women.[42]

In the early twentieth century Swiss architect Le Corbusier, arguing that architecture and urban planning should reflect the capitalist spirit, advised that "[r]evolution can be avoided" through good architecture. Hence, he contended, the chaos and inhumanity of Victorian cities should be replaced with a rationally planned built environment in which a worker's home would be a "machine for living in," an abode wherein the worker would be subject to the same kinds of spatial disciplining as might be found in a factory but that through which workers could find freedom from want and turmoil.[43] Such paternalism was also evident in his plans for a "Radiant City" in which workers would live in apartment blocks wherein communally run kitchens and laundries would provide each family meals and clean clothes. The result was an urban landscape in which the architect and planner provided "patriarchal authority, the authority of a father concerned for his children," so that its inhabitants might order their lives more efficiently.[44]

At a yet larger spatial scale, entire towns and cities have also been planned with the intent of shaping social relations through spatial engineering. Certainly, company towns fit into this category, and there have been myriad such examples built for quite different reasons.[45] For instance, believing that an individual's character is shaped by physical environment, the early nineteenth-century utopian socialist Robert Owen built several communities in both the United Kingdom and the United States designed to improve their inhabitants' moral and economic condition through good spatial planning, whereas French socialist Charles Fourier developed plans for utopian cities in which, he hoped, the physical layout would encourage the solidification in space of humanist principles and so bring about a new social order.[46] Although company towns have been built in many eras (tracts of housing for weavers were established in the fourteenth century in Ghent, for example), their construction peaked as industrial production developed from the mid-nineteenth century to the mid-twentieth, when hundreds were built across the globe.[47] These included Pullman, Illinois (founded by George Pullman for workers making his railroad cars), Bourneville, England (established for chocolate workers), Potlatch, Idaho (set up by the Potlatch Lumber Company), Vandergrift, Pennsylvania (built to house local steel workers), as well as the examples discussed in the chapters of this book.[48] In all of these towns spatial planning was used to secure particular goals, whether it was to avert worker unrest (as in places like Pullman and Vandergrift) or to provide workers with a more bucolic environment in which to work, live, and play (as in places like Bourneville, whose design was influenced by the garden city movement and its goals of transcending the contradictions between town and country).[49]

This time period also saw the establishment of various utopian and experimental communities, with interest in such communities rising and falling largely in relation to the rhythm of the business cycle.[50] As in company towns so in these utopian communities was spatial form often intended to shape social behavior and evoke broader political ambitions. While employers built company towns for purposes of controlling workers and "protecting" them from "harmful" outside influences, many trade unions and other social reformers built cooperative housing for workers as a way to give them greater security from being evicted from homes provided either by their employers or private landlords during periods of industrial unrest or economic recession (when they either would not or could not pay their rents), but also as a first step toward constructing a "workers' city."[51] By the mid-twentieth century, for example, numerous unions in the United States and elsewhere had created housing projects and entire neighborhoods. In New York City, for instance, the International Ladies' Garment Workers' Union, the International Brotherhood of Electrical Workers, the Hat, Cap and Millinery Workers, the Brotherhood of Painters, Decorators and Paperhangers of America, the Amalgamated Meat Cutters and Butcher Workmen, and the United Auto Workers all built cooperative housing that not only provided material comfort for workers but that was also "a symbol of the successful departure of the working classes from the densely packed tenement districts of [places like] Manhattan."[52]

Whereas using urban planning to facilitate the development of model industrial relations or to provide workers freedom from oppressive work environments is evident in the plans for various company towns and utopian communities, other goals have also been pursued quite explicitly through such spatial praxis. For example, in Germany the Nazis unequivocally recognized the power of architecture and spatial planning to express ideological goals and shape citizens' behavior. Albert Speer, the Reichsminister für Bewaffnung und Munition (Minister for Armaments), an architect by training, planned to redesign Berlin so as to "encourage discipline in the city's inhabitants" and to "remind them of their 'heroic' past through [the] 'heroic' scale" of the built environment he would create. The city would be remade through the construction of numerous large buildings with large open spaces for mass rallies which would emphasize the smallness of the individual in the face of the concrete manifestation of the state.[53] More broadly, the Nazis' goal was to create the landscape as a spatial expression of their ideology. Consequently, the Reichsstelle für Raumordnung (Office for Spatial Planning) developed plans for the architectural Germanification of Eastern Europe and the creation of German-style communities as a spatial expression of the *Volksgemeinschaft* (people's community), with numerous sociologists, landscape planners, and geographers working on the project.[54] Likewise, Italian fascist leader Benito Mussolini planned to reconstruct Rome and other cities in order to invoke through spatial form a direct link between the Rome of the Caesars, especially Augustus, and his own fascist party.[55]

In more general terms, city planning and zoning codes have been used either to prevent certain types of social behavior, such as the "mixing of the races" in many U.S. cities and countries like *apartheid* South Africa, or to encourage it, as with the promulgation of the heteronormative nuclear family through allowing only single-family-type housing in particular neighborhoods.[56] What is significant here, though, is that the built environment's path dependence means that some of these practices have a longer impact upon the landscape than do others. Hence, housing built for middle-class, white nuclear families and protected through restrictive deed covenants or other discriminatory practices can easily be occupied by middle-class, black nuclear families once those covenants are lifted or practices are discontinued. On the other hand, such housing's internal layout will generally make it more difficult for nonnuclear family households of whatever race to utilize. The physical structure of a neighborhood's single-family homes, then, may limit the ability of families with an extended structure to access certain neighborhoods, at least until significant redevelopment takes place.[57]

Finally, there are instances of attempts to reengineer whole landscapes in the pursuit of certain social goals. Usually these have resulted out of revolutionary moments, when a new political power has sought quite literally to erase the landscapes that existed prior to the revolution's occurrence. Hence, in the case of Cambodia, the Khmer Rouge sought to remake the landscape so as to erase vestiges of French influence. Rather than to recreate the precolonial landscape, which reflected feudal social relations, they wanted to create a landscape that served as launching pad for the new Communist society they desired to build and the physical expression of that society.[58] As James Tyner has suggested, for the Khmer Rouge the creation of the new society "entailed the complete annihilation of all non-Communist social relations and material practices. It required that Cambodia be literally wiped clean" of its pre-revolutionary landscape.[59]

Similarly, in the early 1920s in the Soviet Union there was significant debate over how the pre-revolutionary urban landscape should be superseded by a new landscape reflecting "socialist" values but also providing the appropriate environment for the "New Soviet Man" to emerge.[60] In the 1930s Soviet planners set about remaking the countryside through agricultural collectivization. Influenced by modernist ideas about the benefits of large-scale farming, they believed that farms could be laid out more rationally than the pre-revolutionary peasant plots and expected such a spatial reformulation to increase efficiency and thereby help deliver the standards of living that socialist revolution promised. Socialist revolution, in other words, required a new socialist landscape within which the new Soviet citizenry would live and work. Significantly, though, part of the planners' goal was also to make the landscape more "legible" to Communist Party administrators. Standardized designs for state and collective farms allowed agricultural engineers to know what workers were supposed to be doing at any particular time of the day, even if they could not observe them directly. This limited workers' abilities to avoid work and increased the state's capacity to have such farms produce food.[61]

Interestingly, such ideas were not confined to the Soviet Union. The Fordist ideas of large-scale production that appealed to farm designers in the USSR in the 1920s and 1930s also appealed to U.S. farm designers, and there was much cross-fertilization of ideas between the two, with both groups admiring aspects of the others' operations — Soviet designers envied U.S. designers' access to capital and other resources, while U.S. designers often pined for the absolutist power that Soviet planners engaged in establishing collective farms had for putting their experiments into operation.[62] Moreover, the fact that two U.S. agricultural engineers were able to plan a large wheat farm for an area south of Moscow while sitting in a hotel room in Chicago for two weeks in 1928 is indicative of the way in which designers imagined they could ignore the particularities of the extant landscape so that new social relations of production could be put in place.[63] That this farm was ultimately a dismal failure, though, is perhaps testament to the difficulties faced by social engineers seeking to impose abstract plans for engineered spaces onto pre-existing material landscapes.

CONTRADICTIONS OF SPATIAL ENGINEERING

Company towns, then, are part of a continuum of deliberate efforts to shape the built environment in particular ways, ranging from the most micro of scales (the individual office) to the most macro (entire landscapes). In all of these instances, the principal goal is to encourage particular types of behavior and identities through consciously designing the built environment in particular ways. However, as with all political proposals, they rarely go exactly according to plan. There are, it seems, two principal reasons for this.

First, those actors seeking to emplace new social relations in the landscape through the creation of new spatial structures do not start with a clean geographical slate. Rather, the social relations and attendant spatial structures of the past that are embedded in the landscape shape the possibilities for, and contexts within which, new spatial structures are laid down. Hence, even in the case of radical transformations of the landscape as attempted by, for instance, the Khmer Rouge, completely removing all vestiges of previous landscapes and social relations is never possible, with the result that any new landscapes are still palimpsests.[64] To amend slightly Marx's famous aphorism about the difficulties of creating a new society out of revolution, then, even when they are being erased, the landscapes of all the dead generations continue to weigh like a nightmare on those of the living, shaping how new landscapes are formed.[65]

Second, the setting in place of new built environments and landscapes is never done without resistance from, and reinterpretation and reworking by, those who will inhabit them. Hence, as Mosher argued in her study of Vandergrift, spatial "visions are seldom smoothly and inexorably translated into [physical] design[s] and then into [actual built environments] — even when shepherded along by politically or economically powerful individuals."[66] In the case of company towns, for instance, even if they are laid out entirely according to the wishes of their designers, their inhabitants frequently find ways to subvert such designers' intents. Equally, we must ask the question of whether workers and others interpret symbols and aesthetics in the ways in which they are intended. Hence, although German architect and Bauhaus School founder Walter Gropius in 1911 suggested that a worker would "find that a room well thought out by an artist, which responds to the innate sense of beauty we all possess, will relieve the monotony of the daily task and he will be more willing to join in the common enterprise [and] the productivity of the firm will increase," what corporate designers and managers may think is a pleasant work environment is often not understood that way by workers.[67] Thus, workers often contest the layout of workplaces designed to make them more productive. For example, as Anna Vemer Andrzejewski highlights, when the U.S. Post Office Department in the early twentieth century sought to better observe workers so as to limit their malingering in toilets or locker rooms, workers simply developed other forms of work avoidance, like developing mail-sorting techniques that merely made them look busy.[68] Moreover, the designs that facilitate surveillance of workers frequently also allow workers to better watch managers, and so workers more readily know when they are or are not being watched. The practice of surveillance, then, is much more complex than the kind of unidirectional gaze suggested by the concept of the panopticon, for surveillance frequently opens opportunities for counter-surveillance.

There are, though, other forms of contradiction within efforts to engage in spatial engineering, ones that involve not so much resistance as a consideration of what is present and what is absent in the landscape. Hence, whereas a number of scholars (e.g., Sewell) have argued that with the correct cultural "decoding tools" buildings can be read like texts to reveal the underlying intents and worldview of their designers, Thomas F. Gieryn has argued that this is only part of the story, for buildings "do as much to structure social relations by *concealing* as by revealing, and therein lies their distinctive force for structuring social relations and practices."[69] Thus, Gieryn maintained, once completed, "buildings hide the many possibilities that did not get built, as they bury the interests, politics, and power that shaped the one design that did." There are also questions about how the various technologies that people like Foucault have discussed as central to the exercise of power over individuals might operate at different spatial scales. Consequently, whereas Foucault emphasized that both partition and enclosure are important elements in using space for purposes of social control, these might work differently depending upon the specific spaces upon which we are focused — although an entire landscape might easily be partitioned, it is, perhaps, a bit more difficult to imagine how it might be enclosed in the same manner in which might a factory or office.

What such issues point to is the fact that in any kind of spatial praxis what is imagined ahead of time and how it is implemented and understood in practice will virtually always be somewhat different. As Lefebvre suggested, the dynamic nature of capitalist accumulation means that space is always in a state of flux, constantly being made and remade. However, this renewal is always contested, for in the reproduction of capitalist — or any other — social relations "there is no purely repetitive process."[70] Thus, it is not the case that company town founders can simply build the towns and then leave them to function as the founders imagined they would. Rather, such places must continue to be supervised lest their inhabitants start to subvert their spatialities by developing alternate geographies of social life, even within the physicality of the constraints laid down by the town planners — as when workers use parks that were initially designed as spaces of respite from the grind of daily work instead as places for large-scale rallies to oppose company plans. Such is the nature of the continuous struggle over space.

NOTES

1. Robert Fishman, *Urban Utopias in the Twentieth Century: Ebenezer Howard, Frank Lloyd Wright, and Le Corbusier* (New York: Basic Books, 1977), 7.

2. Andrew Herod, *Labor Geographies: Workers and the Landscapes of Capitalism* (New York: Guilford Press, 2001).

3. Gerard Naddaf, *The Greek Concept of Nature* (Albany: State University of New York Press, 2005).

4. Patrick Geddes, *Cities in Evolution* (1915; rpt., New York: Oxford University Press, 1950); John Ruskin, *The Seven Lamps of Architecture* (London: Smith, Elder, 1849).

5. Henri Lefebvre, *The Production of Space* (French ed., 1974; English ed., Oxford: Blackwell, 1991), 53, 59.

6. Due to space constraints I provide only a brief outline of each of these iterations in the text below. Readers interested in a fuller accounting should consult Herod, *Labor Geographies*, chapter 2.

7. Several authors were involved in this theorizing, but some of the most notable works in this regard are the following: David Harvey, "Revolutionary and Counter Revolutionary Theory in Geography and the Problem of Ghetto Formation," *Antipode* 4 (1972): 1–13; Doreen Massey, "Towards a Critique of Industrial Location Theory," *Antipode* 5 (1973): 33–39; David Harvey, *Social Justice and the City* (London: Edward Arnold, 1973); David Harvey, "Labor, Capital, and Class Struggle around the Built Environment in Advanced Capitalist Societies," *Politics and Society* 6, no. 3 (1976): 265–95; Manuel Castells, *The Urban Question: A Marxist Approach* (Cambridge, Mass.: MIT Press, 1977); Manuel Castells, *City, Class and Power* (London: Macmillan, 1978); Richard Walker, "Two Sources of Uneven Development under Advanced Capitalism: Spatial Differentiation and Capital Mobility," *Review of Radical Political Economics* 10 (1978): 28–37; and Richard Walker, "A Theory of Suburbanization: Capitalism and the Construction of Urban Space in the United States," in *Urbanization and Urban Planning in Capitalist Society*, ed. Michael Dear and Alan J. Scott (London: Methuen, 1981), 383–429.

8. Edward Soja, "The Socio-Spatial Dialectic," *Annals of the Association of American Geographers* 70, no. 2 (1980): 207–25.

9. David Harvey, *The Limits to Capital* (Oxford: Blackwell, 1982); David Harvey, "The Urban Process under Capitalism: A Framework for Analysis," *International Journal of Urban and Regional Research* 2 (1978): 101–31, 124.

10. Doreen Massey, *Spatial Divisions of Labour: Social Structures and the Geography of Production* (1984; rpt., London: Macmillan, 1995).

11. Doreen Massey, "Introduction: Geography Matters," in *Geography Matters! A Reader*, ed. Doreen Massey and John Allen (New York: Cambridge University Press, 1984), 1–11, 4.

12. Massey, *Spatial Divisions of Labour*, x.

13. Massey, "Introduction: Geography Matters," 6.

14. See, for instance, Jamie Peck, *Work-Place: The Social Regulation of Labor Markets* (New York: Guilford, 1996); Jane Wills, "Space, Place and Tradition in Working-Class Organization," in *Organizing the Landscape: Geographical Perspectives on Labor Unionism*, ed. Andrew Herod (Minneapolis: University of Minnesota Press, 1998), 129–58; Bradon Ellem and John Shields, "Rethinking 'Regional Industrial Relations': Space, Place and the Social Relations of Work," *Journal of Industrial Relations* 41, no. 4 (1999): 536–60; Herod, *Labor Geographies*; Andrew Herod, Jamie Peck, and Jane Wills, "Geography and Industrial Relations," in *Understanding Work and Employment: Industrial Relations in Transition*, ed. Peter Ackers and Adrian Wilkinson (Oxford: Oxford University Press, 2003), 176–92; Bradon Ellem, "Re-placing the Pilbara's Mining Unions," *Australian Geographer* 34, no. 3 (2003): 281–96; Noel Castree et al., *Spaces of Work: Global Capitalism and Geographies of Labour* (London: Sage, 2004); and Kevin Ward, "Thinking Geographically about Work, Employment and Society," *Work, Employment and Society* 21, no. 2 (2007): 265–76.

15. For an empirical example of how such differing spatial visions played out in the U.S. cargo-handling industry, see Andrew Herod, "On Workers' Theoretical (In)Visibility in the Writing of Critical Urban Geography: A Comradely Critique," *Urban Geography* 15, no. 7 (1994): 681–93; and Andrew Herod, "Discourse on the Docks: Containerization and Inter-union Work Disputes in U.S. Ports, 1955–1985," *Transactions of the Institute of British Geographers*, n.s., 23, no. 2 (1998): 177–91.

16. Lefebvre, *Production of Space*, 33–39, original emphasis. Although in the book's 1991 translation the term "representational spaces" is used, Stuart Elden, *Understanding Henri Lefebvre* (London: Continuum, 2004), 206, suggests that "spaces of representation" is a better translation of the original French phrase *les espaces de représentation,* a position with which I am in agreement. See also Ceri Watkins, "Representations of Space, Spatial Practices and Spaces of Representation: An Application of Lefebvre's Spatial Triad," *Culture and Organization* 11, no. 3 (2005): 209–20.

17. Lefebvre, *Production of Space*, 38.

18. For instance, how U.S. cities were laid out in the early nineteenth century, with their grid patterns reflecting ideas about rational thinking, was very different from how they were laid out in the early eighteenth century.

19. Lefebvre, *Production of Space*, 40.

20. Elden, *Understanding Henri Lefebvre*, 190.

21. Lefebvre, *Production of Space*, 54, emphasis added.

22. Michel Foucault, *Discipline and Punish: The Birth of the Prison* (French ed., 1975; English ed., New York: Pantheon Books, 1977), 201.

23. Ibid., 141.

24. Ibid., 143.

25. The term "*gouvernementalité*/governmentality" is derived from *gouverner* (to govern) and *mentalité* (mode of thought). See Michel Foucault, "Governmentality," in *The Foucault Effect: Studies in Governmentality,* ed. Graham Burchell, Colin Gordon, and Peter Miller (Chicago: University of Chicago Press, 1991), 87–104.

26. Marx famously remarked that "Men make their own history, but they do not make it just as they please; they do not make it under circumstances chosen by themselves, but under circumstances directly encountered, given and transmitted from the past. The tradition of all the dead generations weighs like a nightmare on the brain of the living." Karl Marx, *The Eighteenth Brumaire of Louis Bonaparte* (German ed., 1852; English ed., New York: International, 1963, 2004 printing), 15.

27. Harvey, "Urban Process under Capitalism," 124.

28. By way of example, we might think about how the urban landscapes of nineteenth-century cities were built around the railroads but were then swept away in the twentieth century as the truck replaced the train as the dominant mode of transporting goods from city to city.

29. Anna Vemer Andrzejewski, *Building Power: Architecture and Surveillance in Victorian America* (Knoxville: University of Tennessee Press, 2008), includes a number of photographs of such wall-less and doorless facilities (see Figs. 2.27 and 2.28).

30. Lindsay Prior, "The Architecture of the Hospital: A Study of Spatial Organization and Medical Knowledge," *British Journal of Sociology* 39, no. 1 (1988): 86–113.

31. Andrzejewski, *Building Power*, 73, notes that the manager at the Greenfield Tap and Die Corporation in the early twentieth century believed that office efficiency was improved by some 20 percent when he turned the typists' desks away from the supervisor. Whereas typists facing the supervisor could tell when they were being watched, after the desks were turned around the typists had to assume they were being constantly watched as they worked.

32. Juriaan van Meel, *The European Office: Office Design and National Context* (Rotterdam: 010 Publishers, 2000), 25–27.

33. Cliff Kuang, "Evolution of Office Spaces Reflects Changing Attitudes toward Work," *Wired Magazine* 17, no. 4 (March 23, 2009), www.wired.com/culture/design/magazine/17-04/pl_design (accessed January 9, 2010).

34. Frederick Winslow Taylor, *The Principles of Scientific Management* (New York: Harper, 1911); Mary Jo Hatch, *Organization Theory: Modern, Symbolic, and Postmodern Perspectives* (New York: Oxford University Press, 1997).

35. Lindy Biggs, "The Engineered Factory," *Technology and Culture* 36, no. 2, Supplement (1995): s174–s188.

36. Biggs, " Engineered Factory," 179.

37. van Meel, *European Office*, 25–26.

38. Umberto Eco, "Function and Sign: Semiotics of Architecture," *Via* 2 (1973): 131–53.

39. van Meel, *European Office*, 29–33.

40. Dolores Hayden, *The Grand Domestic Revolution: A History of Feminist Designs for American Homes, Neighborhoods, and Cities* (Cambridge, Mass.: MIT Press, 1981).

41. Andrzejewski, *Building Power*, 98–117.

42. Hayden, *Grand Domestic Revolution*, 55–58.

43. Le Corbusier (Charles-Édouard Jeanneret-Gris), *Towards a New Architecture* (French ed., 1923; English ed., London: John Rodker, 1931), 289, 4.

44. Le Corbusier, *The Radiant City: Elements of a Doctrine of Urbanism to Be Used as the Basis of our Machine-Age Civilization* (French ed., 1933; English ed., New York: Orion Press, 1967), 152.

45. John Garner, introduction to *The Company Town: Architecture and Society in the Early Industrial Age*, by John Garner (New York: Oxford University Press, 1992), 3–14, distinguishes between "company towns" and "model industrial towns." The distinction is that whereas in the former a single company usually owns all the community's facilities, in the latter individual workers and business owners may own their homes or shops, but the town has been laid out to pursue some predesignated social agenda. Here I use the term "company town" to describe both of these collectively, as I am less interested in definitional issues than the point that their spatial layout is often designed to shape social behavior.

46. Jonathan Beecher, *Charles Fourier: The Visionary and His World* (Berkeley:

University of California Press, 1986); Kenneth Frampton, *Labour, Work and Architecture* (London: Phaidon Press, 2002); John Harrison, *Robert Owen and the Owenites in Britain and America* (1969; rpt., New York: Routledge, 2009).

47. Garner, Introduction.

48. Stanley Buder, *Pullman: An Experiment in Industrial Order and Community Planning, 1880–1930* (New York: Oxford University Press, 1967); Edward Cadbury, *Experiments in Industrial Organization* (London: Longmans, Green, 1912); Keith Petersen, *Company Town: Potlatch, Idaho, and the Potlatch Lumber Company* (Pullman: Washington State University Press, 1987); Anne Mosher, *Capital's Utopia: Vandergrift, Pennsylvania, 1855–1916* (Baltimore: Johns Hopkins University Press, 2004).

49. On the garden city idea, see Ebenezer Howard, *To-morrow: A Peaceful Path to Real Reform* (London: Swan Sonnenschein, 1898, republished in 1902 as *Garden Cities of To-morrow*). Margaret Crawford, *Building the Workingman's Paradise: The Design of American Company Towns* (New York: Verso, 1995), 71, details how George Cadbury, worried that his company's domination of Bourneville might be deemed too paternalistic by his employees, encouraged non-Cadbury workers to move to the town, such that by 1895 nonemployees constituted half of the town's inhabitants.

50. Brian Berry, *America's Utopian Experiments: Communal Havens from Long-Wave Crises* (Hanover, N.H.: University Press of New England, 1992). See also Robert P. Sutton, *Communal Utopias and the American Experience: Religious Communities, 1732–2000* (Westport, Conn.: Praeger, 2003) and *Communal Utopias and the American Experience: Secular Communities, 1824–2000* (Westport, Conn.: Praeger, 2004); and Arthur E. Bestor, *Backwoods Utopias: The Sectarian and Owenite Phases of Communitarian Socialism in America, 1663–1829* (Philadelphia: University of Pennsylvania Press, 1950).

51. On efforts by garment workers to imagine and implement in the landscape a workers' city in early twentieth-century New York City, see Leyla Vural, "Unionism as a Way of Life: The Community Orientation of the International Ladies' Garment Workers' Union and the Amalgamated Clothing Workers of America" (PhD diss., Rutgers University, New Brunswick, 1994); for more on the German labor movement's building of worker housing in Berlin in the years after World War I (some 10 percent of all housing constructed in some years), see Klaus Homann and Ludovica Scarpa, "Martin Wagner, the Trades Union Movement and Housing Construction in Berlin in the First Half of the Nineteen Twenties," *Architectural Design* 53, no. 11/12, (1983): 58–61.

52. Quote is from R. Plunz, "Reading Bronx Housing, 1890–1940" in *Building a Borough: Architecture and Planning in the Bronx* (New York: Bronx Museum of the Arts, 1986), 70–76, 49. See Herod, *Labor Geographies*, 291, for more on various union housing projects.

53. Benjamin Warner, "Berlin — The Nordic Homeland and the Corruption of Urban Spectacle," *Architectural Design* 53, no. 11/12 (1983): 73–80, 76; see also Stephen D. Helmer, *Hitler's Berlin: The Speer Plans for Reshaping the Central City* (Ann Arbor, Mich.: UMI Research Press, 1985); Albert Speer, *Architecture, 1932–1942* (Bruxelles: Archives

d'Architecture Moderne, 1985); and Jochen Thies, "Nazi Architecture — A Blueprint for World Domination: The Last Aims of Adolf Hitler," in *Nazi Propaganda: The Power and the Limitations*, ed. David Welch (London: Croom Helm, 1983), 45–64.

54. Mechtild Rössler, "'Area Research' and 'Spatial Planning' from the Weimar Republic to the German Federal Republic: Creating a Society with a Spatial Order under National Socialism," in *Science, Technology and National Socialism*, ed. Monika Renneberg and Mark Walker (New York: Cambridge University Press, 1994), 126–38.

55. Dennis Doordan, "The Political Content in Italian Architecture during the Fascist Era," *Art Journal* 43, no. 2 (Summer 1983): 121–31; Dawn Ades et al., *Art and Power: Europe under the Dictators, 1930–45* (London: Thames and Hudson, 1995).

56. Heteronormativity is the acceptance of heterosexuality as normal and, consequently, homosexuality as abnormal. See Michael Frisch, "Planning as a Heterosexist Project," *Journal of Planning Education and Research* 21, no. 3 (2002): 254–66, on how planning codes have often incorporated heteronormative assumptions. In terms of racial segregation in planning, although a 1917 U.S. Supreme Court decision found racial zoning to be unconstitutional, there have been many other ways in which municipalities have designed zoning codes to limit minorities' ability to move into certain neighborhoods, such as with increasing minimum lot sizes to make housing more expensive.

57. Ellen Pader, "Housing Occupancy Standards: Inscribing Ethnicity and Family Relations on the Land," *Journal of Architectural and Planning Research* 19, no. 4 (2002): 300–318.

58. James Tyner, *The Killing of Cambodia: Geography, Genocide and the Unmaking of Space* (Aldershot, Eng.: Ashgate, 2008).

59. Tyner, *Killing of Cambodia*, 119.

60. James Bater, *The Soviet City: Ideal and Reality* (Beverley Hills, Calif.: Sage, 1980).

61. James Scott, *Seeing like a State: How Certain Schemes to Improve the Human Condition Have Failed* (New Haven: Yale University Press, 1998), 196–201.

62. Deborah Fitzgerald, *Every Farm a Factory: The Industrial Ideal in American Agriculture* (New Haven: Yale University Press, 2003).

63. Scott, *Seeing like a State*, 201.

64. The term "palimpsest" refers to parchments from the Middle Ages wherein the parchment was reused by scratching off the surface layer of writing, thereby providing a relatively clean surface on which new writing could occur. However, in most cases the scratching off was never complete, so that certain words or phrases from previous writings would remain and could be seen through the lines of whatever was subsequently written. In the case of landscapes, we can imagine a palimpsest as a landscape in which vestigial traces of older landscapes remain, even when that landscape has essentially been cleared of most of its pre-existing elements.

65. Marx, *Eighteenth Brumaire*, 15.

66. Mosher, *Capital's Utopia*, 3.

67. Quoted in Reyner Banham, *A Concrete Atlantis: U.S. Industrial Building and European Modern Architecture, 1900–1925* (Cambridge, Mass.: MIT Press, 1986), 201.

68. Andrzejewski, *Building Power*, 89.

69. William Sewell Jr., "A Theory of Structure: Duality, Agency and Transformation," *American Journal of Sociology* 98, no. 1 (1992): 1–29; Thomas F. Gieryn, "What Buildings Do," *Theory and Society* 31, no. 1 (2002): 35–74.

70. Lefebvre, *Production of Space*, 11.

CHAPTER TWO

From Company Towns to Union Towns

Textile Workers and the Revolutionary State in Mexico

AURORA GÓMEZ-GALVARRIATO

Company towns have existed throughout the world where profitable business opportunities have required the locating of people in isolated and unpopulated areas. Because it is costly to relocate workers and provide their living facilities, this only happens when the nature of the business involves the exploitation of natural resources in distant and vacant areas. Normally these types of ventures are related to mining, agriculture, or forestry. However, in Mexico, company towns were also prevalent in manufacturing enterprises during the nineteenth century. This gave Mexico's industrialization and capital-labor relations distinctive features that are well worth analyzing.

Mexico had a mechanized textile industry as early as the 1830s, before any other country in Latin America.[1] The mills were located far away from cities because they relied on hydraulic power from waterfalls or rivers rather than mineral coal deposits. Early mills such as La Constancia Mexicana (1835) on the Atlixco River in Puebla or La Magdalena Contreras (1836) on the Magdalena River near Mexico City had company housing, a company store, and other features common in later company towns.[2] The pattern of building mills away from urban centers continued as long as the industry relied on hydroelectric power generated on site by the companies themselves. The size of the mills and the number of workers, however, increased significantly by the late nineteenth century. Large mills employed between one thousand and three thousand workers, more than ten times the number in the largest mills earlier in the century. The task of providing workers and their families with adequate housing and urban services grew proportionally. The complexity of the urban, social, and political problems of company towns also increased.

In this chapter I examine the evolution of two of the largest industrial company towns in Mexico in the late nineteenth century: Río Blanco and Santa Rosa. They were established by the two largest textile companies in Mexico at the turn of the century, the Compañía Industrial de Orizaba (CIDOSA; Industrial Company of Orizaba) and the Compañía Industrial Veracruzana (CIVSA; Industrial Company of Veracruz), which were also the major industrial companies, because textiles was the most important sector.

This chapter explores the ways by which the firms, the workers, the unions, the communities, and the government sought to solve the problems they encountered, and how their actions and interaction changed the company towns as a social and physical space. It studies how the growing power of workers transformed the mill towns from company towns into union towns. First, it illuminates the arrival of the textile companies, the resulting demographic changes in the region, and the birth and evolution of the company towns in physical and political terms. Second, the essay focuses on the development of Santa Rosa as a company town and its transformation into a union town. It summarizes how the company built the infrastructure and established urban services and then discusses the evolution of company housing, stores for the provision of basic needs, and access to education as a result of the increasing power of the unions in the town's governance. The rich archival material available for Santa Rosa, both in company and union archives, allows for a detailed analysis. Unfortunately, CIVSA restricted the access to much richer archives for Río Blanco, which means that it is mostly used as a comparison case. The chapter also draws on the histories of other communities in the Orizaba Valley to enrich the analysis.

RÍO BLANCO AND SANTA ROSA

The Orizaba Valley in the state of Veracruz became one of Mexico's most important industrial regions in the late nineteenth century, widely known at the time as the Mexican Manchester. The railway linked the valley to the port of Veracruz, then Mexico's most important connection to the world economy, and to Mexico City, the country's capital and main commercial center. The valley also had an abundance of water power, which attracted industrial investment. The Compañía Industrial de Orizaba and the Compañía Industrial Veracruzana chose the location to establish large new mills: Río Blanco and Santa Rosa. These mills were far enough from the next city, Orizaba, to force the companies to provide housing for the employees and to create an urban infrastructure. Each mill had a company town with houses for managers and employees, stores, schools, municipal buildings, and churches, giving the company extensive control over the daily lives of the inhabitants. During the first decades after their establishment, the companies undertook most public works and controlled the municipal governments, but as workers' power increased, unions played an even greater role in the provision of public services.

Beginning in the 1830s, the Orizaba Valley was a preferred site for the establishment of the nascent mechanized cotton textile industry. The proximity to the port of Veracruz facilitated the supply with cotton, machinery, chemicals, and other necessary imports, and it was relatively easy to ship the manufactured yarn and cloth to Mexico City, which was both the largest consumer market and home to the most important wholesale stores distributing goods to the rest of the country. Cocolapan, the largest of Mexico's early textile mills, was founded in 1837 near the city of Orizaba. In 1873, the region gained an additional advantage with the opening of the Mexican Railways line connecting Mexico City and Veracruz via Orizaba. Two additional mills opened in the old colonial town of Nogales near Orizaba: San Lorenzo in 1881 and Cerritos in 1882. CIDOSA, founded in 1889, acquired and subsequently modernized the Cocolapan, Cerritos, and San Lorenzo mills and opened the new and even bigger Río Blanco mill in the district of Tenango. In 1896, CIVSA built the Santa Rosa mill in the nearby district of Necoxtla.[3] Other industries established themselves in the Orizaba Valley, such as the jute bags factory of Santa Gertrudis (1892) and the brewery Cervecería Moctezuma (1894).

The original mills sat on greenfield sites, but in the decade following their creation the adjacent settlements of workers' houses became real towns. The prime examples for this transition from an isolated mill in an agricultural area into an urban space were Santa Rosa, where the mill began production in 1898, and Río Blanco, inaugurated in 1892. From 1900 to 1930, the population of Mexico grew by 22 percent and that of the state of Veracruz by 40 percent, while the population of Santa Rosa grew by 213 percent and that of Río Blanco by 92 percent. This rapid population growth around the textile mills created a sudden demand for housing and urban services that the government could not satisfy. The companies had to create the necessary urban infrastructure, although over time the unions took charge, with the support of the municipal governments.

Since very few people lived near the mill sites, the textile companies had to attract migrant workers from other places to the Orizaba Valley. In 1899, the CIVSA board reported to the annual shareholders meeting that production had suffered "because, among other things, they had faced great difficulties in finding workers capable of running the machinery."[4] Yet they were gradually able to hire enough workers: 1,441 by 1900, another 2,156 by 1906, and 2,189 more by 1913, the highest number for a single year during this period. The company looked for workers over a wide area, although most came from states across the central plateau: 40 percent from Puebla, 20 percent from Oaxaca, and 10 percent from Mexico. Only 14 percent of the weavers were originally from the Orizaba Valley, and another 2 percent were from other regions of Veracruz.[5] The rest came from other states, some as distant as San Luis Potosí or Jalisco. The company hired foreigners as technicians to assemble the machinery and as the superintendents of weaving, spinning, bleaching, printing, and engraving. Most were from France, but they also recruited some English technicians.[6] The jobs one echelon below the department heads and superintendents, however, all went to Mexicans. They even held highly skilled jobs such as that of loom fixer.

Some of the workers who came to Santa Rosa must have been peasants, perhaps driven from their small plots as the result of the expansion of haciendas, but many had worked at other textile mills and moved to Orizaba because of higher wages. By 1890, decades of mechanized textile manufacturing in Mexico had created a pool of textile workers for the new mills to draw on. At least 41 percent of weavers hired by CIVSA came from cities and towns that had textile mills and were already equipped with industrial skills and the experience of living in an industrial setting. Millhands in Río Blanco and Santa Rosa had more formal education than the average Mexican at the time. In 1900, the municipalities of Tenango and Necoxtla had male illiteracy rates of 46 percent and 55 percent, respectively, which compared favorably to the 74 percent male illiteracy rate in Mexico as a whole.[7]

Only about 5 percent of the textile workers at Santa Rosa were female. Although the mill dominated the town, and although most of its workers were young males, 49.6 percent of Santa Rosa's population was female by 1910. Apparently the young, single workers at Santa Rosa did not generally live on their own but rather with their families. The women may have worked as seamstresses for two finished clothes factories in the region, or they prepared food for workers who paid to eat at their houses.[8] Similarly, at the three CIDOSA mills, only 2 percent of the 4,163 workers were female in 1920.[9]

Santa Rosa and Río Blanco were immigrant towns with people from diverse regions and environments, which shaped their character. In contrast to most established towns in Mexico, where traditional values and hierarchies mattered greatly, Santa Rosa and Río Blanco had a very young population that was more liberal and open to new ideas.

Textile workers from the Orizaba mills soon began to organize for improvements of their working conditions. In 1906 they created a large labor confederation, the Gran Círculo de Obreros Libres (Great Circle of Free Workers), which included most Mexican textile workers. However, it was brutally crushed by the government with the use of military power. The labor movement in the Orizaba Valley grew stronger during the Mexican Revolution (1910–20). From loose and semiclandestine associations known as "clubs" or "societies" emerged labor unions, which then joined regional federations and national confederations. In 1919, the Orizaba textile unions joined the Confederación Regional Obrera Mexicana (CROM; Mexican Regional Confederation of Workers), which became the most powerful workers' organization in the country in the 1920s.[10] The emergence of strong unions had a profound impact on the company towns.

Río Blanco and Santa Rosa were hotbeds of the fast-growing labor movement. The revolution drastically changed the balance of power in these mill towns: they evolved from company towns into union towns. During the Porfiriato — the government of President Porfirio Díaz (1876–1911) — the state gave full support to the textile companies and repressed workers' organizations. Revolutionary leaders, on the other hand, sought the support of workers for practical and ideological reasons. They tolerated and often encouraged workers' organization and passed laws in favor of labor.[11] The unions in the Orizaba Valley took control of public services initially provided by the companies, assumed leadership in the construction of public facilities, and elected workers as municipal presidents. As Río Blanco and Santa Rosa grew, independent stores established a presence in the region and began supplying many of the goods and services for which the workers previously had relied on the companies. By the late 1920s, the government gained an increasing presence in a space dominated by the companies and the workers' organizations.

In the following sections we explore how the growing power of workers changed different aspects of the company towns: their urban infrastructure and the housing, commercial, and educational facilities, which together encompass the transition of the company towns into union towns.

THE BUILDING AND TRANSFORMATION OF A COMPANY TOWN: SANTA ROSA

Santa Rosa provides an excellent example of the birth and evolution of textile company towns of the Orizaba Valley. Given the abundance of information available for Santa Rosa, the study focuses on this town but provides information about other towns whenever it is possible.

The narrow valley that the town of Santa Rosa (now Ciudad Mendoza) would come to occupy was open land before the construction of the textile mill. At the time the municipal government (*cabecera*) resided in the small Indian town of Necoxtla in the hills overlooking the Santa Rosa Valley. Ever since the opening of the mill CIVSA had pressured the state government to create a new municipality around the factory, pledging to construct the necessary infrastructure. Initially the government preferred to change municipal borders so that Santa Rosa would belong to the municipality of Nogales, whose head town was closer to the mill. The CIVSA board opposed that plan, however, because its competitor CIDOSA controlled the Nogales municipal government. On April 25, 1898, Santa Rosa became the seat of government for the municipality of Necoxtla despite protests by the Necoxtla Indians.[12] CIVSA paid for and supervised the building of the municipal palace of Santa Rosa following a design proposed by state governor Teodoro Dehesa. The company also paid for the construction of the local Catholic church and gave twelve pesos weekly for the support of the priest.[13]

CIVSA also saw to improving public transport and communications between Santa Rosa and the rest of the country. In 1897, it signed a contract with the local tramway company to extend a line that previously ended in Nogales all the way to Santa Rosa.[14] In 1899, CIVSA made a deal with the minister of communications in order to install a telegraph office in Santa Rosa. CIVSA built the offices, and the federal government covered the expenses for the installation of the telegraph lines. CIVSA also provided housing for the telegraph operator and messenger, and it paid them a monthly salary whenever the telegraph office did not make enough money to pay them.[15] In 1897, CIVSA built a branch line to connect Santa Rosa to the network of the Mexican Railways company. It donated the land, built the local station, paid the wages of the railroad employees, and established loading and unloading platforms close to the "Crucero de Santa Cruz."[16] In 1928, CIVSA, CIDOSA, and the Cervecería Moctezuma each contributed about fifteen thousand pesos to the construction of the Mexico-Veracruz highway. To justify the expense, the CIVSA director argued that the highway would increase competition and thus diminish railroad tariffs.[17]

CIVSA initially provided all essential urban services. It built the streets, the town hall, and the church. Since 1906 it provided street lighting for Santa Rosa and did not charge the municipality for the electricity until 1929. In 1917, at the request of the municipality, CIVSA laid pipeline to supply drinking water. The municipality wanted factory workers, the main beneficiaries, to provide volunteer labor for the installation, but CIVSA decided to contract out all the work in order to remain "the sole owner of the installation and distribution of water, and to avoid future problems."[18] These pipelines reached only part of the town. In 1928, CIVSA paid twelve thousand pesos as advance payment on taxes to enable the municipality to provide drinking water for the whole town. In the

1920s, CIVSA also financed the building of Santa Rosa's central plaza and its municipal market through a combination of donations and loans.[19] The situation in Río Blanco was not much different. In 1922, CIDOSA owned the local Catholic church and the market, which it rented to the municipality.[20]

Until 1916 Santa Rosa's municipal presidents had all been CIVSA employees with company backing. Before 1916, municipal presidents of the various mill towns in the Orizaba Valley had normally been white-collar employees from the factories. This gave companies direct power in these towns. Workers considered this power equivalent to "including justice in the company's inventory and making authority a blind instrument to quiet the voice of those workers who had the energy to complain against daily abuses."[21] With the authorities' support it was easy and common for companies to imprison workers for no legal reason.

The municipal presidents after 1917 were CIVSA workers, too, but they were blue-collar workers with union support.[22] The union assembly chose a candidate for municipal president, usually someone who had already held leadership positions and had represented the union at the regional or national federations. In the 1920s the unions ran their candidates through the Partido Laborista (Laborist Party, LP), and most of the time they won. All municipal presidents of Santa Rosa from 1916 to 1958 were workers from the Santa Rosa Mill. Orizaba had only one nonlabor local government between 1916 and 1933. Río Blanco had its first labor local government in 1918, and Nogales in 1914.[23]

The workers' newly won political power did not please the company. When Santa Rosa elected its first blue-collar municipal president in 1916, the CIVSA board complained: "we have a weaver as municipal president and only one gendarme for police, [so] it is not from respect for these authorities that workers will stop stealing."[24] The law gave municipal presidents an important role in labor-capital disputes, which led the CIVSA board to suggest that "in Santa Rosa [the municipal president] is nothing but the puppet of labor unions, and in consequence we will never win any case."[25]

The shift in the political control of the municipal government was followed by a growing role of the union in the town's construction projects. Over the course of the 1920s, the CIVSA union asserted a greater presence in providing public services for Santa Rosa. The union built the school (1927), the sports field (1927), and the movie theater and public library (1949).[26] After 1930, the government played an increasingly important role. In contrast to the early twentieth century, when CIVSA took full responsibility for the construction of urban projects, the municipality now led the way, although the company still provided loans for some projects.

COMPANY HOUSING

The lack of urban development obliged the textile companies to build dwellings for mill workers, white-collar employees, and managers. The construction plans for the Santa Rosa mill from the outset included living quarters for workers. In June 1897, CIVSA built eighteen rows of brick houses. In February 1898, it built three more rows with a total of twenty houses, all made from wood due to a temporary lack of bricks.[27] Most CIVSA workers lived in Santa Rosa, but only a relatively small percentage of them in company housing. By 1900, the payrolls showed only 155 workers paying rent for company housing, less than 12 percent of the total workforce. By 1911, almost one quarter of CIVSA workers lived in company houses, a share that remained steady thereafter.[28] The remaining workers either owned houses, usually of a lower standard than company housing, or rented from private landlords.[29] Many lived in tenement houses (*patios de vecindad*), a common feature of Latin American towns and cities in the late nineteenth and early twentieth centuries during a wave of urbanization caused by industrial growth. Such tenement houses consisted of "a number of small rooms around a common courtyard, where basic cooking and bathing facilities were located."[30]

CIDOSA workers faced similar housing conditions. In 1909, Graham Clark wrote: "at Río Blanco the operatives live in rows of long wooden barracks, which are kept neatly painted and are furnished with water and light by the mill." Clark described the conditions as far better than in other regions of the country: "Orizaba operatives' living surroundings are certainly better than those to be seen anywhere else in Mexico, as the mills in this section build neat wooden or adobe houses that are kept in good repair."[31] Both CIVSA and CIDOSA created enclosed neighborhoods to accommodate employees in supervisory positions and built sports facilities as well as bars with billiard and bowling tables for entertainment. Both companies owned houses for those employees who lived with their families and dormitories for single employees.

Between 1900 and 1930 the comfort of company housing improved substantially. In 1900, most workers' dwellings in Santa Rosa were wooden houses with only one room and no drinking water, electricity, or toilets. By 1910, they had all these amenities. By the late 1920s, the majority of houses were three-room brick houses. CIVSA began supplying the worker houses with electricity in 1906 and started deducting the charges for electricity from each worker's payroll in 1908. Originally each row of houses shared a water faucet and toilets (most probably latrines), but in 1910 CIVSA began installing water faucets in every house and water closets for each row of houses.[32] Workers requested showers, and in 1920 the company installed public baths that workers and their families could use for a small fee. Public showers for workers at Cocolapan and Cerritos were built in 1924.[33]

The first law to regulate company housing in the state of Veracruz was the state labor law of 1918. It required companies with more than one hundred employees to provide "comfortable and healthy" housing for their workers at a monthly rent of no more than 0.5 percent of their registered value, a clause also included in Article 123 of the Constitution.[34] Despite the new regulation there was little increase in the availability of company housing. Rather than build new houses for its workers, CIVSA in the 1920s invested heavily in improving the existing stock. The CIVSA board reported in 1924 that by the end of the year it would replace the last wooden houses with brick houses that could be "judged by the most modern precepts of hygiene."[35] The new brick houses had thick walls and high tile or sheet-steel roofs. Not counting the small patio, they had forty-seven square meters (154 square feet) of living space divided up into a bedroom, a living room, and a kitchen.[36] The inhabitants still had to use the shared toilets and took showers in the public bath. The company added bathrooms to the individual houses only in the late 1940s, using part of the patio.[37]

Over time neighborhoods of workers who owned their houses (*colonias de obreros*) took shape. Workers founded neighborhood associations, such as the Unión Central de Colonias de Obreros y Campesinos de Santa Rosa (Central Union of Neighborhoods of Workers and Peasants of Santa Rosa) in 1923, which had five hundred affiliated individuals by 1927.[38] CIDOSA sold plots of land to workers who wanted to build a home. In 1923, it sold twenty lots in the so-called Barrio Motzorongo, and in 1925, 132 workers purchased lots that they agreed to pay for in four hundred weekly installments.[39] In 1927, such "*colono* payments" amounted to more than CIDOSA received for company housing rents. In 1928, a year with fewer sizeable down payments, "*colono* payments" to the Río Blanco mill amounted to 56 percent of company housing rents.[40] Also in 1928, at its workers' request, CIVSA devised a "colonization project" to sell plots of land to workers in the factory's surroundings. The company board believed that it was in the mill's interests to create a stable nucleus of inhabitants around the factory.[41]

The threat of land expropriation for the purpose of building housing made CIDOSA, a major landholder in region, more likely to sell plots. The threat of expropriation under the agrarian reform in the state of Veracruz and the strength of the tenants' movement facilitated expropriations. In early 1923, the *Comisión Local Agraria* (Local Agrarian Commission) started a legal battle with CIDOSA in order to have part of its land expropriated to be distributed among the population. In April, the municipality gave possession of some company land to peasants under the 1920 Ley de Tierras Ociosas de la Federación (Federal Law of Vacant Land). A few months later, the land became an *ejido*.[42] Moreover, the Veracruz Rent Law of April 8, 1923, provided for the expropriation of urban lands for the purpose of housing construction.[43] In 1924, the state government asked owners of empty lots to cede the property for the building of cheap wooden houses for workers. CIDOSA kept its most valuable lots close to the railroad and sold the rest to the government at tax value plus 10 percent.[44]

FROM COMPANY STORES TO COOPERATIVE STORES

One of the most salient features of company towns was the company store. With its monopoly power, it adversely affected workers' living conditions because the owner could charge higher prices or provide lower-quality goods. That monopoly power rested on the company's decision to pay part of the salary in scrip redeemable only in the company store and the lack of alternative options at a reasonable distance. The degree of monopoly power that company stores held in Río Blanco and Santa Rosa diminished over time, and it had never been as great as generally assumed in the historiography on company towns.

During the Porfiriato, all textile mills in the Orizaba Valley had a company store. Employers' greed does not appear to have been the main motive for the creation of company stores. In 1897, with the Santa Rosa mill still under construction, the CIVSA board saw an urgent need to establish a provisional store for lack of commercial facilities in the area. The board wanted to make sure that workers "do not lack what they need or waste time by having to go to find it as far away as Orizaba."[45] By the end of the nineteenth century, the store at Nogales serving CIDOSA's San Lorenzo mill was the only one outside of the city of Orizaba. By 1898, Santa Rosa had a tramway line to Orizaba through Nogales, but even then it must have taken at least an hour to travel the eleven kilometers to Orizaba at an expense that strained the workers' budgets.[46] By early January 1899, with store construction nearly completed, CIVSA leased it to the Fuentes family for a monthly rent of 150 pesos plus 5 percent commission on sales.[47]

Although some companies maintained monopolies by paying their workers mostly in scrip, in the Orizaba Valley workers received most of their wages in silver coins, as evident from the correspondence from the mills to Mexico City demanding large amounts of coins to pay weekly wages and reporting on their remittance or arrival.[48] Scrip existed as an advance on wages due the following payday. The company accepted scrip at its full value to pay for merchandise or at 90 percent of its value for cash.[49] The companies retained the amount advanced

Figure 2.1 General Store "El Juguete" in Santa Rosa, Veracruz, ca. 1930. Museo Comunitario de Ciudad Mendoza, Veracruz.

as scrip from the workers' wages to pay to the company store — after deducting its 5 percent commission.

In 1900, there still were few alternatives to company stores. But with the Orizaba Valley's increasing urbanization, the monopoly power of these stores diminished. By 1907, Santa Rosa had several new commercial establishments. There was the dry goods store "El Modelo," a Singer sewing machine agency, and at least one other store in Santa Rosa owned by the Ortega family. Traveling salesmen known in the town as the "Italians" and "Hungarians" regularly came to Santa Rosa from Orizaba with boxes full of merchandise.[50] By 1910, Santa Rosa had twenty general stores that sold staples (corn, flour, beans, meat, chili, milk, cheese, vegetables, and fruit) and some items of daily necessity such as coal, candles, cloth, dishes, and pots. Two stores sold shawls (*rebocerías*), and there were two bakeries and a drugstore.

The leaseholder of the Río Blanco company store, Víctor Garcín, was the major wholesaler of the region and sold merchandise to the other local stores.[51] He thus had the power to undermine other stores if they offered too much competition, a power he apparently used to shut down two small local grocery stores: "El Gallo Real" and "El Puerto de Veracruz."[52] Garcín did not enjoy complete monopoly power, however. In 1908, there were at least three other stores in town: "El Infiernito," "El Chin-Chun-Chan," and "Mi Tienda."[53] These stores also sold merchandise on credit, but the company stores held one major advantage: the factory guaranteed their credits.

Events in January 1907 brought the company stores of the Orizaba Valley into the national spotlight. The labor confederation Gran Círculo de Obreros Libres had grown strong, but neither the industrialists nor the government were willing to yield to its increasing power. The conflict led to a lockout by the national textile companies that left most textile workers without pay for several weeks. President Porfirio Díaz tried to settle the conflict by decreeing general regulations for textile mills that appeared to grant concessions to both sides. The regulations did not satisfy many Orizaba Valley workers, and they decided not to return to work on January 7. Instead, they gathered at the mill gates, where some got into a fight with the employees of the Río Blanco company store. After a store employee opened fire and killed one worker, the striking workers first sacked and burned the store, and then they marched along the Calle Real looting and burning all the stores run by Víctor Garcín as well as several pawn shops. On January 7 and 8, the military repression killed about seventy workers and imprisoned another two hundred.[54] After the massacre the local and national workers' movement focused on the issue of abusive company stores.[55]

The CIVSA board responded on January 12 by instructing the mill manager to pay the money owed to the company store and stop charging the 5 percent commission on worker's purchases. The board also wanted the accounting books doctored to hide the company's close involvement with store practices from government inspectors. The CIVSA manager received instructions to advance some money to needy workers, but "under no circumstances should they be charged any percentage for it."[56] After June 1908, CIVSA no longer deducted worker debts with the company store from the payroll, thus ending the company store's special advantage over its competitors. In August 1910, it reduced the rent charged for the store from 150 to 120 pesos per month.[57] As time went by, the rent diminished further.[58] Víctor Garcín left the region and sold his property to his former partner, the Spaniard Manuel Diez, who reopened the former Río Blanco company store in June 1908. A worker wrote a story on the reopening that urged his fellow workers to be alert when they made purchases in this former company store because the previous experience with that store had cost them dearly.[59]

Nearly all the labor laws passed by revolutionary governments in the 1920s explicitly prohibited company stores. The Textile Workers' and Industrialists' Convention of July 1912 had included such a prohibition in its factory regulations.[60] Article 14 of decree No. 11, passed by the governor of Veracruz, Cándido Aguilar, on October 19, 1914, forbade any business from establishing *tiendas de raya* to guarantee freedom of trade.[61] Article 123 of the 1917 Constitution stipulated that wages had to be paid in currency and not in scrip, coupons, or merchandise. Finally, the Veracruz Labor Law contained articles that outlawed company stores and forbade paying salaries in company scrip.[62]

Conditions of consumption and credit worsened as a consequence of the scarcities and high inflation rates caused by the revolutionary conflict, and workers soon realized that the end of the company stores did nothing to improve the situation. They decided to organize consumer cooperatives in order to provide goods at better prices. The governor and military commander of Veracruz, Agustín Millán, received a letter from the Cocolapan mill workers to inform him that on December 4, 1915, they had created a cooperative association "to free ourselves from the merchants who have extorted us so much with the pretext of the revolution, considering that the revolution is not blamable for the swindle of merchants to the proletarian people, and to avoid it, or at least to defend us against it."[63] The letter indicates that the cooperative had a president, vice president, and secretary, but unfortunately we know little about its daily operations or those of other cooperatives in the Orizaba Valley before 1920.

In November 1920, the Federación de Sindicatos del Cantón de Orizaba (FSCO; Federation of Unions of the Orizaba District) and employers of the Orizaba Valley held a series of meetings that resulted in the creation of consumers' cooperatives aimed at "lowering the price of basic products."[64] The companies, instead of granting the 100 percent wage increase that workers demanded, agreed to fund the creation of consumers' cooperatives with fifty thousand pesos. They also provided the premises for such cooperative stores at no cost, helped the stores with the transportation of merchandise, and provided them with cheap cloth for resale. Unions wanted absolute control over these cooperatives, but they apparently agreed to supervision by the state government proposed by the companies.[65] Cooperative stores opened near the Santa Rosa, Río Blanco, Mirafuentes, San Lorenzo, and Santa Gertrudis mills.[66]

Following the French example, the cooperative stores in 1922 formed a federation, the Sociedad Cooperativa de Consumo Obreros Federados (Consumption Cooperative Society of Federated Workers). In June 1924, the Sociedad Cooperativa opened a head office store in downtown Orizaba in a building donated by the Tenants' Union (Sindicato de Inquilinos). Workers from the Cervercería Moctezuma, la Constancia, Cocolapan, Cigarreros, Cerritos, Sta. Gertrudis, Sta. Rosa, Mirafuentes, San Lorenzo, Río Blanco, and Cervecería

Orizaba joined as members. The Santa Rosa union decided that all its members would automatically become shareholders.[67]

The cooperative stores sold groceries, crockery, clothes, and footwear, and those at Río Blanco and San Lorenzo also carried milk, bread, and meat.[68] Workers could buy goods on credit, and some did not repay their debts for months or even years.[69] Cooperative stores spread from Orizaba to other parts of the country. By 1927, they had become so important for labor unions that CROM decided at its eighth convention to create a Department of Cooperatives.[70] At least for some years, the cooperatives apparently achieved their objective to provide cheaper goods for workers. In 1929, *Pro-Paria* reported that private merchants had raised the prices of basic goods while the cooperative store in Río Blanco kept them lower and stable. The article suggested that soon afterward the private merchants lowered their prices again as a result of the competition by the cooperative store. The author concluded that "the cooperative stores, when managed, as they are now, by *compañeros* that are aware of the needs of working people, fulfill a high mission that benefits all."[71]

SCHOOLS

The shift from company to union power that took place in the Orizaba Valley also generated important changes in the provision of education in the region, which substantially increased and improved during the 1920s as a result of the direct participation of organized workers.

A prominent demand workers made in their letters to the press and later through their associations and unions was for better schools. By 1906, Santa Rosa had two small schools, each with only one teacher. The Josefa Ortiz de Domínguez school taught girls, and the Enrique C. Rébsamen school, maintained by the municipal government, served the boys. These schools did not have the capacity to provide basic education for all the children of Santa Rosa. The 1900 census counted 512 children between six and ten years of age and 309 children between eleven and fifteen years in the municipality.[72] Workers complained about the way the schools were run. A letter to *El Paladín* in 1908 suggested that the boys' school teacher, Mr. Ricaño, a former priest, taught the children only Catholic doctrine and how to sweep the floor. "Between nothing and Ricaño, nothing was always better," the letter stated.[73] His replacement, a "lyrical teacher," was no better, and by February 1908 the school had no teacher at all. Workers complained bitterly not least because from 1906 to 1908 the tax for public instruction increased from 0.13 to 0.39 pesos.[74]

Figure 2.2 Construction of the "Escuela América" financed by the Santa Rosa Workers' Union. Museo Comunitario de Ciudad Mendoza, Veracruz.

The citizens of Santa Rosa organized to improve their schools and reshaped the company town in the process. In 1909, Camerino Z. Mendoza, the owner of a local store and a future revolutionary leader, formed a Junta Patriótica to raise funds to construct new buildings for the two schools. That year, the schools taught the first to third grades of elementary school.[75] The government had no resources for schools, but companies did, and the communities pressured them to donate funds for education. In March 1913, the recently formed local board of elementary education (Junta de Instrucción Primaria) sent a letter to CIVSA asking for a monthly donation to support the Santa Rosa schools. CIVSA complied.[76] The CIDOSA Cerritos mill created the Escuela Mixta de Cerritos (Co-ed School of Cerritos) in 1914. The company had donated the premises for the school to the municipal government and paid the schoolteacher, one Natalia Rivera, 50 pesos a month. She charged parents 10 cents weekly per child to complement her wage.[77] Initially the school only went up to second grade, but in 1915 it added a third grade. That year, the school taught 48 children, a low figure considering that the Cerritos mill employed around 430 workers.[78]

CIDOSA did not establish elementary schools in its other mill towns, which all had municipal schools of the kind that existed in Santa Rosa. All CIDOSA did was to make material donations when the municipality made such requests. In Río Blanco, CIDOSA donated the land and helped with the construction of an ad hoc building for the school for boys and girls. It made the necessary repairs to this school as well as to the other municipal schools at no cost to the municipality.[79]

In the 1920s the unions took up the issue of education. In August 1922, the Santa Rosa union asked CIVSA to support building a school, but the company refused, with the argument that such assistance had to be channeled through the government.[80] CIVSA workers created the school nevertheless, named the Centro Obrero Primario Federal "Acción" (Federal Elementary School "Acción"). In 1923 it taught students in all six grades of elementary school. Initially the school had nine teachers apart from its director, Prof. Manuela Contreras de Carballo, who had come to the region as a member of a cultural mission during campaigns initiated by the federal minister of education, José Vasconcelos. The enthusiastic Prof. Carballo worked with the union's pro-school committee to realize the project. Funding came mostly from the union.[81]

In 1926, Prof. Contreras and the union's pro-school committee under the leadership of a weaver by the name of Acisclo Pérez started a campaign to build new premises for the Centro Obrero Primario Federal "Acción."[82] They bought a plot of land measuring over seven acres (28,452 square meters) and raised funds for the construction by charging Santa Rosa workers 0.5 percent of their weekly wages. The workers' contributions made up 73.3 percent of the school's total costs, while federal and state governments covered only 9.4 percent. Donations from local merchants contributed 7.4 percent, donations from other individuals 4.3 percent, and charity events (fairs, bullfights, baseball games, and musical and literary evenings) organized by the pro-school committee 3.1 percent. The rest came from other sources including fines imposed by the union on workers who did not attend night school.[83] The union organized groups of volunteer workers, who helped build the school for their children — a two-story building more spacious and beautiful than most public schools in Mexico today.[84]

In 1930, the Centro Primario Obrero Federal moved into the largely completed building under the name of Escuela América. Children received technical instruction in occupations such as blacksmithing, tinwork, mechanics, carpentry, ceramics, tailoring, and dressmaking. The school's workshops had excellent equipment, and their production was of an exceptional quality as evident in photographs from the yearly exhibitions.[85] In 1934, a junior high school (from seventh to ninth grade) opened on the same premises with a schedule designed to facilitate attendance by mill workers. It was a school for children during the day and became a school for workers in the evening.[86]

Night schools had been a long-standing workers' demand. In July 1907, workers from Santa Rosa petitioned the mill manager to establish a night school for the instruction of workers, which, they claimed, had been promised by the president of the Republic.[87] Workers kept making the demand, and between 1912 and 1916 several night schools opened in the Orizaba Valley. In 1912, one opened at the San Lorenzo mill in Nogales on the premises of the Miguel Hidalgo elementary day school.[88] The municipality reported to CIDOSA that attendance was greater than expected: seventy-five students were enrolled, and more were ready to join the program. By 1916, night schools had opened in Río Blanco and Santa Rosa.[89] In Río Blanco, the school had been an initiative of the union, the Sindicato de Obreros y Similares de Río Blanco (Union of Workers of Rio Blanco). It established the school in buildings that CIDOSA had previously rented out to *pulquerías*, taverns serving pulque — a fermented drink made from maguey juice. The unions saw this change from tavern to school as a powerful symbol of their fight for education, which empowered the workers, and against alcoholism, which they condemned as an oppressive vice.

Santa Rosa's union took a strong stand on workers' education. It believed that illiterate workers did a disservice to the union and that they should receive compulsory education. The pro-school committee fined workers who did not attend school daily and punished them with days of suspension from work.[90] In 1916, CIVSA estimated that it employed 200 illiterate workers at the mill and that 150 of them attended night school.[91] CIVSA paid part of the teachers' wages, provided a house to accommodate them, and supplied free electricity for the night school.[92] In 1928, the Santa Rosa night school for male workers had 245 students, and the night school for female workers had 30 students.[93]

By 1930 the mill towns of the Orizaba Valley had larger and better educational facilities than any other town of their size in the country. The educational opportunities available in the region were outstanding even when compared with those available in many of Mexico's largest cities during that period. This was the result of the way communities in the textile mills organized to obtain educational benefits and is closely related to the important role unions gained during the previous decades in the governance of those towns.

The study of Santa Rosa and Río Blanco from 1890 to 1930 illustrates the ways in which the growth of the textile industry in Mexico transformed urban space and the daily life of working families. Whereas in many other Latin American countries industrial manufacturing began in established cities, in Mexico factories and mills with company towns were a common feature. In a country with few suitable rivers, manufacturers moved their mills to remote locations in search of water power. The textile companies established themselves in places that were both physically and institutionally unoccupied, constructed urban infrastructure, provided housing and basic items of necessity, and assumed duties of the state such as keeping public order. In areas of established settlement, specialized private agents or the state would have assumed these responsibilities, but the relatively weak Mexican state could not expand its presence sufficiently fast to provide effective government in the Orizaba Valley.

During the Mexican Revolution the labor movement gained strength, and unions came to replace the company in the mill towns as provider of basic services. The political change that swept the municipal governments reinforced that change. Whereas before 1916 most municipal presidents had been white-collar employees loyal to the company, after 1916 most of them were blue-collar workers who had been chosen as candidates by union assemblies. The prominence of unions in the government of mill towns generally improved the workers' lot. Better housing and educational facilities as well as cheaper goods from consumer cooperatives made the lives of workers and their families more comfortable. Union initiatives led to the creation of new recreational facilities such as cinemas, theaters, and sports fields. Until the end of the 1920s, the state played a small role in the transformation of these communities. The municipal governments acted mostly as a means to carry out the union's goals rather than as an autonomous power.

The shift from company towns to union towns that took place in the Orizaba Valley from 1900 to 1930 was partly the result of the Mexican Revolution. However, it was also an important force that shaped the nature of the Mexican Revolution itself. Although the Mexican Revolution is generally understood as an agrarian revolution, industrial workers also played a relevant role in shaping its nature, as this chapter shows. The study of the evolution of industrial company towns from 1900 to 1930 provides an excellent vantage point from which to view the transformation in capital-labor relations that took place during the revolutionary decade and the radical labor laws and policies of the revolutionary and postrevolutionary governments. It allows us to better understand the evolution of Mexico's industrial capitalism during this period.

NOTES

1. Rafael Dobado, Aurora Gómez-Galvarriato, and Jeffrey Williamson, "Globalization, De-industrialization and Mexican Exceptionalism, 1750–1879," *Journal of Economic History* 68, no. 3 (2008): 1–53.

2. Estevan de Antuñano, *Obras: documentos para la historia de la industrialización en México, 1833–1846* (Mexico City: Secretaría de Hacienda y Crédito Público, 1979); Mario Trujillo, "La fábrica Magdalena Contreras (1836–1910)," in *Historia de las grandes empresas en México, 1850–1930*, ed. Carlos Marichal and Mario Cerutti (Mexico City: Fondo de Cultura Económica, 1997), 245–74.

3. Aurora Gómez-Galvarriato and Bernardo García Díaz, "La Manchester de México," in *Historia e imágenes de la industria textil mexicana*, ed. Leticia Gamboa Ojeda (Mexico City: Cámara de la Industria Textil de Puebla y Tlaxcala, 2000), 123–37.

4. Archivo de la Compañía Industrial Veracruzana (hereafter CV), Ciudad Mendoza, Veracruz, Actas de la Asamblea General (hereafter AAG), July 2, 1899.

5. Percentages are based on a sample of 625 weavers from 1906 to 1907.

6. CV, Actas del Consejo (hereafter AC), January 3, 1898, February 14, 1898, May 30, 1898, and April 2, 1900.

7. México, Dirección General de Estadística, *Censo y división territorial del Estado de Veracruz verificado el 28 de octubre de 1900* (Mexico City: Oficina tip. de la Secretaría de Fomento, 1901–6), 198–99; and Instituto Nacional de Geografía y Estadística, *Estadísticas históricas de México*, 2 vols. (Mexico City: INEGI, 1986), 90, 102.

8. Programa de Historia Oral, Proyecto Veracruz, PHO7, Interview with Concepción Andrade de Sarmiento and Gudelia Cebada by Olivia Domínguez Téllez, Río Blanco Veracruz, August 1975.

9. Archivo de la Compañía Industrial de Orizaba (hereafter CD), Río Blanco, Veracruz, Correspondence (hereafter CR), Cuestionario sobre trabajo, San Lorenzo, Cuestionario sobre trabajo, Río Blanco, Cuestionario sobre trabajo, Cocolapan, Cuestionario sobre trabajo, Cerritos, July 12, 1920.

10. Aurora Gómez-Galvarriato, "The Impact of Revolution: Business and Labor in the Mexican Textile Industry" (PhD diss., Harvard University, 1999).

11. Jeffrey Bortz, *Revolution within Revolution: Cotton Textile Workers and the Mexican Labor Regime* (Stanford: Stanford University Press, 2008).

12. CV, AC, July 4, 1898; Bernardo García Díaz, *Un pueblo fabril del porfiriato: Santa Rosa, Veracruz* (Ciudad Mendoza: FOMECA, 1997), 69.

13. CV, AC, September 5, 1898, January 15, 1900, February 6, 1899, September 18, 1899, February 16, 1903, April 15, 1907, December 1907; July 1, 1911; April 29, 1913; and March 23, 1920.

14. Ibid., June 7, 1897.

15. CV, AAG 1899, March 15, 1900.

16. CV, AC, May 22, 1897; CV, AAG 1906, April 2, 1907; CV, AC, October 24, 1906.

17. CV, AC, September 18, 1918.

18. Ibid., November 5, 1918.

19. Ibid., August 7, 1928; CV, AAG 1906, April 2, 1907; CV, AC, May 14, 1929, July 4, 1922, November 29, 1927; CV, October 15, 1929. The municipality paid the company back through deductions on municipal taxes on land and patents.

20. CD, CR, Manifestaciones de fincas urbanas a la Receptoría de Rentas del Edo. en Río Blanco, October 1, 1922, and October 15, 1926.

21. *El Paladín*, January 18, 1906, and February 6, 1906.

22. Delgado, "El sindicato de Santa Rosa," 40; Sindicato de Trabajadores en General de la Compañía Industrial Veracruzana S.A., "Bodas de Oro" (Ciudad Mendoza: Pro-Paria, 1965), 46, quoted in Delgado, "El Sindicato de Santa Rosa," 228; Bernardo García, *Textiles del Valle de Orizaba (1880–1925)* (Xalapa: Universidad Veracruzana, 1990), 144; Marjorie R. Clark, *Organized Labor in Mexico* (Chapel Hill: University of North Carolina Press, 1934), 193 and 229; CV, CR, CIVSA-CCP, December 5, 1916.

23. Programa de Historia Oral, Veracruz, Interview with Delfino Huerta by Ana Laura Delgado Rannauro, August 1975, Nogales, Veracruz.

24. CV, CR, CIVSA — Advisory Committee in Paris, December 5, 1916.

25. Ibid., July 28, 1917.

26. Ana Laura Delgado Rannauro, "El sindicato de Santa Rosa y el movimiento obrero de Orizaba, Veracruz" (BA thesis, Universidad Veracruzana, Xalapa, 1977), 85 and 89.

27. CV, AC, June 7, 1897, and February 21, 1898.

28. CV, Lista de Trabajadores; CV, AC, September 7, 1904, July 10, 1905, and July 17, 1905.

29. For example, M. Diez y Cia, the owner of the "Rio Blanco" and "El Fenix" stores, owned several wooden living quarters for workers close to Santa Rosa from 1907 to 1922. CV, AC, July 25, 1922.

30. Andrew G. Wood, "¡Viva la Revolución Social! Postrevolutionary Tenant Protest and State Housing Reform in Veracruz, Mexico," in *Cities of Hope: People, Protests, and Progress in Urbanizing Latin America, 1870–1930*, ed. Ronn Pineo and James A. Baer (Boulder, Colo.: Westview Press, 1998), 91.

31. U.S. Department of Commerce and Labor, Bureau of Manufactures, *Cotton Goods in Latin America*, by William A. G. Clark, Part 1 (Washington, D.C.: Government Printing Office, 1909), 26.

32. CV, AAG 1906, April 2, 1907; CV, AC, November 8, 1910; CV, AAG 1911, April 9, 1912.

33. CV, AC, April 6, 1920; CD, CR, Rio Blanco (hereafter RB) to Mexico City offices (hereafter MX), May 2, 1924.

34. "Ley del trabajo del Estado Libre y Soberano de Veracruz-Llave," January 14, 1918, in Gobierno Constitucional del Estado de Veracruz-Llave, *Colección de leyes, decretos y circulares año de 1918)* (Orizaba: Edo. de Veracruz, 1918); CD, CR, RB to Francisco V. Lara, January 24, 1918.

35. CV, AC, November 14, 1917, and March 23, 1920; CV, AAG 1924, June 7, 1924.

36. García, *Un pueblo*, 83. The description of the houses is based on an on-site observation of the surviving houses. Originally, there were 324 homogeneous brick houses arranged in twenty-two rows.

37. Interview with José Carrasco Abrego, Santa Rosa, Veracruz, June 8, 1998.

38. Bernardo García Díaz, "La escuela Esfuerzo Obrero," *Cuadernos del Museo Comunitario de Ciudad Mendoza*, no. 1 (1998).

39. CD, CR, Fraccionamiento del terreno Barrio Motzorongo, January 1923. The second sale was noted in the public registry on August 12, 1925. CD, CR, Manifestación, CIDOSA makes of mortgages it holds in Rio Blanco, Nogales, and Santa Rosa, January 31, 1930.

40. CD, CR, RB, Resident Payments (*colono* payment) 1927–28 and rent of RB houses and commercial property 1927–29.

41. CV, AC, September 4, 1928.

42. CD, CR, *Gaceta Oficial*, 28, March 6, 1923; CD, CR, Ramón Carrillo E. to RB CIDOSA, March 7, 1923, March 18, 1923, RB to Ramón Carrillo E., April 18, 1923, RB to Ramón Carrillo E., May 9, 1923, RB to Ramón Carrillo E., October 27, 1923, and Ramón Carrillo E. to RB CIDOSA, October 29, 1923.

43. Wood, "¡Viva la Revolución Social!" 115.

44. CD, CR, RB to RB Márquez, May 16, 1924, Ramón Carrillo E. to CIDOSA MX, May 18, 1924, and CIDOSA MX to Ramón Carrillo E., May 19, 1924.

45. CV, AC, January 2, 1897.

46. Jiménez built the tramway line with a credit from CIVSA ($5000), which he paid back in reduced freight rates. CV, Actas del Consejo, April 21, 1897.

47. CV, Caja Santa Rosa, 1900–1918.

48. CD, CR, A. Reynaud to Río Blanco, several letters; CV, CR, Mexico City—Santa Rosa, August 30, 1910.

49. *El Paladín*, May 16, 1907; Accounts by Alberto Lara Rojano and Ernesto Casillas Rojas, Centro de Estudios Históricos y Sociales del Movimiento Obrero (CEHSMO; Center of Historical and Social Studies of the Labor Movement) oral history project, *Historia obrera* 2, no. 6 (September 1975): 33–34.

50. García, *Un pueblo*, 67.

51. Víctor Garcín had been in the region for several decades since 1897. Eduardo Garcín, his brother, was the CIDOSA manager in 1903 and a member of the CIDOSA board in 1905 and 1906. CV, AC, February 25, 1897, October 25, 1897; CD, Asamblea General Ordinaria, March 23, 1905, March 22, 1907, April 3, 1908; Banamex Archive, R.G. Dunn & Co. private reports from August 28, 1899, to January 11, 1904, 97.

52. *El Paladín*, May 16, 1907.

53. Ibid., February 13, 1908, April 5, 1908, and May 7, 1908.

54. Rodney Anderson, *Outcasts in Their Own Land: Mexican Industrial Workers, 1906–1911* (Dekalb: Northern Illinois University Press, 1976), 157–69.

55. Patrice Gouy, *Pérégrinations des "Barcelonnettes" au Mexique* (Grenoble: Presses Universitaires de Grenoble, 1980), 63.

56. CV, CR, Mexico City — Santa Rosa, January 12, 1907.

57. Ibid., Mexico City — Santa Rosa, August 30, 1910.

58. CV, Caja Santa Rosa.

59. CV, AC, April 8, 1907, May 24, 1908.

60. Archivo General de la Nación (AGN), Departamento del Trabajo (DT), 15/11.

61. Felipe Remolina Roqueñi, *El Artículo 123* (Mexico City: Ed. Del V Congreso Iberoamericano del Trabajo, 1974), 69–70.

62. Gobierno de Veracruz, *Colección de Leyes y Decretos año de 1918*, 189, 194.

63. Archivo General del Estado de Veracruz (AGEV) Caja 99, Exp. 70, 1915 Cocolapan. Carta de Pedro Baroja, Nicolás Jiménez y Gumersindo Soriano, al Ciudadano Gobernador y Comandante Militar del Estado de Veracruz, Sr. Agustín A. Millán, December 25, 1915.

64. CV, AC, November 23, 1920.

65. CV, CR, letter from C. Maurel to Santa Rosa (hereafter SR), November 10, 1920; and CV, AC, January 4, 1921.

66. In 1928 there were seven cooperative stores in the Orizaba Valley. *Pro-Paria*, special ed., January 7, 1928, with photographs of all the stores.

67. *Pro-Paria*, July 5, 1924.

68. Ibid., September 23, 1931, 4. Advertisement of the Cooperativa "Obreros Federados"; *Pro-Paria*, August 10, 1929, 8, and March 30, 1929.

69. *Pro-Paria*, "Proyecto para la Reorganización de la Cooperativa O. Federados," January 27, 1928, 7.

70. Ibid., "Creación del Departamento de Cooperativas de la CROM," December 30, 1927. Workers in Orizaba textile mills affiliated with the CROM, the most powerful confederation in the 1920s.

71. *Pro-Paria*, "Demostración práctica de los beneficios que trae el cooperativismo," March 16, 1929.

72. Censo y División Territorial del Edo. de Veracruz verificados en 1900, 116–17.

73. *El Paladín*, February 2, 1908. The letter took the form of a satirical poem signed by "Melchor, Gaspar and Balthasar," a reminder that workers had been killed on January 7, the day after Three Kings Day.

74. Ibid., February 9, 1908.

75. Delgado, "El Sindicato de Santa Rosa," 76.

76. CV, AC, March 4, 1913.

77. CD, CR, MX to RB, August 16, 1923; CD, CR, Natalia Rivera to RB, May 4, 1915.

78. CD, CR, Natalia Rivera, Cerritos, to José Reynaud, RB, January 21, 1915, Durán RB to Natalia Rivera, February 11, 1915, Natalia Rivera to José Reynaud, February 17, 1915; CD, Cuestionario de Salarios, August 1921.

79. CD, CR, MX to RB, August 16, 1923.

80. CV, AC, August 29, 1922.

81. Delgado, "El sindicato de Santa Rosa," 80–81; García, "La escuela," 13; Archivo del Sindicato de Santa Rosa, CR, Elliezer Ollivier to the Sindicato de Santa Rosa, March 20, 1926, cited in García, "La escuela," 10.

82. Acisclo Pérez Servín had been a textile worker since childhood. He joined the Ejército Libertador del Sur led by Emiliano Zapata and returned in 1919 to work as a weaver in CIVSA. He was municipal president of Santa Rosa from 1922 to 1923 and president of the pro-school committee of the Santa Rosa's union from its inception. García, "La escuela," 11–16.

83. Ibid., 11–17.

84. Delgado, "El sindicato de Santa Rosa," 85.

85. Ibid., 20.

86. García, "La escuela," 19–20.

87. *El Paladín*, July 7, 1907.

88. CD, CR, Fco G. Vazquez, head of the Comisión de Instrucción Pública in Nogales to E. Ropiot, Administrator of San Lorenzo, January 3, 1912, and San Lorenzo to Ayuntamiento de Nogales, January 4, 1912. In March they insisted that CIDOSA charge the tax for instruction; again the factory answered that they could not charge any tax in their factories; CD, CR, Río Blanco to Romero, March 4, 1912.

89. Ibid., Avelino Bolaños, Consejero de Instituciones para Escolares, Veracruz to Río Blanco, San Lorenzo, Cerritos and Cocolapan, January 13, 1916.

90. Delgado, "El sindicato de Santa Rosa," 78–79.

91. CD, CR, CIVSA to CIDOSA, 4 February 1916.

92. Ibid., Ezequiel Pérez Palacios to RB Administrator, September 4, 1918. Ezequiel Pérez Palacios to RB Administrator, October 2, 1918, and RB Municipal President to Spitalier, October 15, 1918. Ezequiel Pérez Palacios, to Pedro Durán, January 3, 1919; CV, AC, July 30, 1918.

93. Archivo del Sindicato del Santa Rosa, folio 800, January 3, 1928, quoted by Delgado, "El sindicato de Santa Rosa," 121.

CHAPTER THREE

The Port and the City of Santos

A Century-Long Duality

FERNANDO TEIXEIRA DA SILVA

> The port is the driving force of this city. The city will die if one
> day the port dies. It dies, and there will be nothing else.
> —*Interview with B, former employee of the port administration*

On the eve of World War I, the city of Santos was known as the "Brazilian
Barcelona" because of the uncontested hegemony of anarchists in the local labor
movement. Between World War II and the military coup in 1964, Santos became
known as the "Brazilian Moscow" and its harbor as the "Red Port" because of
the strong presence of Communists in unions and the city's politics. The port
workers took pride in these epithets. They were the bedrock of Santos's working
class with an emblematic influence on national politics. The special connection
between port and city played an important role in the emergence of this strong
labor movement between the end of the nineteenth century and the 1960s. The
monopoly power and intransigence of the Companhia Docas de Santos (CDS;
Santos Docks Company), in control of most port operations, strengthened the
ties of solidarity among the workers and gained support for their strike movements among the people of Santos. The employees of CDS, and in particular the
stevedores, forged a culture of work that shaped city life and allowed for the
creation of institutions to unite different categories of workers.[1]

The Santos Docks Company determined the economic fate of the city, but
Santos was no classic company town. It was neither a planned community nor
in an isolated location. The company never introduced the paternalist welfare
programs so characteristic of company towns, in which the community appears as an appendix to the company. Santos was never — strictly speaking —

a single-industry town with a "system of domination" powerful enough to control the workers' social relations both in the port and the urban space beyond. Still, Santos is best understood as a city dependent on one industry, as its local economy and its labor market were a function of the port. The economic power relations in Santos thus resembled those of classic company towns, but the city's history of urban development did not. The case of Santos highlights that the classic company town constitutes an extreme form of an urbanity where the economic power relations between a dominant company and its workers shape social life.

Since the late nineteenth century, the Santos Docks Company pressured the city and its people to submit to the logic of the port as a capitalist enterprise. It tried to gain control over all loading and unloading operations and to "immobilize" the labor force by eliminating casual work, hoping to make port operations more efficient. The company's strategy violated the workers' sense of freedom and independence, their notion that they were "workers without bosses" for lack of a permanent employment relationship. The company portrayed casual labor as the cause for the workers' uprootedness and their supposed disregard for social institutions such as family, regular work, and a steady home. It blamed casual work for moral ills such as a lack of discipline, urban violence, alcoholism, and worker radicalism. Thus, the fight against casual work had a moral dimension, even if the Santos Docks Company did not pursue a broader agenda of moral reforms.[2] If successful, the company's campaign to eliminate casual work would have diminished the daily presence of the port workers in the city. The workers resisted this attack on their independence, however, and the stevedores in particular maintained a strong presence in the urban space that connected house, street, and port.

THE PORT AND THE CITY

Santos was eminently a port city with characteristics unlike most cities historians of labor have studied closely. Even more than for other Brazilian coastal cities, the Santos port was the engine of the local economy and its principal source of employment. Maritime commerce shaped the urban, economic, and demographic development of the city since the late nineteenth century. Santos had few large factories and some smaller industrial firms in food processing and civil construction. They produced for a city in rapid expansion whose economy closely followed the impulses from the port.[3] From 1850 onward, the extraordinary advance of coffee cultivation in the interior of São Paulo integrated the port into the world economy, turning it into a key element of the agro-export trade. To reduce costs and speed up the transport of coffee, the British-owned São Paulo Railway Company built a line from Santos to Jundiaí, inaugurated in 1867, which handled most shipments from the plateau.[4]

In 1888, Brazil's imperial government had contracted a company to oversee and carry out the construction of a modern port. Two of the company's directors, Cândido Gaffreé and Eduardo Guinle, subsequently incorporated it as a joint-stock company: the Santos Docks Company.[5] The Company, as it came to be known, retained control of the port and would shape the city's economic fortunes until 1980. The creation of the modern port and the arrival of the railway triggered investments in urban infrastructure and accelerated the growth of the city. Its urban design and architecture changed rapidly, driven by the interests of agro-export capital, which turned the city into a commercial center.[6] By the 1920s, Santos had become the most important port in the country, both in volume and value of goods shipped.

Santos experienced a demographic explosion during the initial economic boom. The population tripled between 1890 and 1900 and doubled again by 1920 to reach 102,589.[7] Santos was by then the second-largest city in the state of São Paulo.[8] Mass immigration in the late nineteenth and early twentieth centuries created an ethnically heterogeneous population. In 1913, no less than 42.5 percent of Santos's inhabitants were foreign-born. The main "foreign colonies" were Portuguese, Spanish, and Italian. The "whitening" by immigration depressed the share of blacks: 86.8 percent of the population was categorized as "white."[9] The unsanitary conditions in a city with a fast-expanding population led to epidemics and an elevated death toll. More than 27,000 people died in the 1890s alone, and many others fled the city.[10] The state government responded with sanitation policies that redrew the urban map. Its main project, the creation of drainage canals, opened up new land for settlement and connected both the port area and the city center with the beaches in-between.[11]

Santos became divided into three major zones: the port, the commercial center, and the oceanfront.[12] The development of the railroad, the modernization of the port, and urban improvements triggered a new type of land use. In the first phase of Santos's urban expansion, the population occupied primarily lots in the city center in an area adjacent to the port. Dockers and other workers commonly lived in tenement houses. There were 771 of them by 1890, but they were torn down not long thereafter.[13] The city center, meanwhile, could no longer sustain the demographic growth. The rich moved to the oceanfront, where they built stately art-nouveau mansions. Residences in the center made way for commercial establishments, and after 1880, many of the former inhabitants moved to new neighborhoods such as Vila Macuco and Vila Matias, which had the highest concentration of workers in the city. By the mid-1930s, the city stretched from the hills to the beaches: 60 percent of the municipality's land area was settled.[14] Population growth, tourism, and the economic diversification of the region led to the reordering of the city starting in the 1940s and 1950s. The mansions on the boulevards near the beach made room for highrises. Neighborhoods such as Macuco, Vila Belmiro, and Campo Grande attracted a growing middle class but still remained home to many workers. The lowland and the hills surrounding the city center became densely populated working-class neighborhoods, with high concentrations of migrants — from the Northeast and Minas Gerais — who had found employment in the port.[15]

The period before the 1930s established the city's economic characteristics. The port was the engine of the local economy and accounted for the largest share of the local labor market. In 1913, with about 90,000 inhabitants, the economically active population stood at 37,179, with 22.7 percent working in the port as longshoremen, stevedores, carters, porters, and coffee sackers. That share rose to 32 percent in 1920. Port workers were the largest contingent in the city, together with workers employed in urban services and construction. The census for 1940 indicates that the sector of "transport, communications, and warehousing" retained the greatest share in the labor market.[16] The urban and industrial expansion of São Paulo after 1940 changed the Santos region. The presence of a broader range of companies producing consumer goods in neighboring municipalities led to a diversification of the regional industrial geography. Urban development and demographic change also led to an expansion of local transport, communication, and service sector jobs. The value of industrial manufacturing in Santos, however, remained low. In the 1960s, it accounted for only 1 percent of the overall production in the state of São Paulo.[17] By 1970, the port was more dominant than ever: it provided direct or indirect employment for 56,136 people, or 45.1 percent of all workers.[18]

"DOCKOPOLIS"

The relationship between a city and its port depended above all on the organization of the latter. Port administration could be decentralized or centralized, private or public, and the particular institutional arrangement largely determined the linkages between the economy of the port and local urban development. The port's institutional arrangement also configured the local labor market. Work could be casual or permanent. Gang work, union control over hiring under the closed shop, and the self-organization of loading and unloading operations characterized the port as an industry. Most of the work was not structured by the rhythm of a machine, and neither the cargo nor the dimensions of the ships were standardized. The efficiency of work depended in large part on the skill of the workers. Work in groups allowed for regular conversations, which enabled workers to resist exploitation and the whims of the foreman. The pressure on the shipowners to have their vessels leave the port quickly made time the workers' most precious ally. Their most effective weapons were brief stoppages or the slowing down of work, which forced the employers into negotiations in order to speed up the departure of the vessel.

Port administrators everywhere tried to streamline operations by eliminating casual work. They blamed the casual nature of work for a bad work ethic, but their real goal was to undermine the bargaining power enjoyed by casual workers. Such efforts ran up against the power of the intermediaries, however, who controlled the hiring — the most delicate aspect of this industry.[19] The demand for labor fluctuated with the intermittent arrival of ships, and their owners rarely employed the workers directly because it was too costly to maintain a permanent contingent in every city where their vessels called. The owners adopted a practice of hiring through intermediate firms, shipping companies, or import-export houses, which explains the physical and institutional dispersion of units in most ports. This lack of a central agency conspired against the formation of a permanent workforce.[20] It was the intermediaries who built close relationships with the workers, marked by mutual trust, by favoritism, by political loyalties, or by relations of friendship or kin. Control over hiring gave the intermediaries considerable power in this "system of fluid boundaries," since they decided who could work, for how long, and under what conditions.[21] Systematic "decasualization" began only after World War II.[22] The workers opposed more regular work arrangements because they feared an elimination of jobs and resented being subject to only one or very few contracting firms.

The Santos Docks Company, however, aimed to monopolize control over all loading and unloading operations in the first decade of the twentieth century, an atypical organization of work that would have transformed the port into an integrated and centralized complex, giving the CDS control over hiring and further strengthening its already dominant position in the city. Such centralization required large-scale investments and carried tremendous financial risks for a private company, but protection by the state aided private initiative in the case of Santos.[23] The Company benefited greatly from land expropriations and tax exemptions. It occupied all the waterfront lands that enclosed the developed urban area to the north and east of the city, effectively controlling the access from the city to the shore at the expense of local interests.[24] For over a century, the municipality had no authority over the port and could not even levy property taxes. As early as 1892, the Company's capitalization equaled "the combined capitalizations of the seventeen largest industrial companies in Rio de Janeiro and São Paulo."[25]

In the early twentieth century, the local press coined the terms "Dockopolis" and "Octopus" to evoke the Company's tentacles in the life of the city. Guilherme Guinle, CDS director, commented with notable frankness in 1926 on the "difficult relations that exist between the port and the city: [The] latter must adapt to the requirements of the former and often that adaptation comes at great sacrifice, be it for the municipal coffers, be it for who bears the expenses of port construction, not to mention the series of losses, every one of them small, but accumulating in number, that individuals suffer who are forced to move, at great inconvenience, and then they too have to undergo the necessary adaptation to the situation that the development of the port has created for them."[26] Inside the port the Company took advantage of labor conflicts to strengthen its position. After the general strike in 1891, CDS gained the upper hand in a dispute with the export houses over the control of coffee transport and obtained exclusive rights to handle both imported goods and those destined for export, giving it full control over the gangs of porters. During the violent general strike in 1897, the Company "triumphed in that battle against its rivals [the export houses] and turned them into its customers; there were no longer any independent warehouses after the 1897 strike. All trade went through customs on the docks."[27]

After these initial successes, CDS expanded its tentacles into ship maintenance, electrical generating, and warehousing, and it operated its own railway around the docks. In 1908, it began to perform all transport services for coffee inside the port, thereby excluding the carters and coffee sackers.[28] In competition with owners of wagons and general warehouses, CDS offered transport and warehousing services beyond the docks, attracting those who "resort to the Docks Company because they discover the advantages of its rates."[29] The Company held power over workers in loading and unloading gangs as well as warehousing, crane operators, railway yardmen, foremen, locomotive engineers, firemen, and sailors for harbor vessels. It also employed workers in mechanical and electrical maintenance and in the paint shop, as well as brick masons and helpers, office staff, guards, and inspectors. After the strike for the eight-hour day, in 1908, only the stevedores — who worked inside the ships and were the most powerful category — escaped the absorption of their services. The situation in Santos was thus very different from decentralized ports with fragmented control over operations. The Company maintained a permanent body of workers, which enabled it to impose work discipline more effectively.[30]

Of the six strikes between 1889 and 1912, only the one in 1889 brought results that were fully satisfactory for the workers. In the other shutdowns, CDS adopted a hard line, hired scabs, and called on the police. In the 1891 strike, for example, it used ex-slaves — who had fled to the city in the last years of bondage — as scabs.[31] The export houses and the Company portrayed the struggle between strikers and scabs as expression of the immigrants' "racial prejudice," but the issue was in fact the chronic problem of an industrial reserve army.[32] In July 1917, during a massive general strike in the city of São Paulo, CDS requested that the minister of the navy dispatch warships as a preemptive measure. He complied promptly.[33] Yet another example of the Company's extraordinary power to demobilize labor occurred during the longest shutdown of the port (sixty-seven days) in 1920. In an operation that Afonso Schmidt called a "man hunt," the Company used its packing houses and warehouses as prisons for workers and had them "tied up like dogs."[34] To break the strike CDS hired more than two thousand new workers, the majority of them brought in from Rio de Janeiro. These workers were employed at much lower pay and subjected to terrible abuses.[35]

The Company imposed ironclad discipline. One important means of control was the gang foremen, who displayed a perverse kind of distrust toward workers. In the words of one former docker: "they watched us even when we went to the bathroom: they were afraid that someone would be eating fruits [*chupar fruta*]." In the washrooms the Company had installed a humiliating device, which "released the water from the tank flushing the toilet after a preset time," drenching its user.[36] The foremen cultivated a reputation for toughness and boasted symbols of manliness in ritualized "games" to reaffirm their masculinity. They used physical confrontation, verbal abuse, and intimidating gestures to establish distinctions between competence and ineptness, strength and weakness, man and woman.[37] The division of the port in sections, with varying pay and conditions of work, served to distinguish "good" from "bad" workers, "newcomers" from "old hands," the "hard-working" from the "backsliders." The newcomers and the "backsliders," for example, were sent to the sixth section, where the work was harder and unhealthy.[38]

The nature of the work imposed limits, however, on the Company's attempt to organize the port like a factory and establish even more pervasive control of labor. The dockers who worked in loading and unloading on land were divided into gangs that rendered services specific to the type of good, the layout of the port, and the available means of transport. This was what Marx called "simple cooperation," an organization of work in which workers carry out their tasks concurrently, in one or several interconnected production processes. The technical division of labor imposed by machines played a subordinate role, notwithstanding the fact that the port required large capital investments. In the lifting of a load, social power brought itself to bear in the simultaneous action of many arms in an operation with a very limited division of labor. The social contact caused an "emulation and a stimulation of *animal spirits*" but also led to the group exercising control over behavior.[39]

The workers' roles in the gangs in effect implied familiarity and a set of expectations vis-à-vis fellow workers with respect to keeping one's job, family life, alcoholism, and so on. These expectations were one of the many forms of brotherhood in everyday life on the docks. The workers expected their coworkers to carry out their tasks to the best of their ability. A man who brought to the port his share of energy, experience, and ingenuity demonstrated his sense of community, making the work less difficult and dangerous for all involved. Thereby work thought of as harsh and degrading could become "a morally creative experience," forming "small cooperative societies."[40] In the words of a former docker, "this is something interesting about the work in gangs; there is always an affinity among the members of the gang. . . . Just imagine that these men, working together for a long time, begin to have feelings of friendship towards each other. Taking into account the harsh nature of the work and the rigid supervision by the foremen, one understands why these bonds would only grow stronger."[41]

The nature of work, the vast distances inside the port, and the resulting sense of anonymity fostered the formation of informal groups, creating links that were crucial for the survival of the workers and served as an apprenticeship for secret forms of resistance: "lift it this way, waste time, work slowly, there is the boss and here is where we hide."[42] According to a former longshoreman, "the older ones had great experience on the job, and we are also warier. One would say to the other: 'careful, don't do it like that' — and he wouldn't do it. We helped each other, taught each other, and handled the goods in a way so that nobody would get hurt."[43] And it is true that the likelihood of accidents was smaller among those working full-time compared to casual labor.[44] The workers also drew on personal and familiar ties, not least in the hiring process, building multiple loyalties and traditions of work passed on from generation to generation. A former employee of CDS recalled that "we ha[d] entire lineages in here: grandfather, great-grandfather, son, grandson."[45] Some of these lineages came with a tradition of militancy and union struggles.[46]

The networks of relations reinforced actions that served as protection against the hostility of the foremen. One way was to exploit their tolerance with respect to an everyday aspect of work in the port: jokes. According to the recollections of Celso de Lima, "a spirit of humor that borders on insult was a fixture among these workers. . . . Nobody escaped having a nickname, often mocking:

workers, foremen, warehouse managers, and so on. The nicknames bordered on insult: Cara-de-Gato [catface], Cabeça-de-Cavalo [horse-faced], Mãos-de-Vaca [hoof-handed], Cabeção [bighead]."[47] He remembered the jokes as "very daring" because they often targeted foremen. As they had witnessed these "improper" games as workers, or even participated in them, however, foremen usually handled such provocations well. These games were part of a language particular to the port, in which collegiality found expression in obscene gestures, friendly insults, and offensive nicknames that created a sense of unity among port workers and set them apart from a hostile outside world that saw them as men of low reputation.[48] The Company accepted the humor and the talk as ways to make the conditions of work bearable, with benefits for the work flow.

This tolerance by the bosses extended to other, more dangerous liberties, such as small-scale pilfering. Customs guards held watch at the cold storage rooms on the docks and would not let the workers out of their sight "even for one minute." The guards themselves, however, "hid bags underneath their characteristic wide blue overcoats that they filled with fruits, and only the best. They freely entered the cold chambers; very well-behaved, they told us: 'you can eat as much as you want, but watch out for your foremen. Just don't cause us difficulties.'"[49] Collusion, veiled support, and surreptitious participation in petty theft were a part of the social relations that resulted in reciprocities, mutual protection, and the exchange of favors among the workers. Between vigilance and tolerance, the workers created means for increasing their earnings. In the words of one former docker, "the port workers were not considered to be thieves, but rather 'untighteners.' . . . They were tight on money and went out to sell something. This was even a joke amongst us: 'you are untightening, right?' There was no stealing. He was 'untightening'!"[50] Thus, when they were "tight" for money, they would create an informal, parallel economy of stolen goods, giving them some income beyond their wages.[51]

But these small transgressions were not always sufficient to deal with issues of control and discipline. Tensions were often "resolved" by physical aggression, and they could take the form of denunciations and demands in the public sphere, thus placing limits on arbitrary power. The workers' pressure in assemblies made the foremen leave the port workers union, in 1959, since "any demand by the foremen that was brought up at the union would be rejected by the workers in the loading and unloading gangs."[52] Many foremen did not think of themselves as "workers," but rather as a distinct group and part of the administrative staff. Faced with the polarity of identities, "us-them," a divide emerged at the level of union representation. A "great majority of workers in the assemblies believed that it was not right that the foremen, who had come from the workers' midst, then forgot their origins and began to act in the name of the administration once they had moved on to the other side."[53]

Personal affinities, everyday acts of solidarity, and the informal communication networks created promising terrain for collective action, such as a shutdown of work in the entire port, sometimes without any previous organization or officially formulated demands. Irregularities at work could quickly lead a gang to stop working; on other occasions, informed by word of mouth, all the workers would act in solidarity with a movement that had begun in isolation; in some cases, militants who traveled all over the port forced the shutdown. Informal channels of communication functioned in defiance of supervisors who tried to stamp them out. The port workers created a sense of unity, represented in machine metaphors: "a functioning machine ordinarily counts on parts of the most diverse variations and functions. However, when only one of these parts jams, the others will consequently jam as well, and the machine comes to an immediate halt. With us, it is the same thing. If one group of workers stops work because a just demand has not been attended to, even though that category of workers has only 100 members, the other seven or eight thousand workers should join [the stoppage], and that is how the machine in our unit will never get jammed again."[54]

Over the course of the port's history, there were numerous episodes that demonstrated this kind of support among different groups of workers. Even in the absence of open demonstrations of solidarity, the synchronized nature of the work process usually made it possible to bring all operations to a halt, above all when the stoppage occurred in one of the main loading sectors, stevedoring (on the ship) or unloading on the dock (on land). There the workers found themselves in permanent physical proximity and a relation of absolute interdependence. It is not by accident that stevedores and longshoremen were the main targets of the Company, which sought, in a first step, to absorb the stevedores and then to eliminate the distinctions between the two occupations.[55]

WORKERS WITHOUT BOSSES

CDS tried to weaken the labor movement in Santos by submitting the stevedores to company norms, but they resisted that effort. The casual nature of the work shaped the stevedores' trade culture, habits, and beliefs, and they showed little interest in regular employment.[56] Greater independence compensated for the disadvantages of casual employment, such as unstable pay. They did not experience their work as routine or monotonous because of the variation in ships and cargo, the fluctuation of trade volume, the mobility between different occupations, the regular breaks from work, and not least the back and forth between home, the streets, and the docks. Since they worked for different companies, they did not identify their trade with any one firm, and their allegiance was instead to the trade itself. The lack of a boss was a source of pride and of an acute sense of freedom: "I enjoyed the freedom to say: 'look, I don't want to work [today],' and I didn't go. . . . I did not go to work, I had no obligations, and I did not have a boss. I knew that I would then have to work hard to make up for what I had lost, but I thought that it was a nice freedom, and I liked it."[57]

The Company, however, did not like it. The work of the stevedores was the only part of port operations that it failed to control. In the early twentieth century, stevedores worked for master stevedores, who subcontracted the service from the shipping companies and the export houses. In the 1910s, CDS undercut the "unconnected" stevedores during strikes by organizing its own gangs of stevedores who offered services to shipping companies at "more favorable prices."[58] The stevedores fought for the control of the labor market, however, and scored a partial victory. In the 1920s, many shipping companies still preferred independent and unionized stevedores, which led more than half of the Company stevedores to "desert the docks in search of better-paid work."[59] From 1930 on, the union held absolute control over the labor market after eliminating the Company as competition. It was in part a political victory. After the "Revolution of 1930," the union forged an alliance with the *tenentistas*, a faction of the government, championing corporatist unions and in support of the closed shop. What the Communist stevedore leader Oswaldo called the "the miracle of solidarity" also played a decisive role.[60] The Company's stevedoring employees refused to work in a show of solidarity with the stevedores. CDS would never again get to hire stevedores. Its director, Guilherme Guinle, lamented that stevedoring no longer "had a unified command." He believed that the stevedores union "subverted the natural order of things" because it placed itself "in the position of the shipowners' obligatory agent. The union thereby exercised a function of the employer, which is fundamentally wrong."[61]

The union monitored how the work was carried out and effectively assumed control over the work process. The new work rules reshaped power relations in a way that resembled the efforts of skilled workers in other industries to control the organization of production. The lament of Rio de Janeiro's port superintendent pointed to the source of the stevedores' power: it resided in "the nature of the task, which is pressing and must be completed in the short term, under the threat of severe losses for the shipowner, who is dealing with workers who are not subject to the norms of work discipline that prevail in factories, shops, etc., and who has no power to oppose the unjust and improper demands; either he accepts them, or he incurs even greater losses because of the delays for his ship in port."[62] The stevedores imposed and negotiated lasting rules to regulate hiring and work inside the ships, which reduced the power of the bosses.

The stevedores further expanded their power in a series of surprisingly long-lived victories over the Company. One of the most important, besides the closed shop, was the organization of work by turns in order to distribute employment opportunities equitably among all unionized stevedores, a regime that came into force after World War II. It eliminated the favoritism that had privileged a minority to the detriment of the majority in the daily hiring of workers. In 1956, the Brazilian Senate approved a law that instituted the system of turns for the general foremen. The representatives of the shipowners lost the privilege of selecting preferred candidates, and the stevedores came to perform these duties on a rotating basis for sixty days at a time, which gave everybody the opportunity to earn the higher foremen pay.[63] The implementation of the system of turns reinforced the pride of "not having a boss," since the stevedores could simultaneously be workers, inspectors for the union, and foremen.

Militancy was important to ensure that the clauses of the union contracts were upheld. Every stevedore had the right to serve as foreman for sixty days, but the union established firm rules of conduct. The foreman had to show respect for the coworkers, control alcoholism, and be responsible for "good performance" at work. The stevedores had a strong incentive to fulfill these duties to the best of their ability to defend the favorable conditions of work.[64] Many of the stevedores' victories were the result of the actions of the Communists. Without getting into the details of the remarkable role the Partido Comunista do Brasil (PCB; Communist Party of Brazil) played in the port from 1945 and 1964, it is worth noting that the party enjoyed its greatest support in Santos among the stevedores.[65] The Communists understood the workers' everyday life experiences and displayed an extraordinary capacity to organize and "extract rights." It was up to them to "pacify stevedoring," which meant creating political, contractual, and institutional mechanisms that allowed for a more equitable distribution of employment opportunities and pay in the postwar period. That created conflict with some union directorates, which had — by means of favoritism and intimidation — perpetuated their control to the detriment of the rank-and-file.

THE PORT WORKERS IN THE CITY

The stevedores fostered a culture of solidarity in Santos, which found expression in several labor movements that garnered wide attention and had a significant impact on national politics between the 1950s and the military coup in 1964. The mobility of these workers, on the docks and beyond, was the key ingredient for closer ties between port and city, and it shaped the urban characteristics of Santos as well as the port workers' place in the urban space and its culture. The casual nature of work shaped the interaction between port and city. Neighborhoods close to the harbor saw a heavy concentration of dock workers, who could get to work quickly and without transportation costs, which to an extent made up for comparatively poor housing conditions. In the absence of a formal system of information about the need for workers in particular locations, the information spread in taverns or through neighbors and kin, effectively constituting a type of informal Port Gazette.[66] Those who lived further away from the port had to wait for work near the docks, where employment would be offered several times a day. Those not contracted would wander around the docks or await another opportunity for work in the bars near the port. In the 1930s, the Café Evaristo in the city center "was always the stevedores' preferred hangout," a "practically free territory," the meeting spot for union leaders and a place to settle disagreements in fistfights or even shootouts.[67] The bars were not simply spaces of licentiousness but functioned rather as "social clubs for working men" where they could relax and seek refuge.[68]

This suggests that the case of Santos does not fit the "theory of the isolated masses," which posits that the geographic and social isolation of certain categories of workers, such as miners, port workers, and sailors, forges a "worker subculture."[69] The Santos port and the port workers were not separated from the rest of the city. The financial and commercial center of the city was close to the docks, which made for a more heterogeneous society in those areas than suggested by the image of the "closed community." The life of port workers was far from insular and was profoundly shaped by a strong urban culture, as working-class politics invaded spaces previously closed to workers' political expression. The Guarani Theatre, usually reserved for performances by renowned drama companies, featuring actresses such as Sarah Bernhardt, was also the scene of abolitionist and republican rallies, as well as celebrations and meetings of working-class associations.[70] The port workers' mobility extended into public spaces, propelled by their unique sense of freedom and independence.[71]

Santos did not have segregated working-class neighborhoods. The precariousness of accommodations, the seasonality of the work, and the scant material resources led to high residential mobility. This inhibited radical attempts at housing reform to settle and discipline the port workers in spaces that would be defined and organized following the principles of social reformers and employers who believed in scientific management. It was extremely rare in port cities to see any initiatives to build company housing in order to establish and maintain a permanent labor force. The port workers' way of living created a dual sense of identity. On the one hand, there were the social relations developed at work, in the neighborhood, and with kin that reinforced a sense of community and of belonging to a particular occupational group. On the other hand, the port workers' interaction with workers from other sectors nourished strong class cohesion. Calling work stoppages with little preparation time was possible because the port workers had built relations with other workers. Reluctant to replace its striking employees with their neighbors and colleagues, the Santos Docks Company resorted to the more expensive temporary solution of bringing in large contingents of scabs from São Paulo and Rio de Janeiro.

The workers of Santos had no history of strong internal divisions in contrast to other ports around the world, where a strict separation by occupations often nurtured a group identity rather than the sense of belonging to a social class. In the port of New York, for example, the occupational and residential segmentation (into distinct blocs) and the mosaic of unions mirrored the rivalries between Irish, blacks, and Italians.[72] The port of London was a showcase for residential compartmentalization as a result of professional and ethnic discord: these divisions created a "vast archipelago of small communities of workers." As a result of these strong ethnic, racial, and religious identities, large-scale strikes remained rare.[73] In Santos, on the other hand, port workers built networks of sociability. The workers, mostly male, young, and single, gathered every day in eateries and boarding houses. The Portuguese Consul in Santos noted that "the majority of workers take their meals in restaurants."[74] The regular contacts in these settings reinforced the solidarity in the case of strike movements. The Communist Celso de Lima, who lived in a boarding house shared by port and railroad workers, remembered an episode that illustrates the dynamic. When he commented in the boarding house that the railroad workers had been called upon to "rat" during a dock workers strike in 1945, the innkeeper, Miloca, fired a shot in the direction of the docks' fences and called on the retired railroad workers, "like a mother would do with her children," to return home immediately.[75]

In Santos, workers of different occupations were each other's neighbors, and so were the unions. They all had offices in the city center, which allowed for the organization of unified movements. The port worker Leonardo Roitmann, a Communist leader, recalled that in 1929 he accompanied his brother to the assemblies of "almost all the unions." The association of carters had its offices less than thirty meters from his house.[76] The anarchist militant Manuel Marques Bastos saw a connection between Santos's relatively homogenous economic structure and the fraternity of the workers before World War I. "Santos in 1912 only had the wharves of the Docks Company and small-scale retail trade. The workers had their Federation, in the Rua General Câmara. . . . Next to the Federation operated the Union of Construction Workers, the Coachmen's Resistance, the respective Unions of Stone-Masons, Railroad Workers, Coffee Sackers, and Dock Workers. . . . This made workers' unity more feasible and effective."[77]

The organization of movements took place in cultural associations, sports clubs, unions, and neighborhoods. In the postwar period, the Communists created dozens of cells, popular democratic committees, and district committees in the working-class neighborhoods of Santos and supported dances and popular festivals as well as lectures and rallies, all to tighten the links between workplaces and living spaces.[78] These micro-sociabilities forged in everyday life, as diffused and fragmentary as they were, created broad-based solidarities in conflicts or in support of demands. When the workers occupied the city center, they (re)created spaces of sociability. The close contacts between different groups of workers may explain why Santos was the only Brazilian city that experienced regular solidarity strikes and even general strikes.[79] The 1891 shutdown, for example, was the first citywide general strike in Brazil.[80] In 1960, the port workers led a work stoppage in the entire city of Santos in solidarity with thirty-one workers at the Moinho Santista, who had been threatened with a transfer to another state. Two years later, the entire city stopped again in solidarity.with the petrochemical workers in Cubatão: "not even the leaves of the trees moved," in the words of Domingos Garcia, president of the stevedores union at the time.[81]

THE PORT WORKERS' CITY

How did the port workers see their place in the city as well as their impact on the national economy and the Brazilian labor movement? They portrayed themselves as a magnetizing force for other workers. According to one port worker who had been a militant since the 1950s, "there were port workers in every corner of the city. . . . We kept the city going; [after all], the port was at the heart of the city's life. . . . The city stayed alive because of the port worker, didn't it?"[82] Another worker put it this way: "the main force really was the docks, it was the docks that had the power . . . because when the docks stopped, the city practically stopped."[83] For the port workers, their toil to supply the domestic and international markets was the cradle of the city. Foreign currency entered and left the country by their hands. This gave rise to notions of merit and dignity. To be a "good worker" and to work for the wealth of the nation required, in turn, recognition of their efforts and a share in the fruits of their labor. The indispensability of the work in the port served as justification for labor movements, as the workers saw themselves as "agents of progress." "We cannot bring this to a halt. . . . Have you ever seen development without a port? We are the lever for exports."[84] The demonstrations of solidarity sustained the port workers in this reading of their role. They boasted of their strikes in solidarity with "weaker groups of workers." "We needed to help the workers . . . who had no power vis-à-vis their bosses. By themselves they could not have done anything."[85]

A strike in the port caused considerable losses that affected the entire city. Whenever the movement of goods through the port stopped, local banks, restaurants, and retail trade immediately felt the effects. "A strike in the port was a major event for the community" and secured the support of the population and the press, "which was a rare feat in other Brazilian cities."[86] In a dramatic port workers' strike in 1920, the shop owners collaborated and offered free meals to the strikers.[87] The writer Affonso Schmidt suggests that "the evil deeds of the police ended up rallying the people of Santos fully behind the dock workers. I even witnessed bourgeois merchants . . . stop in at newspaper offices to recount the events with great and profoundly justified indignation."[88] And as Maria L. Gitahy highlights, "what are we to say about the strike of the tram conductors, for example, when working-class children in the neighborhoods threw stones at strike-breakers?"[89]

When coffee exports stopped, the ripple effects were felt at the most sensitive points of the national economy. One Communist port worker remembered: "[T]he closeness in which he lives with his fellow workers and the awareness of his own importance in the national economy determined the port worker's readiness for struggle. The press contributed to the emergence of this consciousness, making the workers' struggles national news and revealing the 'astronomical losses' caused by every work stoppage."[90] The port workers' insertion in national and international labor movements reflected their position in the economy. Regular contacts with militants from other cities and countries were possible because sailors played the role of messengers, transmitting political news "first hand."[91] The port workers held a key position in facilitating the entry of militants from elsewhere into the city, after they had established relationships with the respective crews, "where one could always find a sailor of the same creed."[92] Many leading militants among the port workers had been sailors themselves. Wherever the workforce had been recruited from among sailors or other itinerant workers, the labor movement tended to be better organized and more combative.[93]

In addition to strong intraclass relations, the port workers also built alliances with other social groups. The political police gathered detailed information on the frequency of workers and union leaders visiting the homes of lawyers, intellectuals, and professionals, as well as on stays in the city's best hotels.[94] The record of strikes in the port of Santos since the late nineteenth century refutes the general claim that port communities did not establish links with "members of the middle class" and that their struggle always took the path of direct action, without institutional mediation "from outside the working class." Strike movements in Santos often saw mediation by lawyers, journalists, politicians, or police chiefs.[95] In short, port work facilitated the formation of a broad network of relationships in the urban space.

The port workers had to confront employers who at the same time contended and cooperated with each other. To the extent that the port was, institutionally, an intermediary between the market and the companies, it brought together competing interests, but it also created synergies capable of attracting a high volume of trade of great value.[96] Because it established a connection between the regional, national, and international economies, with ramifications into its hinterland, the port followed a complex political and business logic and became the object of various strategies to upgrade its infrastructure. As David Montgomery observed, "the waterfront of a great port dramatized both the organizational achievements and the social chaos of industrial capitalism."[97] The port's integration into the city, however, was laden with conflict. The interests of various groups tied to this century-long duality, above all the entrepreneurs' overriding concern with the circulation of goods, caused a divide between the port and the inhabitants in the city. It fell to the workers to tame predatory capital, and they left the mark of their presence on the urban space of Santos. Far from being something that was "given" to the local working class, the port workers constructed that connection themselves.

THE GLOBALIZED PORT

Over the last forty years, the culture of solidarity forged by these workers has been gradually undermined. During the period of military dictatorship (1964–85), the "Red Port" bore an ever greater stigma, above all for the city's middle classes, who closed their eyes to what they considered to be the subversive and uncivilized world of the port. The dictatorship led to social and political exclusion of the workers. The port also underwent profound technological change, most importantly the switch to containers, which drastically reduced the labor force and altered the tradition of work based on physical strength and individual skill. The administration of the port passed into public hands after the end of CDS's lease in 1980, which paved the way for a further reconfiguration of the port, its labor relations, and its ties with the city. The laws for the "modernization of the ports" put an end to the closed shop, undoing one of the workers' proudest victories and undermining one of the foundations of the stevedores' power.

The privatization of the port and the globalization of capital have resulted in a greater separation of port and city. The Santos port, like others around the world, has become a functional piece in the private management of a global circulation of goods, cutting off — in the words of Gerardo Silva and Giuseppe Cocco — "the institutional and political channels that could have sustained an administration of both port and city in the public interest." The increasing specialization of port services in the hands of private companies obeys above all the interests of global corporations, to the detriment of the social and economic needs of the city. The "isolation of the port as a strategy to increase the value of the infrastructure of circulation," Silva and Cocco argue, "complicates the port's assimilation as part of the local community's everyday life."[98] The technical change and the increased specialization have resulted in the decentralization of the port as industry, a deregulation of work, increased unemployment, a weakening of unions, and the management of the labor market by the Órgão Gestor de Mão-de-Obra (OGMO; Unit for Workforce Management), an institution largely controlled by the entrepreneurs.[99] The duality port/city has made room for the duality port/world.

NOTES

Translated by Oliver Dinius. The author would also like to thank Michael M. Hall for help with the final revision of the English text.

1. Fernando Teixeira da Silva and Maria Lucia Gitahy, "The Presence of Labor in the Urban Culture of Santos," in *Space, Culture, and Labor: Brazilian Urban Workers in the Twentieth Century*, ed. Paulo Fontes and Michael M. Hall (Gainesville: University Press of Florida, forthcoming).

2. Such attempts at far-reaching moral reform were common in other ports. See Andrew Parnaby, *Citizen Docker: Making a New Deal on the Vancouver Waterfront, 1919–1939* (Toronto: University of Toronto Press, 2008).

3. Santos shared these characteristics with other port cities such as Liverpool in England and Fremantle in Australia. Sam Davies et al., eds., *Dock Workers: International*

Explorations in Comparative Labour History (Aldershot, Eng.: Ashgate, 2000). The relevant essays are Eric Taplin's "The History of Dock Labour: Liverpool," 442–70; and Malcolm Tull's "Waterfront Labour at Fremantle," 471–93.

4. Maria Lúcia Gitahy, *Ventos do mar: trabalhadores do porto, movimento operário e cultura urbana em Santos, 1889–1914* (São Paulo: Hucitec, 1992), 24.

5. For more detailed studies on the modernization of the port, see Gitahy, *Ventos do mar*, and Cezar Honorato, *O polvo e o porto: a Companhia Docas de Santos, 1888–1914* (São Paulo: Hucitec, 1996).

6. Pedro Rivaben de Sales, "Santos: a relação entre o porto e a cidade" (PhD diss., Universidade de São Paulo, 1999), 127.

7. Gitahy, *Ventos do mar*, 41; Brasil, *Recenseamento do Brasil realizado em 1º de setembro de 1920*, vol. 4, 774–75.

8. Santos, *Recenseamento da cidade de Santos em 31 de dezembro de 1913* (Santos: Prefeitura de Santos, 1913), 89, 93.

9. Gitahy, *Ventos do mar*, 41–42.

10. Maria Valéria Barbosa et al. eds., *Santos na formação do Brasil: 500 anos de história* (Santos: Prefeitura Municipal de Santos, 2000), 36.

11. Carlos R. Andrade, "De Viena a Santos: Camillo Sitte e Saturnino de Brito," in *A construção das cidades segundo seus princípios artísticos*, ed. Camillo Sitte (São Paulo: Ática, 1992).

12. Sales, "Santos," 134.

13. Wilson Gambeta, "Desacumular a Pobreza," *Espaço e Debate*, no. 11 (1984): 17–24.

14. On the urban development of Santos, see Ana Lúcia Duarte Lanna, *Uma cidade na transição: Santos: 1870–1913* (São Paulo: Hucitec, 1996).

15. José R. Araújo Filho, "A Expansão Urbana em Santos," in *A Baixada Santista: aspectos geográficos*, ed. José R. Araújo Filho et al., vol. 3 (São Paulo: Universidade de São Paulo, 1965), 38; Paula Beiguelmam, "Morros Santistas," *Sociologia*, no. 10 (1945): 30–37.

16. Santos, *Recenseamento*; Brasil, Fundação IBGE, *Censo Demográfico de 1940*.

17. Sales, "Santos," 159.

18. Wolfgang Schoeps and Walter Delázaro, *Influência econômica do porto de Santos* (Rio de Janeiro: Livraria Agir Editora, 1980), 44–46.

19. Frederick Cooper, "Dockworkers and Labour History," in Davies, *Dock Workers*, 527.

20. Maria C. Velasco e Cruz, "Portos, relações de produção e sindicato," *Ciências Sociais Hoje* (1986): 143–70.

21. Eric Hobsbawm, "National Unions of the Waterside," *Labouring Men: Studies in the History of Labour* (London: Weidenfeld and Nicolson, 1964), 204–30; Howard Kimeldorf, *Reds or Rackets? The Making of Radical and Conservative Unions on the Waterfront* (Berkeley: University of California Press, 1988), 29.

22. Gordon Phillips and Noel Whiteside, *Casual Labour: Unemployment in the Port Transport Industry: 1880–1970* (Oxford: Clarendon Press, 1985).

23. Velasco e Cruz, "Portos," 37.

24. Sales, "Santos," 129.

25. Honorato, *O polvo e o porto*, 119–20.

26. Quoted in Sales, "Santos," 128–29.

27. Gitahy, *Ventos do mar*, 84.

28. Ibid., 97.

29. Companhia Docas de Santos, *Relatório da diretoria de 1914* (Rio de Janeiro, 1915), 29.

30. The most closely comparable case, albeit in the nineteenth century, was the Compagnie des Docks et Entrepôts de Marseille. William Sewell Jr., *Logics of History: Social Theory and Social Transformation* (Chicago: University of Chicago Press, 2005), 302, 305.

31. Maria Helena P. Toledo Machado, "From Slave Rebels of Strikebreakers: The Quilombo of Jabaquara and the Problem of Citizenship in Late-Ninetenth-Century Brasil," *Hispanic American Historical Review* 82, no. 2 (May 2002): 247–74.

32. Gitahy, *Ventos do mar*, 81.

33. Companhia Docas do Estado de São Paulo, Ofício de G. B. Weinschenck a Ulrico Mursa, July 14, 1917.

34. *A Plebe*, December 13, 1920.

35. Companhia Docas de Santos, *Relatório da diretoria de 1920* (Rio de Janeiro, 1921).

36. Celso de Lima, *Navegar é preciso: memórias de um operário comunista* (São Paulo: Diniz, 1984), 34, 39.

37. Fernando Teixeira da Silva, "Valentia e cultura do trabalho na estiva de Santos," in *Culturas de classe: identidade e diversidade na formação do operariado*, ed. Cláudio Batalha et al. (Campinas: Ed. da Unicamp, 2004), 205–45.

38. See Fernando Teixeira da Silva, *A carga e a culpa: os operários das docas de Santos, 1937–1968* (São Paulo: Hucitec, 1995), 34–37.

39. Karl Marx, "Cooperação," in *O capital*, vol. 1 (São Paulo: Nova Cultural, 1988), 247.

40. Herb Mills and David Wellman, "Contractually Sanctioned Job Actions and Workers' Control," *Labor History* 28 (Spring 1987): 167–95; Stanley Aronowitz, Introduction to *Longshoremen: Community and Resistance on the Brooklyn Waterfront*, ed. William DiFazio (South Hadley, Mass.: Bergin & Garvey, 1985), xvi.

41. Lima, *Navegar é preciso*, 34.

42. David Montgomery, *Workers' Control in America: Studies in the History of Work, Technology and Labor Struggles* (Cambridge: Cambridge University Press, 1979).

43. Quoted in Silva, *A carga e a culpa*, 29.

44. Klaus Weinhauer, "Dock Labour in Hamburg: The Labour Market, the Labour Movement and Industrial Relations," in Davies, *Dock Workers*, 503.

45. Interview with J., former employee of the port administration. Unless otherwise

noted, the interviews were conducted by the author between 1989 and 1991 as part of the research for his master's thesis, published as Silva, *A carga e a culpa*.

46. Two novels include narratives of the forging of relations of family, friendship, and godparenthood among the port workers of Santos: Ranulpho Prata, *Navios iluminados* (São Paulo: Scritta, 1996); Alberto Leal, *Cais de Santos* (Rio de Janeiro: Cooperativa Cultural Guanabara, 1939).

47. Lima, *Navegar é preciso*, 42.

48. Robert Cherny, "Longshoremen of San Francisco Bay," in Davies, *Dock Workers*, 116–17; Anna Green, "New Zealand Waterside Workers in Auckland, Wellington and Lyttelton," in Davies, *Dock Workers*, 263.

49. Lima, *Navegar é preciso*, 40.

50. Interview with L., former dockworker.

51. See Peter Linebaugh, "Crime e industrialização: a Grã-Bretanha no século XVIII," in *Crime, violência e poder*, ed. Paulo Sérgio Pinheiro (São Paulo: Brasiliense, 1983).

52. Interview with C., former foreman.

53. Interview with B., former dockworker.

54. Ata da assembléia extraordinária, May 6, 1962.

55. Beginning in the 1920s, port administrators in Hamburg attempted to abolish the distinction between longshoremen and stevedores. Weinhauer, "Dock Labour," 502.

56. Phillips and Whiteside, *Casual Labor*, 271.

57. Quoted in Carlos Oliveira, "Quem é do mar não enjoa" (PhD diss., Pontifícia Universidade Católica de São Paulo, 2000), 80.

58. Companhia Docas de Santos, *Relatório da diretoria de 1911* (Rio de Janeiro: 1912), 11.

59. Herndon Goforth, "Labor Difficulties on the Wharves at Santos, Brazil," January 18, 1924; Records of the Department of State relating to internal affairs of Brazil, 1910–1929, General Records of the Department of State (RG 59), National Archives, College Park, Md.

60. Interview given at the occasion of the "Memória sindical da Baixada Santista," Faculdade de Filosofia de Santos, on May 17, 1990 (recorded by the author).

61. Guilherme Guinle, *Projeto de regulamento do serviço de estiva* (Rio de Janeiro, 1939), 23–27.

62. Quoted in Guinle, *Projeto de regulamento*, 19–20.

63. See Fernando Teixeira da Silva, *Operários sem patrões: os trabalhadores da cidade de Santos no entreguerras* (Campinas: Ed. da Unicamp, 2003), chap. 4.

64. Silva, *Valentia*, 235.

65. See Fernando Teixeira da Silva, "Direitos, política e trabalho no Porto de Santos," in *Na luta por direitos: estudos recentes em história social do trabalho*, ed. Alexandre Fortes et al. (Campinas: Ed. da Unicamp, 1999).

66. David Montgomery, *The Fall of the House of Labor* (Cambridge: Cambridge University Press, 1995), 87–88.

67. Tribunal do Júri da Comarca de Santos; Antonio André Carijo [réu], no 2.587, caixa 208, 1931.

68. Mariam Panjwani, "Space as Determinant: Neighbourhood, Clubs and Other Strategies of Survival," in Davies, *Dock Workers*, 756.

69. Clark Kerr and Abraham Siegel, "The Inter-industry Propensity to Strike: An International Comparison," in *Labor and Management in Industrial Society*, ed. Arthur Kornhauser (New York: Doubleday, 1954). For an application of this theory to port cities, see Raymond Miller, "The Dockworker Subculture and Some Problems in Cross-cultural and Cross-time Generalization," *Comparative Studies in Society and History*, no. 11 (1969): 302–14.

70. Gitahy, *Ventos do mar*, 44.

71. On this issue among the port workers of Liverpool, see T. S. Simey, "La comunidad portuaria y el sindicalismo," in *Estructuras sindicales*, ed. Torcuato di Tella (Buenos Aires: Nova Visión, 1969), 69–78.

72. Kimeldorf, *Reds or Rackets?* 42–46.

73. Erik Nijhof, "Les syndicats de Dockers de Londres, du Havre, de Rotterdam et de Hambourg," in *L'invention des sindicalismes*, ed. Jean-Louis Robert (Paris: Sorbonne, 1997), 77–78.

74. Ministério dos Negócios Estrangeiros de Portugal, *Inquérito consular*, 1934, 4, maço 468.

75. Lima, *Navegar*, 26–30.

76. Interview with Leonardo Roitmann, Centro de Memória Sindical de São Paulo, August 30, 1980), 2.

77. Quoted in Edgar Rodrigues, *Nacionalismo & cultura social* (Rio de Janeiro: Laemmert, 1972), 127.

78. Rodrigo Tavares. "A "Moscouzinha" Brasileira: cenários e personagens do cotidiano operário de Santos (1930–1954)" (PhD diss., Universidade de São Paulo, 2004).

79. Cf. Gitahy, *Ventos do mar*; Silva, *A carga e a culpa*; Silva, *Operários sem patrões*; Ingrid Sarti, *O porto vermelho: os estivadores Santistas no sindicato e na política* (Rio de Janeiro: Paz e Terra, 1981).

80. Gitahy, *Ventos do mar*, 79–82.

81. Quoted in Silva, *Direitos, política e trabalho*.

82. Interview with M., former loading and unloading worker.

83. Interview with M., former warehouse worker for CDS.

84. Former longshoreman in interview with Maria Célia Paoli, *Desenvolvimento e marginalidade* (São Paulo: Pioneira, 1974), 88.

85. Interview with B.

86. Gitahy, *Ventos do mar,* 123.

87. Edgar Rodrigues, *Trabalho e conflito: pesquisa, 1906–1937* (Rio de Janeiro: Arte Moderna, s.d.), 282.

88. Affonso Schmidt, *A Plebe*, December 18, 1920.

89. Gitahy, *Ventos do mar,* 121.

90. Arlindo Lucena, *Bagrinhos e tubarões* (São Paulo: Fulgort, 1964), 20.

91. See Silva, *Operários sem patrões,* 141.

92. AESP, Setor DEOPS, Prontuário da Delegacia Auxiliar de Santos, n. 561, vol. 1.

93. Kimeldorf, *Reds or Rackets,* 20.

94. Silva, *Operários sem patrões,* 142.

95. Citahy, *Ventos do mar,* 103; Silva, *Operários sem patrões,* chaps. 3, 6–8.

96. See Thierry Baundouin, "A Cidade Portuária na Mundialização," in *Cidades e portos: os espaços da globalização,* ed. Gerardo Silva and Giuseppe Cocco (Rio de Janeiro: DP&A, 1999), 34–36.

97. Montgomery, *Fall of the House of Labor,* 97.

98. Gerardo Silva and Giuseppe Cocco, eds., "Introdução," *Cidades e portos,* 16, 21.

99. Carla Regina Diéguez, "De OGMO (Operário Gestor de Mão-de-Obra) para OGMO (Órgão Gestor de Mão-de-Obra): modernização e cultura do trabalho no porto de Santos" (PhD diss., Universidade de São Paulo, 2007).

CHAPTER FOUR

Whitened and Enlightened

The Ford Motor Company and Racial Engineering in the Brazilian Amazon

ELIZABETH ESCH

Shades of Tarzan! You'd never guess these bright, happy, healthy school
children lived in a jungle city that didn't even exist a few years ago.
— "The Ford Rubber Plantations"

A look at the world of the Ford Motor Company in the decades after World
War I reveals just how thoroughly the company had been able to create what it
described as an "empire." The war had, of course, played a massive role in this,
spreading not just Ford's products and production methods across the globe,
but also those of the United States. As Ford workplaces appeared around the
world — assembly shops, manufacturing plants, and car dealers — so too did
the residential areas Henry Ford himself fantasized would one day include all
nonfarm workers: "Ford towns," as they came to be called first in Michigan.
Amazingly, such "Ford towns" were not just part of the company's narrative
of life and work in the United States; they were increasingly part of a global
geography. By the mid- to late 1930s an expanding and border-crossing network linked Ford City, California, to Ford City, Tennessee, both "Ford towns";
Pequaming, in the Upper Peninsula of Michigan and purchased by Ford in 1923,
sent its timber to Iron City, Michigan, where Ford owned and ran a timber
camp including one of the world's most advanced sawmills; further south but
in a country to the north of the United States was Ford City, Ontario, Canada,
itself linked by imperial geography and company schemes to Port Elizabeth,
South Africa, already nicknamed the "Detroit of South Africa," where would-

be workers built a community called KwaFord from the company's discarded packing crates.

Perhaps the most startling example of the international "Ford town" is to be found at Fordlândia, the first of two plantations the Ford Motor Company operated in the state of Pará, Brazil. Here the company linked the imperative to grow and process rubber to the imperative to create new people, urged by a state that, by the middle of Ford's tenure in Brazil, had linked its ideas of modernity and progress to those promoted by the company in the Northern Amazon and across the globe. While the history of Fordlândia can be used to reveal narratives of many kinds, some more fantastic than others, it is particularly useful for thinking about the relationship of racial engineering to social engineering and the relationship of each to the built environment of the plantation.[1]

In his wonderful reflection on the relationship(s) between social and spatial engineering included in this volume, Andrew Herod skillfully directs us to consider the — perhaps obvious but nevertheless often overlooked — significance of built environments to relations of power. Most importantly, Herod draws attention to the dialectic that links workers and their struggles to the landscapes they inhabit, considering company towns in the continuum of housing and living arrangements that are both imposed on workers and created by them. He writes, "The physicality of landscapes is a reflection of the social interests of those who construct them but also . . . [the way in which] landscapes are made shapes how social relations subsequently unfold [t]he social and the spatial, in other words, are mutually constituted and constituting." To Herod's insight this essay adds a further consideration, that is, the desire for and commitment to racial improvement that allowed the Ford Motor Company to build common cause with modernizers in Brazil. In pursuit of what Ann Laura Stoler has called "racial rationalization," company men and Brazilian elites saw in the very materiality of plantation living possibilities for social engineering.[2]

DIEGO RIVERA'S DREAM

In 1932, when he was invited by the Detroit Institute of Arts to cover the four walls of its courtyard with frescoes of his choosing, Diego Rivera chose the Ford River Rouge plant as the centerpiece for his vibrant series "Detroit Industry." Though commissioned by the Institute of Arts, the project was underwritten by Edsel Ford, a patron of the arts and decided disappointment to his father, Henry. The main frescoes marvelously portray the intimate processes of mass production on the River Rouge assembly line, and Rivera used them to represent the idea that industry's "development" of the natural world would provide the basis for human liberation. These two large and detailed frescoes of the work process are surrounded by twenty-five other, smaller frescoes depicting the bounty and beauty of the natural world, the worlds of science and invention, and several characters who represent what Rivera called the "four elements of the world."[3] These elements formed the basic ingredients in steel, which for Rivera was the key to modern manufacturing possibility, particularly as represented by skyscrapers and cars. Of these differently colored figures Rivera said: "The yellow race represents the sand, because it is most numerous. And the red race, the first in this country, is like the iron ore, the first thing necessary for the steel. The black race is like the coal, because it has a great native aesthetic sense, a real flame of feeling and beauty in its ancient sculpture, its native rhythm and music. So its aesthetic sense is like the fire, and its labor furnished the hardness which the carbon in the coal gives to steel. The white race is like the lime, not only because it is white, but because lime is the organizing agent in the making of steel. It binds together the other elements and so you see the white race as the great organizer of the world."[4]

The explicit link between race and industrial production that Rivera articulated verbally and through his art was one that Henry Ford made as well. Writing in his first memoir that his company's product was not so much cars as men, Henry Ford had gained notoriety through his multifaceted attempts to "rebuild" human beings. Most significant was his five-dollar-a-day wage, introduced in 1914, which required immigrant workers to prove their commitments to becoming American through a range of behaviors they practiced outside of the workplace. Sobriety, cleanliness, marriage, speaking English, participating in religious worship (preferably Christian) all counted toward earning the wage. Though it lasted only about a decade, Ford's efforts to claim a unique set of behaviors and norms as "American" and to link those to the regime of production practiced in his factories would soon be applied not just to the peoples of the world as they came to Ford but also to the peoples of the world as Ford came to them.[5] By 1925, the company had expanded to more than twenty countries, and its particular involvement in Latin America was seen by Rivera as having significance other than as an imperial power in the region. The future of the Americas — its modernity — for Rivera was found in the unique coming together of the technoculture of the hyperdeveloped north, or the United States, with the resilience of traditional indigenous cultural production across the Americas.

Though the enormity of Ford's impact on the planet is evident in Rivera's frescoes, in speaking about them he emphasized not the troubling emergence of U.S. industrial dominance but instead the emergence of a new world. The only people living outside of the United States represented in Rivera's frescoes were Brazilian rubber tappers. In the paintings the Amazon is connected to the Rouge plant by water, rubber on one side being tapped from trees, smoothly transported from the Amazon River across the Atlantic Ocean up the Rouge River, where it would be transformed into tires. In the frescoes, the rubber tappers represent the process Rivera wished to celebrate, in which human labor and intellect could transform raw materials into goods whose use would be freeing. They are also suggestive of Rivera's internationalism, learned in the surrealist and Communist movements, which saw industry as bringing liberation to people worldwide. Interestingly, however, the rubber tappers find no place in Rivera's imaginary chart of the races of the world, being actually neither yellow nor red, neither black nor white. While this may have been an oversight on Rivera's part, the "in-betweenness" the rubber tappers represent is precisely what Ford relied on when it decided to build its rubber plantations in the Brazilian Amazon.[6]

The choice to locate its rubber plantations in the Amazon linked Ford both to the politics of the Brazilian state and its homegrown commitment to turn "savages" and other "substandard" people into real Ford men. We cannot understand the decision to build the plantations if we do not understand the world economic circumstances that led to it. This chapter describes how techniques that are often described as "Americanizing" were used in Brazil in order to "Brazilianize" the indigenous people Ford sought to run its plantations. Thus while this was an imperial venture on the part of the U.S. State Department and Ford, it was also embraced by local Brazilian elites who believed in the promise of "new men."

HENRY FORD'S DREAM

When Ford launched the project that would result in two rubber plantations being carved out of the Amazon region of Brazil, only one part of its ideal was to grow and process rubber. Company records reveal an intense interest — and belief — in racial progress, which it relied on as it attempted to "proletarianize" and "civilize" rubber tappers living in the region. While neither Fordlândia nor Belterra are company towns specifically, they also did not function merely as plantations, which was part of Ford's dilemma. These two towns should be seen as attempts by Ford to accomplish the goals of a conventional company town in an extractive industry — not unlike a plantation in an agricultural capitalist economy — while bringing to bear a peculiar commitment to the role of white supremacy in making workers.

In the summer of 1928 the Ford-owned *Lake Ormoc* set sail from Detroit for the newly founded Fordlândia in the state of Pará, Brazil. Following the ship was a barge carrying provisions to house and care for the "American staff" for up to two years and to launch the plantation. In addition to a set of tracks and ties for laying its own rail, the company brought with it "[a] filtration plant . . . dock construction equipment . . . medical supplies . . . power house engine room . . . saw mill equipment . . . road machinery . . . tugs and workboats."[7] Though the *Ormoc*'s cargo suggests an extraordinary degree of foresight, subsequent events in the Amazon reveal that the company was absurdly ill-prepared for the project it was undertaking.

Approaching Brazil with the same commitment to social engineering it brought to other contexts, Ford had chosen Pará because its ecology was suitable to growing *hevea brasiliensis*, what the world market called "wild rubber." But what tipped the scales in favor of Brazil, as compared to other regions with equally favorable climates and geographies, was the possibility of recruiting and developing laborers of specific racialized types. This faith in its own capacity to manage both race and nature underwrote the hubris that made Ford's presence in Pará seem all too often like a prequel to Werner Herzog's classic cinematic study of colonial overreach in Brazil, *Fitzcarraldo*.

Carl LaRue, a botanist who scouted plantations for Ford, recommended Brazil because, although "labor is somewhat more expensive than in the East . . . labor is also more intelligent than the average labor in the East." LaRue spelled out a solution to the problem of expenses for the company, arguing that the use of machines on a modern plantation that Ford intended should offset any advantage that the plantations in "the East" might have. LaRue also believed that the laborers whom Ford would recruit in Brazil were themselves capable of being modernized because of what he saw as their racial characteristics. LaRue's report claimed both racial and historical expertise: "The dwellers of the Amazon Valley are of three main stocks: Portuguese, Indian and Negro . . . admixture has gone on so long that it is difficult to distinguish the different types. The mixture is not a particularly good one from a racial standpoint but it is by no means a bad one . . . the fate of these people is more tragic because they are not possessed of the stolidity of the orientals, but have enough of the white race in them to suffer keenly and long intensely for the better things. As it is, their condition is worse than that of any of the coolies in the East, far worse even than that of the average slave in the old days."[8]

That "race mixing" could imply improvement, that is, whitening, was a manifestation of racist thought particular to a Brazilian social context.[9] It reflected neither the "one drop rule" that policed race in the United States, nor the then slightly less draconian model in South Africa, where whites believed "race mix-ing" would lead to the degradation of those whites who participated in it. The different expressions of white supremacy that Ford embraced in different so-cial contexts did not challenge the company's overriding commitment to racial hierarchies. Indeed the idea that the company believed it could tap the desire for consumer goods they believed flowed in the veins of "Amazonian people" is revealing of Ford's very particular ideology of exploitation. As the story of Fordlândia reveals, such thinking was essential to the company's approach to its workforce; LaRue's final recommendation to the company concluded that extending "help" to the destitute of the region and establishing "profitability" were compatible.[10]

Ford's plan to exploit the natural resources in the region and the labor of those who lived in it was part of an overall strategy by the United States to gain control from the British of the rubber market. As the overwhelming consumer of the world's rubber, U.S. industry had a particular stake in its price. Ford did not hesitate when he received in 1923 a letter from H. F. Firestone inviting him to participate in a "conference of international significance." The immediate rationale for the meeting was the 1922 implementation of the British Rubber Restriction Act, which had more than doubled the price of rubber on the world market. According to Firestone, an increase in cost of over $150 million should be expected as a result of the British move, an untenable situation for those, like Ford, who sought to promote "the use of automobiles and the development of highway transportation." Revealing of the globality of the most nation-based realities, low world prices for rubber would matter in a new way to those who consumed cars in the United States. The halting democratization of consump-tion of automobiles thus could undergird calls for low world market prices of the commodities from which they were built.[11]

Within five years of Firestone's appeal, U.S. firms had acquired land for rub-ber production across the globe: Firestone launched the Liberian plantations for which it would become notorious, Goodyear began plantation agricultural experiments in both Sumatra and the Philippines, and Ford bought 2.5 million acres of land, an area just smaller than the state of Connecticut, in the northern state of Pará, Brazil.[12] Signaling the opening of a short but lethal chapter in the history of American imperial adventures, Ford's arrival on the Brazilian coast brought with it commitments to order and progress through which it would confidently try, and fail, to remake the ecology, society, economy, and people of the region.[13]

Ford had already established an industrial presence in Brazil through its as-sembly plant in São Paulo, built to supply the steadily growing Latin American market. Ford's expansion into the North Amazon occurred alongside a social debate that was underway in Brazil about the relationship of scientific management and social progress. In her examination of this process in São Paulo, Barbara Weinstein demonstrates how this debate had been developing, "percolating among industrialists, engineers, social hygienists and educators in São Paulo since the 1920s," and insists that it is necessary to understand elite practices as strategies of social control. "By identifying with new currents in rational organization and scientific management," she writes, "these industrialists, engineers, and educators claimed for themselves the professional authority and technical expertise necessary to modernize Brazilian society."[14] These professionals were highly interested in Fordist process: "advocates of Fordism, while still regarding the factory as the key location for change, believed that the transformation of the workplace required attention to aspects of industrial life beyond the production process."[15]

Ford's arrival in the Amazon could not have been more well-timed from the point of view of these reformers. As modernizers who seemed to have technology and science on their side, Ford's "American staff" was welcomed by Brazilian elites who hoped to use the company's commitments to men-making to further their own goals and to address the wreckage in the countryside caused by the changing rubber market. The experiment in the Amazon reveals the inner workings of the corporation, and the connection between the economic and social, the natural and the global, realms it sought to dominate.

As part of its agreement with the state government in Pará, the company was required to plant at least a thousand trees within one month of the start of the operations. Ford managers had arranged to have these rubber seedlings planted along the river so that production would be underway before the construction of the plantation began. After their arrival, however, the crew was informed that the seedlings had actually been planted in the state of Amazonas, not in Pará where Ford had been given permission to cultivate rubber. Local legislation prevented the transport of the trees from one state to the next. Although they tried to reverse this decision in court, the company failed to secure release of the trees.[16]

So they began again. The first manager of the plantations was replaced, at the urging of Henry Ford, whose hands-on attention bespoke the symbolic import as well as the economic potential of the experiment, by Einard Oxholm. Though Oxholm, captain of the *Lake Ormoc*, knew literally nothing about growing rubber, Ford's arrogant belief that "anyone could learn anything" led to his being put in charge of Fordlândia. Oxholm remained at Fordlândia until the end of 1929; his tenure there reflected the swagger of a company intent on absolutely conquering the very ecology that had nurtured the trees it was there to exploit. Ford's willful ignorance in the face of decades of local knowledge of rubber production, held by the indigenous people Ford saw as untamed racial others, proved fully disabling. The land that Ford had selected was completely unsuited to a mono-crop plantation. Its hilliness limited mechanization; even what the company knew how to do, running sawmills, floundered in the face of hard-wood species that "dulled Yankee saw blades and tended to crack."[17]

By its very structure, plantation agriculture requires a rejection of time-tested knowledge of cultivation and care. Mass production of nature, agribusiness as it has come to be called, relies almost entirely on the transformation of ecologies. The rainforest, which had always been necessary to the growth of rubber, was treated by Ford as a problem: "The first obstacle that confronted Ford was the almost impenetrable tropical jungle. But it had to be cleared and for every 40 acres a clearing gang of 20 native workers was organized." As early as summer 1929, fifteen hundred acres of rainforest had been slashed and burned and then planted with rubber saplings. By 1930 three thousand acres were cleared, and the infrastructure of the plantation — administrative offices, barracks, a clinic, sewerage and water pipes, railroads, and a sawmill — had been constructed.[18]

Of course, it was the rainforest and the ecosystem it represented that allowed the extraordinary growth of latex-producing *hevea brasiliensis* trees. One of the most significant problems Ford created for itself was blight. Grown in their natural environment, rubber trees are protected from the spread of fungus by the shelter of other plant life and the distance in between the trees. Planting rubber saplings on barren land, in straight rows separated only by a few feet, almost guarantees the spread of disease from tree to tree. Plantations in the British and French empires dealt with this self-imposed problem through innovations in hybridization and, ultimately, pesticides. Ford, still intent on using the once highly reliable *hevea brasiliensis* tree, did not learn its lesson until the mid-1930s, when Ford hired its first botanist.[19] As historian Mira Wilkins wrote: "If [Fordlândia] was a "green hell" for its human inhabitants, it was quite as infernal a habitat for the *hevea*. This tree was subject to root diseases, leaf maladies, fruit and flower blights, injuries caused by phanerogamic plants, brown bast, abnormal nodule structure, cortex nodules, abnormal exuadations of rubber pad, chlorosis of the leaves, and numerous other hazards."[20]

The initial assumption, that local people would be as amicable to transformation as the ecosystem, proved equally mistaken. By the mid-1930s the company reported that three thousand people were employed by Ford.[21] Most of those were engaged in the construction of the physical infrastructure of Fordlândia, which by the early 1930s was sprawling and continued to grow. Work on the construction of barracks, sawmills, roads, and a cafeteria distracted even the company from the fact that its primary concern was the cultivation of rubber and, even beyond that, the production of tires. One manager wrote that "a great amount of work has been done . . . and a great deal of money spent . . . very little has been done along the lines of what we came here to do, namely to plant rubber."[22] For all of Ford's "progress," the disarray and destruction brought by the company in at least the initial stages of the project were startling to both American and Brazilian observers, many of whom thought the word "Ford" was synonymous with efficiency. One troubleshooter sent by the company said: "There is a complete lack of organization at the property. . . . Waste is terrible. . . . At present it is like dropping money into a sewer."[23]

The company's particular vision of the men they sought to recruit to work on the plantation contributed to the "urgent" need to develop the built environment. Because workers were seen as a threat to the American managers, the structures — hospital, barracks, cafeteria, and mill — increasingly became part of the method of disciplining and modifying the behavior of those who lived at Fordlândia. The company's understanding of the "improvability" of the *caboclos* (term for "mixed-race people" of Amerindian and European descent) was based on the earliest projections from LaRue, drawn on the contemporary practices of Brazilian social scientists, whose commitments to both white supremacy and racial improvement in the interwar years are brilliantly dissected in Jorge Amado's fiction work *Tent of Miracles* and Jerry Dávila's meticulously researched *Diploma of Whiteness*.[24] Dávila's focus on the place of educational policy, especially during the Vargas regime, in furthering cultural practices and social policies designed to whiten "underclass" Brazilians, brilliantly engages the multiple conversations taking place among planners and ideologues of all kinds before and during the period of the *Estado Novo,* beginning in 1937. Thus Ford's conviction that those who were "really worse off than slaves" were salvageable precisely because their "mixed-race" status brought an imperial dimension to a set of processes that were seemingly local. In Brazil as in the United States, race management would complement rather than challenge scientific management as a hallmark of modernity.[25]

Convincing enough people to live and work on the plantation was the largest challenge Ford faced, and one it was never able to win. The company clearly thought its plan — creating a waged labor force of single men who slept in barracks, punched time clocks, and worked eleven-hour shifts — was not only agreeable but generous in contrast to the quasi-feudal social arrangements on other plantations. At Fordlândia workers were paid in money and not company scrip, and thus they were not tied by debt to the plantation. However, they still were required to work off the costs of their own transportation to the plantation and to pay for their own food, hammocks, and tools. Ford's managers had been certain that "in the beginning plenty of laborers can be recruited on the Tapajos and neighboring rivers. These men when well fed and cured of hook worm, malaria etc. will make good laborers."[26]

Despite the company's stated fears that they might at any minute be swamped by workers seeking an easy life, it is evident that Ford was never able to keep people on the plantation. Through November and December 1930, more people were fired each week than were hired. In one week 218 were fired while just 42 were hired; another week 188 were fired while 87 were brought on. Though in other weeks the numbers were more well balanced, those fired outpaced those hired for more than one year.[27] The company's own racism left little room for it to transcend the sharp limits on its ability to create Ford workers out of the people living in the region and on its capacity to get them to stay at Fordlândia once they were recruited. Acting on a deep connection between knowing race and managing workers developed in the United States, Ford managers ranked the people they encountered in degrees of "savagery" and "tameness." After inspecting workers' villages, one labor recruiter sent a telegram that read, "Even if they were tame they are lazy and undisciplined." The company replied, "Suggest we only take 100 with the distinct understanding that they are subject to discipline or they will be of no value, they must guarantee to do steady work every day or they would be without value and if they cannot talk Portuguese we might be better off without them."[28] Every colonial administration has its own idea of what it means to "tame savages." In Ford's case the measurement was clearly capitalist work discipline. A "tame" worker wore shoes, lived on the plantation, returned to work the day after being paid, and worked for eleven hours, through the heat of the day. The connection of capitalist production and work discipline, so well developed by E. P. Thompson, ethnically inflected in the U.S. histories of Herbert Gutman and intriguingly present in A. Mark Smith's slavery study *Measured by the Clock*, here found another telling variation.[29]

Ford managers projected their white supremacist fantasies onto the bodies of the people among whom they now lived. The Americans at Fordlândia seemed to be in a constant state of fear of the tropics, with the threat coming from both the people and the ecology. This sensibility mirrored the Brazilian eugenic movement, whose major modernizing projects in the 1920s and 1930s focused on sanitation and disease. Upon arrival at Fordlândia each worker was given a medical inspection. Those with malaria or hookworm were sometimes hospitalized, sometimes turned away, though seemingly never immediately hired. Upon being hired new workers were then photographed for company records.

The structured role of the medical department was integral to the shaping of the workforce, again revealing the link between racist civilizing missions and capitalist labor imperatives, and reflecting a long-standing practice of using the clinic in the control of workers in both colonial and noncolonial contexts.[30]

Increasingly, doctors played a significant role in the management of workers on the plantation; the hospital was the place where sick workers were distinguished from the "just lazy" ones; the latter were fired. C. Beaton, the medical officer at Fordlândia, wrote to R. D. McClure at Henry Ford Hospital in Detroit: "Ordinary dressings, medication, injections are given during [work] hours so it is not necessary for men to lose time during working hours. By insisting that all sick men go to hospital . . . and by discharging certain men who were just lazy we have been able to practically abolish the former very large list of absentees from work."[31]

Ford's extravagant commitment to its own ideas about how work should be organized and how workers should be managed, learned over decades in its auto factories in Detroit, made little sense in rubber production. Ford managers did not recognize the fact that their management technique had evolved dialectically through the years in which workers had gradually been trained to accept the imperatives that attended the assembly line (which, of course, they never fully did). Managers seemed to think that if they could impose their form of managerial discipline on rubber tappers, then plantation production would follow. Yet the less appropriate their ideas were to the task, the more tenaciously the company seemed to cling to them. In an exchange of letters with steam whistle manufacturers a manager expressed his concern that the company had not yet found a whistle that could withstand a tropical climate and that was loud enough to allow workers on all sides of the plantation to hear it. Of course, the company had scheduled the whistles at 5:30, 6:00, 6:30, 7:00, 11:00, 11:30, noon, 3:30, 4:00, 4:30, 5:00, and 5:30. But what use, they fretted, is all this precision if no one can hear the whistle? And what good is punching time cards if time is not uniformly understood? As one manager put it, "Owing to the fact that our daily labor are punching time cards it is imperative that time signals be controlled. Otherwise the hours of operation are not uniform throughout the plantation."[32]

Indeed, management thought electric service would be advisable throughout the plantation in order to accommodate time clocks and bells "similar to those in the factory."[33] Electricity, of course, would enable other changes in the lives of those who lived on the plantation. Electricity would make it possible, for example, for Ford to show company-made films to workers. Ford also used prerecorded "American folk music" in its dance classes on the plantation. The company thus imposed mass-produced goods such as records, radios, and imported clothes as well as the technology of industrial management in its "transformation" onto its workers both at work and at home.

A 1930 strike revealed the depth of disgust that workers felt toward the highly controlled living arrangements on the plantation. On December 22, management announced to workers who had gathered for the evening meal that the structure of food service had been changed. Rather than being served food at tables, the men would now line up, cafeteria style. This message was delivered by a supervisor who had earned a reputation among workers as being especially harsh and unfair. When workers were informed of the new plan, they responded by saying they "were not dogs." When they confronted managers about the new policy, they were told that "the Company now and then put new rules into effect but it was always for the betterment of the workers." According to a Brazilian foreman, Manoel Caetano, the manager's comments were "[j]ust as putting a match to gasoline." Not satisfied with the betterment program, the workers immediately banded together as the managers fled by boat.[34]

When the managers returned to Fordlândia, they discovered that a good portion of the company's property had been damaged or destroyed. "Most of the time clocks were completely demolished," R. D. Chatfield wrote. Also targeted for destruction were the cafeteria, the time card racks, and all the trucks. Managers received a list of demands from the workers: the dismissal of a particularly harsh manager, as well as Service Department head Victor Gill, on the grounds that each was unnecessarily harsh and arbitrary in relating to workers; that men be allowed free access to the dock; that men be allowed to live where they chose; that the rule prohibiting the consumption of alcohol be eliminated; that they be allowed to choose their own recreational spaces and activities; and that no one should be dismissed without being given another chance.[35] What the demands reveal about how life on the plantation was ordered reflects the accumulated practices of Ford, in its Americanization programs at Highland Park and in its repressive system of rules in the Rouge plant.

The stakes of the strike ensured dramatic soul-searching by management. As the labor geographer Don Mitchell has written, paraphrasing Karl Marx, "labor makes it own geographies, but not under conditions of its own choosing. . . . As long as labor continues to take hold of geographies and continually transforms them in the name of a justice that, while sensitive to "'the local' is also universal in outlook, the geography of capitalism will always be contested." Ford managers saw no justice in the strike, but plenty of threat at the local and global levels.[36]

Different managers had different ideas about how to make sense of the strike, though all shared a paternalistic belief that they knew better than the workers what was good for them. One felt that while the change in the food service plan may have been "the straw that broke the camel's back," it was "no doubt communism, coupled with ignorance" that caused the riot. Another believed that it was the paying of wages in cash rather than company scrip that led workers to take advantage, thinking that Ford's "kind treatment of them may be based on weakness." A third felt that the men "naturally" resented the placing of restrictions on their liberties though "such rules are only intended for the good of their own health." Another explained that it seemed "apparent" that some men could become "Bolshevistic" in their general attitude toward the company and could "quite easily forget that we were providing them with the best living conditions . . . they had known in all their days."[37] The political and ideological explanations of the strike and attendant violence suggest that Ford believed that at least some of its workers were already "modern," even though the racist fantasies simultaneously held by managers contradicted this. That is, the strike was not blamed simply on savagery and ignorance, but on Bolsheviks and Communists, decidedly modern actors. In response to the strike the company called in the Brazilian military, which arrested more than thirty "ringleaders." After the strike the company agreed to a police proposal to make workers rather than management into Fordlândia's foreigners by creating "passports" for all workers containing their fingerprints and previous police records, in a vivid illustration of Ford's recourse to relying on the Brazilian state even as it had a colonial understanding of Fordlândia as its own possession.

Living and working conditions on the plantation changed little as a result of the strike, and the company continued to have trouble finding enough workers. For the next five years, no rubber was exported, few seedlings survived, and what work was done centered on the creation of the "village" for the American staff. In 1934, after clearing eight thousand acres of rainforest, Ford admitted defeat at Fordlândia. Making a radical shift in strategy, the company abandoned virtually the entire plantation, save what it would use for research purposes, and bought more than seven thousand acres of land eighty miles away. The new plantation, named Belterra, promised better growing conditions and easier access to waterways and roads.

The move to Belterra coincided with another shift in policy as management decided it would allow some men to bring their families to live on the plantation and would build housing for them. Fantastic fears that the plantation would be overrun by poor women and their children who would require care but could not work had driven past policy. But as fewer and fewer men were willing to uproot themselves from communities and families, and as more and more single men left after working on the plantation for periods of time, the company conceded. One manager cabled his field recruiter, "Jovita find out quietly how much it would cost to bring 40–60–70 families . . . labor is so scarce here that we will have to figure on importing families and paying their way stop do this quietly."[38] By this time, although "no likely looking prospect [was] turned away," Ford was still failing to sustain the workforce it needed. The strategy displayed supreme confidence in its own powers, as much as those of Brazilians, of race managers. Having mistaken "savages" for loyal, modern workers, the company rethought but did not retreat; having succeeded in creating neither a "loyal" nor a "disciplined" workforce, Ford set its sights on the workers of the future: children.[39]

In a letter to the Detroit headquarters a manager at Belterra described the "youngsters who are growing up on the plantations . . . who most assuredly are our best prospects for future employees." Again, the connection between workers and the natural world was made clear, with new laborers growing up alongside seedlings. Photos of a visit to the plantation by Brazilian president Getulio Vargas show smiling children waving Brazilian flags — which bear the slogan "Order and Progress." That these watchwords could also have been Ford's reflects the basis on which a nationalizing — and nationalistic — government and a colonizing corporation could coexist. One photo in a Ford promotional brochure bears the caption that opens this chapter: "Shades of Tarzan! You'd never guess these bright, happy healthy school children lived in a jungle city that didn't even exist a few years ago!"[40]

If Fordlândia's project focused mostly on experimentation with *hevea brasiliensis*, Belterra became the new site for fuller experimentation with people. Virtually every activity on the plantation carried within it the potential for Fordist ideas about nationalism, thrift, science, and progress to be shaped into behavior-modifying campaigns. With the introduction of family living at Belterra came the imposition of a multitude of requirements. School was compulsory for adults ("The night shift is reserved for adults and the one who refuses — goodbye") and for children; required uniforms were provided by the company: "boys wore outfits similar to Boy Scouts and girls neat white pleated skirts and white blouses." The decision to provide uniforms to those children who could not afford them was defended by one manager who felt the psychological impact on the children would be too great if they were not able to afford their own uniforms. Working from a textbook called "Moral Education: My Little Friends," children studied Portuguese, geography, Brazilian history, arithmetic and geometry.[41] Living in what was described by one writer as a "children's paradise," residents of Belterra learned American folk dancing, an obsession of

Henry Ford's, and were entertained by Ford-made motion pictures. The company felt this practice was so successful that Edsel Ford proposed making films about the plantations and then showing them at points along the Amazon and northern Brazilian coast.

From the beginning of the plantations in the late 1920s until 1940 no significant amount of rubber was exported from the plantations to Detroit for use in tire production. Despite Ford's poor production record the plantations began to receive a tremendous amount of attention in the early 1940s because of the changed global political situation. The United States, beginning to worry that access to rubber was increasingly under threat, sought to create political support for the Ford project: the *Detroit Times* ran a series of articles on Ford and Brazilian rubber, which were republished as a small booklet in support of the war effort. *Harpers, Cosmopolitan,* and *Business Week* all ran features on the plantations in 1944. The caption under a *Business Week* photo of a time clock read, "And time clocks, incongruous devices in the customarily indolent atmosphere of a steaming Amazon jungle — measure the workers 11 hour days."[42]

In 1941 the company produced a promotional pamphlet. "The Ford Rubber Plantations" told the story of the lucky Brazilian people who were being civilized through the generosity and vision of Ford. Describing both the natural and built environments at Fordlândia and Belterra, the pamphlet seems designed to lure potential managers and scientists as well as investment by the United States. The homey little pamphlet sets out "[t]o give you some idea of the problems that are involved in this vast project and of the methods by which they are being brought to successful conclusion and reminds the reader that The Ford Rubber Plantations of Brazil represent but one of many Ford Motor Company projects for the scientific development and utilization of natural resources . . . projects that in no small measure make possible the building of finer and finer cars at low prices within the reach of more and more people."[43]

The scary specter of "waste" land and the "jungle" features prominently in the story of "natives" being brought into the fold of modernity: "Paved roads, cement walks, comfortable homes, electric lights, telephones — this might be any Midwestern town. But it is Belterra, buried deep in the jungle of Brazil. . . . Yes, There is even a golf course — a sporty 18 holes — at Fordlândia. Beautiful clubhouse, tropical foliage — and 700 miles from civilization."[44]

One journalist was moved to note the participation of the schoolchildren of the plantations in the creation of "Latin-Saxonian unity." Now presumably no longer to be seen as Indian and mixed-race but as "Latins," Ford's rubber workers were fighting the good fight: "Undismayed by isolation these boys and girls are going ahead, playing their part in a great movement that is . . . not only setting an example for satisfied workmen and helping to unify the Western Hemisphere by producing a necessary product for the Americas in the Americas."[45]

In 1941, the company estimated that its plantations "would produce from 30 to 40 million pounds of high quality rubber during the next ten years . . . and thereafter a minimum of 10,000,000 pounds per year." But in 1946 the company left Brazil more abruptly than it had arrived, departing virtually overnight. With the introduction of synthetic rubber in the United States, Ford — and the country as a whole — had found a new solution to their production worries. Ford sold the plantations to the Brazilian government for $250,000, a fraction of the obscene sum of $20 million they had poured into the project.

In kind, "taming savages" or raising children to be workers was not unlike what Ford did in U.S. contexts, where from early on it had tried to link behavior at home to wages at work. Social control goes with the territory of making people do alienating wage labor, but recognizing that both social control and nationalization have relied on and promoted racial categorization allows us to begin to think differently about the staying power of racist practice even when laws change. At Ford, "scientific" evaluation was embedded in the quest for constant improvement, and this commitment to improvement was highly racialized. The line that separates racial from national characteristics in racist thought moves constantly, determined by geography, region, behavior, and timing, not by scientific understandings. In Brazil, Ford managers once felt "it may prove advantageous to hire Chinese laborers, undoubtedly the best of all oriental workmen . . . as there are many worthless fellows among ordinary Brazilian laborers."[46] Yet in Detroit, Chinese laborers were never considered, even as the importation of workers was always on managers' minds. That the overarching goals of production and improvement of men through work could be pursued through such contradictory practices reveals the depth of fantasy that racism requires, the significance of local context to making race have meaning, the enormous power of those who control wealth to control ideas, and the limits set by national histories and peculiarities on how, but not whether, Ford could continually attempt to manage race.

Insofar as the company producing rubber, the short, unhappy history of Ford in rural Brazil continually teetered between failure and farce. As a laboratory for making men, and later families, it was scarcely any more effectual. But as a laboratory for informal U.S. corporate empire building, it cannot be written off so easily. The same hubris that compromised its attempts to understand the ecology and people of the region allowed it to see the latter as malleable racial material, capable, above all, of being managed. Moreover, even during a period of nationalist and populist authoritarian rule in Brazil, Ford could feel confident in building its own "land" there, eliciting the aid of local authorities without having to make constant appeals for the backing of the guns of the U.S. Empire so frequently heard in Central and South America. The projects of racial improvement that it shared with national elites, plus the wealth and promise Ford brought to rural areas devastated by the world market it extolled, could provide a sense that there would be time to develop control over the things it thought consequential: the clock, the school, the clinic and, above all, the pace of labor and lives of laborers.

NOTES

1. This chapter was written before the publication of Greg Grandin's *Fordlândia: The Rise and Fall of Henry Ford's Forgotten Jungle City* (New York: Metropolitan, 2009.) Grandin's book makes several arguments about what Fordlândia can help us understand about the Ford Motor Company specifically and industrial impact on extractive industries more generally. His work is largely uninterested in the role played by racial thinking that forms the core of the research presented here. For more on this see Elizabeth Esch, "Breeding Rubber, Breeding Workers," in "Fordtown: Managing Race and Nation in the American Empire, 1925–1945" (PhD diss., New York University, 2004) and Elizabeth Esch, "'Shades of Tarzan! Ford on the Amazon," *Cabinet: A Quarterly Journal of Art and Culture*, issue 7 (Summer 2002).

2. Ann Laura Stoler, "Tense and Tender Ties: The Politics of Comparison in North American History and (Post) Colonial Studies," *Journal of American History* 88, no. 3 (2001): 861.

3. Diego Rivera, with Gladys March, *My Art, My Life: An Autobiography* (New York: Dover Press, 1991), 116.

4. Quoted in George F. Pierrot, *An Illustrated Guide to the Diego Rivera Frescoes* (Detroit: Detroit Institute of Arts, 1934).

5. The most useful work on Ford's Americanization activities in the United States is Stephen Meyer III, *The Five Dollar Day: Labor Management and Social Control in the Ford Motor Company, 1908–1921* (Albany: State University of New York Press, 1981). A brilliant fictional treatment of the ceremonies associated with the Americanization program at Ford can be found in Jeffrey Eugenides, *Middlesex* (New York: Picador, 2003).

6. On the idea of "in-betweenness" in a U.S. context, see James R. Barrett and David Roediger, "Inbetween Peoples: Race, Nationality and the 'New Immigrant' Working Class," *Journal of American Ethnic History* 16, no. 3 (Spring 1997): 3–44.

7. Unlabelled folders containing the *Ormoc's* provision lists, Box 4, Accession 74,

Henry Ford Archives, Benson Ford Research Center of the Henry Ford, Dearborn, Michigan (hereafter BFRCHF).

8. LaRue, "Living Conditions in the Amazon Valley," May 6, 1927, Vertical File, "Rubber Plantation," BFRCHF, 6, 1, 4.

9. See Anthony W. Marx, *Making Race and Nation: A Comparison of South Africa, the United States and Brazil* (New York: Cambridge University Press, 1998); Nancy Stepan, *"The Hour of Eugenics": Race, Gender and Nation in Latin America* (Ithaca: Cornell University Press, 1991); Carl N. Degler, *Neither Black Nor White: Slavery and Race Relations in Brazil and the United States* (Madison: University of Wisconsin Press, 1991); Agnelo Rossi, *Brasil: integração de raças e nacionalidades* (São Paulo: Companhia Ilimitada, 1991); Maria Luiza Tucci Carneiro, *O racismo na história do Brasil: mito e realidade* (São Paulo: Editora Ática, 1994); and France Winddance Twine, *Racism in a Racial Democracy: The Maintenance of White Supremacy in Brazil* (New Brunswick, N.J.: Rutgers University Press, 1998). For a more recent and critical examination of race, culture, and statecraft in Brazil see Micol Seigel, *Uneven Encounters: Making Race and Nation in Brazil and the United States* (Durham, N.C.: Duke University Press 2009).

10. LaRue, "Living Conditions," 5, BFRCHF.

11. Letter from H. F. Firestone to Henry Ford, BFRCHF.

12. Contemporary scandals about slave labor in Firestone's Liberian plantations made Ford's public commitment to "progress" seem strategic and, apparently at least, heartfelt. See I. K. Sundiata, *Black Scandal: America and the Liberian Labor Crisis, 1929–1936* (Philadelphia: Institute for the Study of Human Issues, 1980).

13. Within a few years of its implementation the British restriction plan was scrapped, owing largely to the refusal of Dutch growers to be cartel-ized. American firms continued to pursue rubber production in spite of this. See John Galey, "Industrialist in the Wilderness: Henry Ford's Amazon Venture," *Journal of Interamerican Studies and World Affairs* 21, no. 2 (1979): 261–89.

14. Barbara Weinstein, *For Social Peace in Brazil: Industrialists and the Remaking of the Working Class in São Paulo, 1920–1964* (Chapel Hill: University of North Carolina Press, 1996), 1–4; Joel Wolfe, *Autos and Progress: The Brazilian Search for Modernity* (New York: Oxford University Press, 2010), which furthers research into the relationships between technology, democracy, and consumerism.

15. Weinsten, *For Social Peace,* 5.

16. Allan Nevins and Frank Ernest Hill, *Ford* (New York: Scriber, 1954), 236. John Galey says quite clearly that the problem was entirely of Ford's making in that the company sought state, rather than federal, exemptions from taxation. John Galey, "Industrialist in the Wilderness: Henry Ford's Amazon Venture," *Journal of Interamerican Studies and World Affairs* 21, no. 2 (1979): 261–89.

17. Richard Tucker, *Insatiable Appetite: The United States and the Ecological Degradation of the Tropical World* (Berkeley: University of California Press, 2000), 259. See also Joe Jackson's recent book, *The Thief at the End of the World: Rubber, Power and the Seeds of Empire* (New York: Viking, 2008).

18. "The Ford Rubber Plantations," n.d., Vertical File, "Rubber Plantations — Pamphlets," BFRCHF.

19. Galey, "Industrialist in the Wilderness," 275. In late 1933 Ford hired its first botanist, who recommended that the company abandon Fordlândia and move to more usable land upriver. See also Grandin, *Fordlândia*, esp. chaps. 20–22.

20. Mira Wilkins, *American Business Abroad: Ford on Six Continents* (Detroit: Wayne State University Press,) 1964, 128.

21. Folder "Proposed — Rubber Plantation Book — Material Instructions," Box 8, Accession 74, BFRCHF. The voluminous literature on comparative and transnational racial systems involving the United States and Brazil centers almost wholly on the black-white color line. For a recent contribution to the debate, see Michael Hanchard, "Acts of Miscegenation: Transnational Black Politics, Anti-Imperialism and the Ethnicentrisms of Pierre Bourdieu and Loïc Wacquant," *Theory, Culture and Society*, no. 20 (August 2003): 5–29. The inclusion of indigenous histories means that the black-white basis of comparison, which is in itself troubling for its reliance on modern racial constructions and therefore limited in its ability to explain how those constructions came into being, is appropriately decentered.

22. Folder "Proposed — Rubber Plantation Book — Material Instructions," Box 8, Accession 74, BFRCHF.

23. Cited in Galey, "Industrialist in the Wilderness," 271.

24. Jorge Amado, *Tent of Miracles* (New York: Knopf, 1971); Jerry Dávila, *Diploma of Whiteness: Race and Social Policy in Brazil, 1917–1945* (Durham, N.C.: Duke University Press, 2003).

25. LaRue, "Living Conditions," 4, BFRCHF.

26. LaRue, "Living Conditions."

27. "Weekly Reports, November, December, 1930," Folder "Companhia Ford Industrial do Brasil — Progress Reports — 1930," Box 2, Accession 74, BFRCHF.

28. "South America, 1927 (Blakely File) Carl LaRue Data," Companhia Ford Industrial do Brasil (CFIDB), Box 1, Accession 4, BFRCHF.

29. E. P. Thompson, "Time, Work-Discipline and Industrial Capitalism," *Past and Present*, no. 38 (1967): 56–97; Herbert Gutman, "Work, Culture and Society in Industrializing America, 1815–1919," *American Historical Review* 78, no. 3 (June 1973): 531–88; and A. Mark Smith, *Mastered by the Clock: Time, Slavery and Freedom in the American South* (Chapel Hill: University of North Carolina Press, 1997).

30. See Stepan, *Hour of Eugenics*; and Michel Foucault, *The Birth of the Clinic: An Archaeology of Medical Perception* (New York: Vintage Books, 1994). On colonial understandings of race and the tropics, see Warwick Anderson, "The Natures of Culture: Environment and Race in the Colonial Tropics," in *Nature in the Global South: Environmental Projects in South and Southeast Asia*, ed. Paul Greenough and Anna L. Tsing (Durham, N.C.: Duke University Press, 2003), 29–46; and Warwick Anderson, "Going through the Motions: American Hygiene and Colonial Mimicry," *American Literary History* 14, no. 4 (2002): 686–719.

31. "Letter from C. Beaton, Medical Officer, Boa Vista, to R. D. McClure, Henry Ford Hospital, October 1, 1929, "Vertical File, Rubber Plantation, BFRCHF. Boa Vista was the name used before Fordlândia was adopted.

32. "The Irradiating Center of Civilization," *Time*, June 1941.

33. Ibid.

34. "Riot at Boa Vista, December 22, 1930," Box 2, Accession 74, BFRCHF.

35. On significance of time clocks see Gutman, "Work, Culture and Society," 531–88.

36. Don Mitchell, "The Scales of Justice: Localist Ideology, Large-Scale Production and Agricultural Labor's Geography of Resistance in 1930s California," in *Organizing the Landscape: Geographical Perspectives on Labor Unionism*, ed. Andrew Herod (Minneapolis: University of Minnesota Press, 1998), 189.

37. Letter from Rogge and Chatfeld to Kennedy; Letter from Kennedy to Carnegie; unsigned report, Box 2, Accession 74, BFRCHF.

38. Radiograms between Jovita and Johnson, "Indian Labor," Box 6, Accession 74, BFRCHF.

39. Proposed rubber book, 11, BFRCHF.

40. "Ford Rubber Plantations," 1941, Vertical File, "Pamphlets: Henry Ford Archives," BFRCHF.

41. "Schools," Box 2, Accession 74, BFRCHF.

42. *BusinessWeek*, 1941.

43. "Ford Rubber Plantations."

44. Ibid.

45. Vance Simmonds, "Schools of the Amazon," *Herald*, n.d.

46. Ibid.

CHAPTER FIVE

The Making of a Federal Company Town

Sunflower Village, Kansas

CHRISTOPHER W. POST

Company towns in the United States in the twentieth century possessed the same fundamental purpose as others throughout the Americas: to keep workers near their jobs so as to maximize labor-cost effectiveness. As with company towns elsewhere, they exhibited tight mechanisms of social control and provided only limited opportunities for employees to improve their conditions. However, unlike their pan-American cousins, company towns in the United States were predominantly private, with little to no government oversight or even church paternalism. This pattern changed, however, with the Great Depression and World War II. A different company town landscape emerged because of the growing importance of public investment in company towns. They differed from their corporate brethren in layout, openness, politics, and social opportunities. They were, indeed, democratized company towns.

This essay complements Andrew Herod's discussion, in chapter 1, of landscape and space by elaborating on the geographic conceptualization of place. Second, it summarizes the landscape conditions of American private company towns, primarily those of the Appalachian and western United States. Third, it introduces the idea of the federal company town that resulted from growing government involvement in the American economy from the 1930s through the 1940s. This started with President Franklin D. Roosevelt's Depression-era New Deal, which led to increased defense industry mobilization during the Second World War. Finally, despite the harshness of the company town landscape in the United States — both private and public — worker residents still developed profound attachments to their communities; they turned the spaces of external control into places of internal meaning. This chapter concludes by investigating the ways in which company towns acted as "places" among their residents, enabling workers to develop attachments and assign meaning to the cultural landscape.

In illustrating these points, this chapter draws heavily on my previous work on the federal company town of Sunflower Village (Kansas) to illustrate how it compared to private company towns in the United States.[1] The Federal Public Housing Administration (FPHA) built Sunflower Village for employees of Sunflower Ordnance Works (SOW), a munitions factory about thirty-one miles west of Kansas City (Missouri). Initially fabricated as a temporary arrangement, Sunflower Village stood the test of time and provided much more safety, mobility, and opportunities for family interaction than many private company towns and even other ordnance works plants. Due to its morphology and functional zonation, Sunflower more easily stimulated such a relationship between workers, their families, and the community, particularly for children. Sunflower's landscape stood at the core of this bond and distinguished it from other company towns, making it the anchor for this synthesis.

PLACE AND SENSE OF PLACE

Andrew Herod provides excellent analyses of the geographical conceptualizations of space and landscape in chapter 1. He adds to what Don Mitchell claims, that every landscape is produced to serve a function, particularly in a modern and global capitalistic world.[2] Complementary to these ideas is that of place. Space tends to keep distance from intimate relationships of the self; it focuses on social, economic, and political interactions. Place, on the other hand, concentrates more on the personal meaning that is produced through living in and experiencing those very same relationships situated in the landscape. In addition to reflecting and reinforcing values, the landscape also provides a means and meaning to its interactors. As geographer Ben Marsh precisely claims in his study of Pennsylvania coal towns, "place is . . . partly the *means* an area provides for its own continuation but also the *meaning* derived from its past for its continuation."[3]

All humans sense the means and meaning of their places through experience. Sensing place incorporates everyday actions and emotions that humans experience; to varying extents, all people can accrue an attachment to their surroundings. Despite spatial control enforced through the company town landscape upon laborers, that very employment does provide a means to human survival for the workers. It puts a roof over the head and bread on the table, as the saying goes. Simultaneously, and because of this relationship, the industrial landscape — despite the pollution, long hours, poor pay, and health endangerment — gives meaning to the lives of those workers as the source of their livelihood. It is this dichotomous situation that creates a series of unique places out of the cultural landscape. And places, like space, do not exist in the ether. They constantly change and shift according to their inhabitants' reproduction of space and landscape.

Over the past twenty years, cultural geographers have turned this study of places, their meanings, and connection to our daily lives — commonly referred to as "sense of place" — into an important field. The approach intends to get closer to the heart of a community by searching for its vernacular qualities and relationships among the residents and between the residents and their environment. The geographer Cary de Wit has proposed a useful working definition for sense of place: "the actual experience of place in all its dimensions: physical, social, psychological, intellectual, and emotional."[4] Kent Ryden, Peirce Lewis, and Richard Shein have all highlighted that individuals and groups convert the spaces they occupy into meaning-rich places as they form the connections that are essential for social life.[5] Social theorists in the fields of geography, philosophy, and anthropology have contributed to this dialogue through a variety of frameworks that address the experience of place.[6] They emphasize structures inherent to society including neo-Marxism and social justice.[7]

Geographer Robert Sack postulates making place as a process of meaning, social relations, and nature. Action defines this process and vice versa: "[p]laces constrain and enable our actions." Though experienced at a different scale, Sack's discussion of control over the construction of place in the home relates to company towns: "As an ideal, the range of control associated with the home provides not only such familiar positive qualities as security and ease, but also a sense of responsibility for that place. Yet, control and responsibility never occur equally or without limit. Children have less of it than adults, and all too often men have more than women."[8]

Intuition tells us that company towns would never be an ideal, even possible, place to which to attach, for the simple fact that worker residents lacked that very control over their own home. However, studies of company towns challenge this assessment as well as others of sense of place, despite their being "hard places" and *seemingly* difficult places to which to attach.[9] Studies of company towns, both public and private, have dealt with this very issue.[10] The remainder of this chapter explores how this has occurred in company towns across the United States.

THE CORPORATE COMPANY TOWN IN THE UNITED STATES

The socially and economically engineered landscape of the corporate American company town directly reflects the foundational points of place, space, and landscape. American company towns also reflect all of the geographic, social, economic, and political objectives of the firm as outlined throughout this book. These towns existed as isolated, simple, temporary, and grid-based communities. American companies provided employees and their families with basic, cheap, and uniform accommodations, utilities, a company store with scrip, health-care services, schools, and churches.[11]

The company towns in the United States certainly shared many cultural attributes with other North American cities when it came to ethnicity, religion, education, and health care. The United States had a long-standing tradition of open borders and since the 1880s was a well-established immigrant nation, which had a tremendous impact on company towns.

Companies frequently hired immigrants for mining, logging, and factory positions because they often could save on labor costs. American Indians and Mexicans sought positions in western camps. Scandinavians worked in midwestern logging towns while Appalachian coal towns attracted large numbers of Eastern Europeans, and southern Colorado coal companies hired Spanish and Japanese immigrants.[12] Ethnic neighborhoods evolved out of segregation policies that either were enforced by the company or evolved out of pre-existing ethnic relations. World Wars I and II hastened this segregation out of fear by white Americans and those European groups they accepted. Greek Town, Austria Town, and "Jap" Town existed in McGill, Nevada.[13]

Religious services and communities provided one venue for company town residents to express this diversity and establish social relationships. As Marsh noted, "churches were the physical and social centers of neighborhoods and communities [in his part of Pennsylvania], and a small town might have had a dozen different congregations."[14] Companies invested in building churches to provide the workers with a moral foundation for peaceful labor relations but did not develop a paternalistic relationship as the Catholic Church did in Volta Redonda (Brazil), as Oliver Dinius reports in chapter 6. Companies hired priests and ministers from regional churches and gave them additional part-time work in the mines or as umpires in community baseball games. The McCloud Lumber Company of McCloud, California, possessed so much diversity in its employee demographics as to erect separate Episcopalian, Catholic, and two different Baptist churches.[15]

Companies realized that establishing social services beyond churches was essential to employee morale and productivity. Schools stood central to the company town experience for youth. American companies built schools and oftentimes lent homes to teachers at the same low rental rates as regular workers.[16] Firms offered employee health care at relatively inexpensive rates since they could lose profits if workers were too sick or injured to work. Companies even built emergency facilities in their towns if the nearest hospital was too far away. Kennecott Copper Corporation built such facilities in McGill, Nevada, in addition to local doctors' offices for everyday care.[17] Finally, businesses constructed recreation facilities such as baseball diamonds to help promote morale and fitness in their towns. Companies even offered teams uniforms and equipment in southwestern Pennsylvania and southern Colorado.[18]

In most company towns a company store dominated retail sales and made employees use extended credit or company scrip.[19] The company allowed no outside competitors, forcing residents to purchase everything at those stores. In some cases, as Aurora Gómez-Galvarriato establishes in chapter 2, this was the workers' best and fairest source for credit. Employees received this credit at the store, and the company deducted an equivalent amount from the worker's next paycheck. The amount deducted, however, because of interest or high fixed prices, oftentimes forced employees to spend more than they earned, ending up in a perpetual cycle of debt to the company that forced them to work longer hours in the mine. When managed greedily by the company, scrip evolved into one of the most crucial aspects of spatial control over workers in the company town landscape. The debt cycle meant less freedom to leave and find work elsewhere for a competitor, who might pay better. Merle Travis, son of a coal miner, famously wrote about the scrip experience in the song "Sixteen Tons." The lyrics, popularized by "Tennessee" Ernie Ford's 1955 cover, illustrated the crippling effect on laborers and the community landscape: "You load Sixteen Tons / whadaya get? / Another day older and deeper in debt / Saint Peter don't you call me 'cause I can't go / I owe my soul to the company store."[20] The spirit of the song and its final line became part of country and blues music as southern sharecroppers experienced the same degrading practice (e.g., the southern rock/blues/jam band Gov't Mule's song "Mule").[21]

There remains one particularly crucial construct of company town culture to discuss. No known evidence purports that company towns implemented any type of community government. Allen explains that civic governments undermined the power of the companies, and that expanding power to employees was not in their best interest.[22] Residents received no opportunity to organize, propose changes to their community, or coordinate with each other simple community services (regardless of the fact that companies may have accepted labor organization in the mine, factory, or field). This power structure affected living conditions and the landscape. This final point defines well the overall private company town experience. It also offers one of the largest differences between private company towns and their public brethren, such as Sunflower Village.

VARIATION: THE FEDERAL "COMPANY" TOWN

In surviving the Great Depression with the New Deal and eventually entering into World War II, the federal government created a different type of company town in America. This section provides examples of three such communities — Sunflower Village (Kansas), Norris (Tennessee), and Boulder City (Nevada) — by addressing why and how these towns existed and by discussing the case of Sunflower Village in greater detail. In the decades before the 1930s, private extraction companies had been putting folks to work in the West in camps, some of which eventually developed into permanent towns. During the Great Depression, the federal government became increasingly involved in putting U.S. citizens to work. In the process, the government established a few company towns whose landscapes differed from those of most private towns despite the same original inspiration: keep employees close by for sake of timeliness and cost effectiveness. In contrast to the private company towns, however, many of these government communities were planned in a progressive fashion inspired by the garden city movement and the advent of suburbia. Moreover, the government provided residents with goods and services through contracted regional companies or co-ops, thus avoiding the potentially abusive scrip system. As a result of these services and landscapes, reflecting departures from most corporate company town plans, these democratized company towns became special places in America.

At its height, Sunflower Village, Kansas, accommodated upward of seven thousand employees of the Sunflower Ordnance Works (sow) munitions plant. The small towns of Eudora and De Soto sat closest to the new plant and community. Lawrence, a college town of just over fourteen thousand residents, lay just fifteen miles further west of the new plant.[23] The Kansas River and the Atchison, Topeka and Santa Fe Railway linked these cities and provided resources for the plant. The government assumed that these neighboring communities would also absorb the influx of employees; thus their plan did not originally include Sunflower Village. Rubber rationing during World War II eliminated long-distance commuting from and to Kansas City as an alternative solution, however. When it became clear that accommodations were necessary, workers first built their own tent city across Kansas Highway 10 (K-10). This grassroots

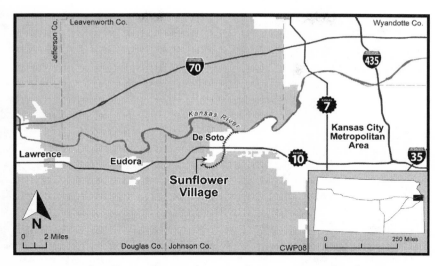

Figure 5.1 Map of Sunflower Village in relation to other communities of northeast Kansas. Map by author.

workers camp eventually evolved into Sunflower Village. First, the FPHA built barracklike dormitories next to the plant for employees without children, but eventually a more permanent solution was needed. In 1943, the administration built Sunflower Village for workers with families. The town remained under federal administration until 1959, when the government sold the land and the buildings to a private investor.[24]

Sunflower Village's layout reflected the progressive urban planning of the time associated with the "garden city" and "greenbelt" town movements. Its distinctive features included winding roads that minimized the impact of the automobile near residential units. The town possessed grid-style roads within a fluid perimeter of curving streets, a pattern that became popular with suburban growth after World War II. One New Deal project, the Greenbelt Program, extensively used this plan. The program created the suburbs of Greenbelt (Maryland), Greenhills (Ohio), and Greendale (Wisconsin).[25]

British landscape architect Ebenezer Howard originated the urban garden city concept in England. Howard's student Clarence S. Stein popularized the plan in the United States by selling it to public planners and implemented it at the private company town of Tyrone (New Mexico). The garden city plan possessed three elements. First, it was designed to create "a town planned for industry and healthy living, of a size that makes possible a full measure of social life, but no larger, surrounded by a permanent rural belt." This objective led to

Figure 5.2 Aerial photo of Sunflower Village taken during World War II. 1943. Photo courtesy of David Rhodes, manager of Clearview City.

the inclusion of "greenbelts," or open spaces used to create a rural environment in an otherwise urban setting. Second, roads possessed specialized purposes. Cul-de-sacs and smaller lanes in residential neighborhoods and larger streets in business districts separated pedestrians and automobiles. Third, the plan implemented clusters of homes (called "neighborhood units" or "superblocks") and businesses that connected to the rest of the community by unobtrusive lanes. Overall, Howard and Stein devised "a town in which people could live peacefully with the automobile — or rather in spite of it."[26] Traditional downtowns and Main Streets were absent in garden cities. Primary roads curved around the town and residential entrances opened to large lawns, with perhaps a sidewalk but no intervening road between facing neighbors.

For Sunflower Village, the main entry road off K-10 — Sunflower Road — wrapped around the west side of the town. The newer eastern half of the village presented a semicircular design with a limb that jutted to the northeast. The dutifully named Army Road divided the village into its two parts: Old (west) and New (east) Villages. Sunflower Village likely introduced such a curvilinear design before anywhere else in Kansas. Other planned communities under the New Deal may have possessed more extravagant designs, but Sunflower was at once both ahead of its time and an impressive accomplishment given that it was conceived and built in little more than a year.[27]

Residential buildings took over Sunflower's landscape. The FPHA originally built 852 one-story homes. Residents adjusted their own personal spaces, but more permanent changes were not made until after the Korean Conflict (1950–53). Only building size separated one residential unit from another. The largest buildings stood 118 feet long and 24 feet wide; the smallest were 72 feet by 24 feet. Square footage varied from just over 1,700 to nearly 3,000 feet. Colors of green, cream, slate, and tan existed as one additional measure of separation of one from another.[28] Original village blueprints and maps show that each residential building originally had as many as six individual units within. A few possessed only four units. The buildings in the New Village addition contained only two units each. Studio apartments were the most common floor plan. These units contained one living room/bedroom, a kitchen, and a closet-sized bathroom, offering only 472 square feet to their occupant. Two-bedroom and three-bedroom units were made available to workers with spouses and children.

Residents expressed their individuality via decorating the walls or moving in their own furniture. Families altered the outdoor landscape with flower plantings and in some cases vegetable gardens. The community also planted a large victory garden of the time. Compared to most corporate company towns in the American West, Sunflower's rent was low, ranging from $29 to $36.50 per month, based on the number of bedrooms.[29] All units possessed kitchen appliances, and residents could rent either a furnished or unfurnished unit. The government provided and delivered gas for water heaters, coal for stoves,

Figure 5.3 Residential unit in Sunflower Village (now in Clearview City) taken in March 2002. Photo by author.

ice, sanitary services, and electricity.[30] Telephone communications were offered originally only through a few pay phones scattered throughout the community. Lines for all units eventually made their way into the village after World War II.

Beyond the residences, the government built a number of administrative, social, and business buildings to provide its residents with the necessities of everyday life. The FPHA first built a community building for the village at Sunflower Road and K-10 Highway. This original structure faced east and housed nearly everything the community needed apart from daily goods: administration offices, a library, and an auditorium used for Saturday night dances and church services.[31] It even served as the schoolhouse until the first of two permanent schools was built behind it.

Sunflower Village's designers erected two single-story commercial buildings facing K-10 on the village's southern edge. This location departed from strict garden city form since it was not central within the community's plan. Instead of implementing a company store with scrip, the government reserved the buildings for private contractors so that residents would not have to travel for essentials such as food, prescriptions, postal service, daycare, or immediate medical attention and thus offered residents nearly anything they could need during a walk to their local "downtown."

These two commercial buildings demonstrate the first example of Sunflower's existence as a democratized federal company town. The Sunflower model clearly went against the basic idea of the firm's making money by providing goods and services to their employees via company-owned stores and withdrawing scrip from paychecks. Instead, the federal government saved money by not operating its own store (such as commissaries on military bases) and also increased the market for regional businesses looking to expand.

The western business building stood first and measured approximately three hundred feet long and sixty feet wide and was white. This building provided residents with daily needs and housed a grocery store (owned by a regional chain), barber shop, drug store (operated by the Walgreen Corporation), soda parlor (located within the drug store), and post office.[32] A Red Cross station, doctor's office, and a daycare also operated out of this first building.[33] The FPHA set up a press for two community papers: the *Sunflower Villager* and the *Sunflower Planet*. The needs supplied by the businesses in this original building — food, health, and daycare — provided services that allowed for efficient employee production. In addition, the proximity of goods and services for residents meant they did not have to travel during wartime rationing.

The FPHA built the second commercial building in July 1945, two months before the end of World War II, and provided more entertainment services for so-cial interaction such as a movie theater, tavern, gas station, Sears catalog center, and bowling alley.[34] Because it was built so close to the end of the war, wartime residents shared fewer memories of this place. This second set of businesses focused on entertainment, which kept morale up. The timing also suggests that Sunflower Ordnance Works and Village was looking at becoming a more per-manent facility.

Though Sunflower Village's business buildings were not physically located at the center of the community's landscape, they were central to the lives of its residents. In particular, these stores offered unique experiences for the youth, whether it was through the obvious time at school or daycare or the more com-plex relationships forged at the soda parlor or at the movie theater with friends and family members. Every resident that I interviewed voiced some opinion about the businesses there and the opportunities they afforded. The larger issue here, however, is that these businesses offered a choice.

The choice and opportunity to travel to surrounding cities for goods and services, such as Lawrence and Kansas City, depended on timing and personal preference. For the first couple of years and before the end of World War II, residents had to go to the cities for some needs such as postal services.[35] As the number of services in the village increased, especially at the end of World War II, residents could choose to spend time and patronize their local services and businesses. Those who had personal transportation, especially after World War II and rubber rationing, traveled to Kansas City for specialty clothes shopping, groceries, or entertainment (the movie theater and Sears catalog center were not built in Sunflower until after World War II).[36] Many informants commented, however, that they utilized Sunflower's commercial buildings with more daily frequency during their various tenures in the community.

The government helped villagers adapt quickly to their new living situa-tion by providing services and activities that maintained efficiency at work and minimized stress. FPHA officials viewed community involvement as a way to speed the process of acclimation and to provide social and physical recreation away from plant work. To this end, the community offered residents a handful of ways to connect with each other and the village. The first three contrast with U.S. corporate company towns to varying degrees.

First and similar to corporate and North American company towns, religion held its vitality to life in Sunflower Village. The FPHA, however, did not imme-diately build a church. Unlike private company towns, or other countries such as Brazil and its historically close association with Catholicism, the govern-ment restrained from building any religious structures. Logic points to the First

Amendment right that separates church from state as an explanation for this. Building a church for one group could have meant building a church for every group represented in the community. Instead, all religious activities occurred in the community building, including both Catholic and Protestant services through World War II. However, a resident Protestant minister arrived in the village in October 1944.[37] No faith-specific meetinghouse existed in Sunflower until after the government sold the Sunflower property.

Second, the government helped establish the two papers: the *Sunflower Planet* and *Sunflower Villager*. The *Planet* reported information for all Sunflower Ordnance Works employees. The *Villager* was specific to village residents. Residents, in collaboration with government officials, edited the *Villager*.[38] Such sources of information may have been welcome in other company towns, but time to write and edit would have been rare, and the editorship would have been strict and not placed in the hands of residents or workers.

Third, in a rare feat for company towns, and defining of such a democratized company town experience, villagers formed their own town council. Organized in 1943, the committee consisted of five neighborhood representatives and one general mayor with the objective of "collaborating with the Housing Authority" to make life in Sunflower as accommodating as possible.[39]

Finally, schools were also crucial to the Sunflower experience. As mentioned, Sunflower established schooling first in the original community building. Eventually, the FPHA built a dedicated school behind that structure. When New Village was developed, a second school was built. Both these schools, however, offered only kindergarten through middle school education. High school students commuted to De Soto.

These legacies of Sunflower's landscape — the businesses, schools, newspaper, town council — became central to it becoming a place among its residents. The memories of former residents clearly indicate this, as discussed more below.[40] Sunflower, however, did not exist on its own as a federal company town. Two more examples provide illustrative comparisons and contrasts with the Kansas community.

The U.S. government started building Hoover Dam in 1931 — the largest American public works project of the time. In 1928, the Bureau of Reclamation (BOR) started Government Survey Camp No. 1 near the dam site in Black Canyon to house surveyors and engineers. Several other campsites, such as McKeeversville and the aptly named Ragtown, sprang up in the region to house workers, both the employed and the hopeful. Eventually, in 1931, the settlements consolidated and evolved into Boulder City, Nevada, a series of dormitories and homes exclusively for dam workers, making commuting from Las Vegas (roughly thirty miles north) unnecessary. The government originally asked landscape architect Saco DeBoer to design the community, but the Great Depression forced the government to minimize his plans while government agents took over the planning process. Similar to the development of Sunflower, the BOR provided everything for Boulder City citizens including churches, a grocery store, and entertainment venues such as a movie theater. Two key contrasts exist, however, between Sunflower and Boulder City. Where schools were a priority for the FPHA at Sunflower, they were secondary in thought at Boulder City, and the schools' organization struggled because of this.[41] In addition, the Kansas community was offered a town government run by representatives from different "neighborhoods." Sims Ely, entrusted by the Department of Reclamation to keep the town clean for productive employees, effectively ran Boulder City single-handedly. Ely prohibited gambling and alcohol sales in his town (labor unions were also prohibited by the Department of Reclamation). After completion of the dam, the Boulder City population dropped but did survive. The city was incorporated in 1960 and exists today as the primary portal to Hoover Dam for visitors.

Norris (Tennessee) provides the third example of a government-run company town. Part of the Tennessee Valley Authority (TVA) born out of the Great Depression and Works Progress Administration, Norris originally existed as a camp for dam workers and provided basic goods and services (mostly through cooperatives), schooling, and its own government. The school, built and staffed by the TVA, was so good that it served as an experimental and demonstration site for the University of Tennessee.[42] The federal government planned Norris, but as the town evolved, it followed through on its plan to be unique with its curved roads, as the case study of Sunflower Village, Kansas, illustrates. The community grew throughout the TVA project but declined upon its completion. Remaining residents commuted to nearby Knoxville for work and for more and better goods and services, but Norris is still incorporated.

Sunflower Village, which offered social and economic freedoms beyond anything seen before, morphed from company town to Clearview City Retirement Village to its current status as a duplex rental community not acknowledged by the U.S. Census Bureau. Nearby De Soto desires to annex the property; several buildings from New Village were actually moved to De Soto. The post office still stands, and the community still retains its own postal code, but no other services survived. Boulder City, run iron-fisted by Sims Ely, thrives with approximately fifteen thousand residents and a median household annual income of just over $50,000. Boulder City profits from the real estate adage of "location, location, location" near Lake Mead. The site between Hoover Dam and Las Vegas brings in retirees for the warm weather, tourists for the dam and Las Vegas, and recreation enthusiasts for the lake. Norris, despite its early success, still serves as a more rural residential community within the Knoxville metropolitan area. The 2000 Census reports the population of Norris at just over fourteen hundred with a median household income of just over $47,000 per year.

Two models of company towns exist in the United States. Privately owned, or corporate, company towns exhibited a great amount of control over residents and limited their opportunities to connect with their communities and environment. The second form is the publicly owned type such as Sunflower, Boulder City, and Norris. Despite the contrasts between these two forms, however, there exists a common thread of contemporary human spatial behavior among these communities: the residents' making of place out of seemingly difficult spaces and harsh landscapes. One need only look at the remaining populations in Sunflower, Norris, and Boulder City to realize this fact. However, even western private corporate towns have survived and continue to operate, albeit usually in different situations. Some towns such as Cripple Creek, Colorado, have taken advantage of their environment and thrived from tourism. Communities including Cokedale (Colorado) and Toluca (Illinois) indeed exist, although as fragments of what they once were.[43] More near-urban company towns have become enveloped by their neighboring metropolitan cities, such as Pullman, Illinois, outside Chicago.

MAKING PLACE IN SUNFLOWER VILLAGE

Researching the place-making process in company towns is not new but is oftentimes too focused on the material landscape. Company towns, as illustrated throughout this volume, present many challenges to their working-class residents. Much of the literature on these communities focuses on this more critical perspective. Ben Marsh writes one of the most thoughtful analyses of place making in the coal-mining communities of Appalachia.[44] In addition, David Mould tells of the impact of long-lasting material culture and its affect on the busted company towns of the brick industry in Ohio.[45] More recently, Geoffrey Buckley utilizes historical photo archives to examine company towns owned by the Consolidation Coal Company in Appalachia. Such records reveal both the material and ethereal attributes of life in these towns.[46] David Robertson's work on Toluca (Illinois), Cokedale (Colorado), and Picher (Oklahoma) looks in great depth at the local processes that forge strong senses of commitment to place in such difficult conditions.[47] Robertson found that place making may be closely associated with movements to memorialize and preserve past experience when faced with the struggles of deindustrialization or the mines running out of minerals. Historians have also contributed to this research. Russell Elliott retells his own experience growing up in the now-defunct copper-mining town of McGill, Nevada, and the extent to which that lifestyle provided a special place in his life.[48] Rick Clyne indicates the distinctly multicultural landscape of Walsenburg, Colorado, and its surrounding coal-mining villages.[49] This literature also concludes that place making can occur even in the most difficult — often western — company town landscape.

Structures such as location, environment, and economics are critical to development of place in company towns. In addition, most scholars agree that time is required for place making to evolve. J. B. Jackson claims, "It is my own belief that a sense of place is something that we ourselves create in the course of time"; he continues, "But [others] . . . believe that a sense of place comes from our response to features which are *already* there — either a beautiful natural setting or well-designed architecture."[50] Yi-Fu Tuan also comments on the time needed for humans to turn space into place, stating that rootedness, not sense of place, results from several generations occupying the same place. Sense of place, he argues, "implies a certain distance between self and place that allows the self to appreciate place."[51] This interpretation makes room for personal and social mobility in the process of sensing place, as the popular adage "distance makes the heart grow fonder" may indicate. Writer Barry Lopez similarly agrees that place making requires time and also supports the crucial element of the natural environment in such a process. Lopez refers to this as "la querencia . . . a place on the ground where one feels secure."[52]

Given this literature about the importance of time in making place, company towns, because of their intentional temporality, become a crucial test of the concept. Companies, or the federal government, intended for these communities to exist for only a short amount of time, and oftentimes they did not possess impressive material landscapes, especially in regard to architecture (simple, rectangular homes with pitched roofs). They offered a challenging life to their residents. Still, and despite these facts, places were made and feelings became attached.

How, then, can place making occur in company towns? I focus on Sunflower Village to answer this question by exploring primarily the memories of former residents of the towns throughout its different phases, particularly during war-time production of World War II and the Korean Conflict. Of utmost importance here is how child residents of Sunflower connected to and made place out of the local landscape in step with, but also beyond, what was frequently experienced by adults. Creativity, independence, and socialization for the youth prove critical and empowering to this increased sensitivity of place that, according to my interviewees, existed much less among SOW workers.

One key component to work with here is the very plan used to design many company towns, particularly those federal towns that implemented a green village plan. The openness of these urban plans and the existent mobility work two ways. On the one hand, the openness of the green village reinforces Lopez's ideas of place making. On the other hand, the opportunities to shop, learn, and interact elsewhere within a logical travel distance could have reduced such a process. Instead, mobility fostered the perspective among residents about their home. Such attachment could be particularly strong among certain cohorts. In Sunflower Village, the impacts were felt especially by the youth of the village and their relationships with each other and their built surroundings. The space offered opportunity for exploration, socialization, mobility, and freedom; all were unavailable to their parents working long shifts.

Lopez's earlier comments about achieving intimacy and security with nature become important. The openness enabled by the garden city movement developed a more open and natural landscape in the urban environment, allowing residents more space to breathe, live, and connect with their natural surroundings, thus intensifying their relationship with the place. One result of Sunflower Village's urban plan and role of its business district was a great focus and a sense of power, independence, and control of place in the hands of children. Sunflower Village, to be frank, revolved around the community's children, who at one time made up half the town's population, leading to nicknames such as "Nursery Junction."[53] For these children it also granted additional play space. The space offered by the government-run town, while maintaining proximity to other communities, empowered villagers to experience that "certain distance between self and place" that, as Tuan points out, is central to place sensing and place making. Residents left, reflected on, and even missed Sunflower. Neither the Village, FPHA, nor the plant controlled or frustrated residents with scrip and little mobility, either physically or economically. Further evidence points to community connections with outside communities. Schooling, shopping, recreation, among other activities, occurred in neighboring towns, even Kansas City, for many residents despite their availability in Sunflower. I interviewed three residents in 2002 who had all lived in the village — through all phases — since moving there during World War II when they or their husbands were employed at the plant. One particular interviewee told me at the time she traveled every weekend to the Kansas City area to visit family, only to return to her home in what is now Clearview City. She succinctly defined her entire adult life in Sunflower Village/Clearview City by saying, "I got roots."[54]

Evidence also suggests that age is crucial in making and sensing place in company towns. The most conscientious, intimate, and positive place associations forged by Sunflower residents were by children who spent their formative years there taking advantage of the opportunities to make place and build relationships. The child's mind, according to Tuan, experiences landscapes with few obstructions and filters, instead seeing only "the present and immediate future" in landscapes where adults often sacrifice their present circumstance to idealize the past or glorify the future. The impact of time even changes for youth. As Tuan explains, children live more in the present and thus make and attach to place quickly. In addition, a child's imagination is "of a special kind. It is tied to activity. . . . [Children] may look matter of factly [sic] on places that to adults are haunted by memories."[55]

The children who came to Sunflower Village with their parents immediately experienced independence. One interviewee who grew up in Sunflower and still lives in northeastern Kansas commented: "We had a red wagon and a bike. Walked around and scavenged. You were very independent, fixed your own meals. Independence was all I knew."[56] Children in Sunflower experienced self-reliance every day their parents worked their long shifts. It was not uncommon for shifts to overlap, leaving children of two working parents entirely alone. "Sleep and Work," as one employee remembered, forced a distance between working parents and their children.[57] Workers frequently dropped their children off at the commercial strip daycare on their way to catch the bus into the plant across the highway. Weekends were the most common time for an entire family to be together. This time saw increased family outings to the local theater, bowling alley, or surrounding towns. This independence, interestingly, was relatively risk free. The Red Cross maintained a nursing station in the commercial strip near other care facilities.

Joining all of this independence, however, was an increased level of responsibility at a young age for these children. School and house chores kept many kids busy and out of trouble. One interviewee recalled his independence coming with much responsibility: "[Mom] worked night hours and kids were on their own. Mom wasn't lax, but she had her orders for while she was gone like chores and things not to do."[58]

Another important element to the youth experience in Sunflower was imagination, which came easily with the village's open plan and especially during the summertime. One interviewee experienced quite a busy summer between school years: "There were some pillars at the entrance, we dug around those and got inside and it was our fort. We brought all our stuff there. I was sad when that came down; I was about six. We brought our stuff there like comic books. That was a summer project. You used your imagination to figure out what to do."[59]

Toys and play structures were limited but did include skates, stilts, and bikes. A popular decision was made one summer when the administration built a temporary roller skating rink. Kids camped out in tents when the weather abided and fished at one of the village ponds. One interviewee who grew up in the village remembered, "There was scouting. There were weekly dances and I wanted to do that but was too young and then we moved. You were on your own for [entertainment], depending on what you had."[60]

Taking advantage of the material landscape built and offered by the FPHA was crucial to the youth experience in Sunflower Village and was inherently easier than it was for adults. As a village youth reported, "Everyone had parents working. There wasn't family activities. It was the kids that were more social. Mom and dad may not be home at the same time. Outside of our family there weren't usual get-togethers."[61] Many families focused their time together at the Village Church, which opened after the Korean Conflict. The church supported many activities for village youth, and they frequently recalled the church more than their older counterparts because of these events. The business strip also accommodated village children and their social skills. The Red Cross nursing station, the soda parlor, a "Teen Town" activity center, the movie theater, and the bowling alley all provided a nexus of activity for the youth.

"An intense experience of short duration . . . can change our lives," reports Tuan.[62] The experience of youth at Sunflower Village exemplifies this very idea. New schools, new colleagues and friends from various parts of the country, and a new natural environment for some, let alone long work days, all coalesced to overwhelm residents and flood their senses with experience. This intensity profoundly impacted its residents and made Sunflower a special place to them.

Finally, and most viscerally for all company towns, communities created out of an industry that contributed to a greater good were also noted for producing a profound sense of attachment. Steel workers in Johnstown (Pennsylvania) took great pride in producing the rails that set across the American West.[63] Miners in Picher, Oklahoma, found dignity in the fact that Allied munitions during World War II were produced from their lead.[64] Residents of Sunflower Village manufactured that lead into arms. Hoover Dam workers felt pride in their building the largest structure in the world that enabled making a living in the desert Southwest in the midst of the Great Depression.[65]

Company towns in the United States have existed in two types: corporate and federal. These communities shared many common plights such as hard work, long hours, and ordinary landscapes. However, they also held that work done and time spent went toward a greater good: building the West, winning the war, powering the country. However, many differences also existed among these places.

Corporate company towns of the United States set out to achieve all of the same goals as those of their pan-American neighbors, and it is easy to be critical of many company towns and the ways by which firms designed them to control the labor force. The cultural landscape reflects and reinforces this objective. Be it through ordinary landscapes or controlling spatial praxis, company store scrip, limited mobility and security, or few to no labor rights, company towns were indeed "hard places."

Federal company towns that arose out of the Great Depression and World War II attempted to part ways with these traditions by becoming more spatially democratic. Town councils, extensive daycare and schooling services, community newspapers, openness and mobility, and the absence of a company store resulted for many not only in a more positive labor and living experience, and memory of it, but also in more permanent places to live such as Sunflower Village (Kansas) or Boulder City (Nevada).

On the surface it would seem that it would be difficult to form an attachment to such spaces, regardless of private or public management, and to make meaning out of them. These limitations, however, do not make the process impossible. Though instances of profound attachment to living in and among a company town landscape would seem rare, scholars show they do exist. What is more, the ability to adapt, socialize, and attach was made particularly possible and became true for Sunflower Village, Kansas. This was due, in part, to the very mobility and security of these communities, along with the pride of knowing that the work being done within that landscape went to a greater good (defeating the Depression or the Nazis). As indicated in the broader discussion of place, inhabitants of private company towns also felt a profound attachment to their town because of the value of their work.

The potential for making place was even more acute for children who grew up in the community. With increased freedom, responsibility, and, in the case of Sunflower Village, an open community design, children there were given opportunities to interact with each other and their environment in ways absent from traditional urban places. Despite the limitations of the American company town, residents, particularly children, enabled themselves to attach to their communities and find both the means and meaning out of what can often be seen as a "hard" American landscape.

NOTES

Sections of this article have been previously published in *Material Culture* and in the *Journal of Cultural Geography*. The author would like to thank the journal editors for their cooperation in granting the necessary permissions.

1. Christopher W. Post, "Company Town Culture: Sunflower Village, Kansas, in the 1940s," *Material Culture* 37, no. 2 (2005): 42–59; Christopher W. Post, "Modifying Sense of Place in a Federal Company Town: Sunflower Village, Kansas, 1942–1959," *Journal of Cultural Geography* 25 (2008): 137–59.

2. Don Mitchell, "New Axioms for Reading the Landscape: Paying Attention to Political Economy and Social Justice," in *Political Economies of Landscape Change*, ed. J. L. Wecoat Jr. and D. M. Johnston (Dordrecht: Springer, 2008), 29–50.

3. Ben Marsh, "Continuity and Decline in the Anthracite Towns of Pennsylvania," *Annals of the Association of American Geographers* 77, no. 3 (September 1987): 337–52, 338, emphasis in original.

4. Cary W. de Wit, "Sense of Place on the American High Plains" (PhD diss., University of Kansas, 1997), 9.

5. Kent C. Ryden, *Mapping the Invisible Landscape: Folklore, Writing, and the Sense of Place* (Iowa City: University of Iowa Press, 1993); Peirce Lewis, "Defining a Sense of Place," *Southern Quarterly* 17, no. 3 (1979): 24–46; Richard H. Schein, "The Place of Landscape: Conceptual Framework for Interpreting an American Scene," *Annals of the Association of American Geographers* 87, no. 4 (1997): 660–80.

6. Edward S. Casey, "How to Get from Space to Place in a Fairly Short Stretch of Time: Phenomenological Prolegomena," in *Senses of Place*, ed. Steven Feld and Keith H. Basso (Santa Fe: School of American Research Press, 1996), 13–52; Edward Casey, *The Fate of Place: A Philosophical History* (Berkeley: University of California Press, 1997); Steven Feld and Keith H. Basso, introduction to *Senses of Place* by Steven Feld and Keith H. Basso (Santa Fe: School of American Research Press, 1996), 3–11.

7. Robert Sack, *Homo Geographicus: A Framework for Action, Awareness, and Moral Concern* (Baltimore: Johns Hopkins University Press, 1997).

8. Ibid., 14, 15.

9. Richard V. Francaviglia, *Hard Places: Reading the Landscape of America's Historic Mining Districts* (Iowa City: University of Iowa Press, 1991).

10. Geoffrey L. Buckley, *Extracting Appalachia: Images of the Consolidation Coal Company, 1910–1945* (Athens: Ohio University Press, 2004); Marsh, "Continuity and Decline"; Post, "Modifying Sense of Place"; David Robertson, *Hard as the Rock Itself* (Boulder: University Press of Colorado, 2006).

11. James B. Allen, *The Company Town in the American West* (Norman: University of Oklahoma Press, 1996); Michael A. Amundson, *Yellowcake Towns: Uranium Mining Communities in the American West* (Boulder: University Press of Colorado, 2002); Russell R. Elliott, *Growing Up in a Company Town: A Family in the Copper Camp of McGill, Nevada* (Reno: Nevada Historical Society, 1990); Marsh, "Continuity and Decline"; Roger M. Olien and Diana Davids Olien, *Oil Booms: Social Change in Five Texas Towns* (Lincoln: University of Nebraska Press, 1980); Buckley, *Extracting Appalachia*; Rick J. Clyne, *Coal People: Life in Southern Colorado's Company Towns, 1890–1930* (Denver: Colorado Historical Society, 1999); Margaret M. Mulrooney, *A Legacy of Coal: The Company Towns of Southwestern Pennsylvania* (Washington, D.C.: National Park Service, 1989), 19.

12. Allen, *Company Town*; Buckley, *Extracting Appalachia*; Clyne, *Coal People*, 49; Elliott, *Growing Up*; Mulrooney, *Legacy of Coal*; Olien and Olien, *Oil Booms*.

13. Elliot, *Growing Up*, 28.

14. Marsh, "Continuity and Decline," 343.

15. Allen, *Company Town*.

16. Ibid., 104.

17. Elliot, *Growing Up*.

18. Mulrooney, *Legacy of Coal*; Clyne, *Coal People*.

19. Allen, *Company Town*; Mulrooney, *Legacy of Coal*.

20. Merle Travis, *Folk Songs of the Hills* (Capitol T-891, 1947).

21. Artists who covered "Sixteen Tons" or cited its lyrics included Johnny Cash, The Platters, Tom Jones, Eric Burdon, Stevie Wonder, and the Eels.

22. Allen, *Company Town*.

23. U.S. Bureau of Census, *1940 United States Census of Population*, vol. 1: *Number of Inhabitants* (Washington, D.C.: Government Printing Office, 1942).

24. John T. Alexander, "A Village Born in War Years Seems Doomed to Die Young," *Kansas City Star*, January 5, 1958. I should also note that between World War II and the Korean Conflict, the ordnance facilities produced commercial farm fertilizers — few adjustments were necessary.

25. Arnold R. Alanen and Joseph A. Eden, *Main Street Ready-Made: The New Deal Community of Greendale, Wisconsin* (Madison: State Historical Society of Wisconsin, 1987); Joseph L. Arnold, *The New Deal in the Suburbs: A History of the Greenbelt Town Program, 1935–1954* (Columbus: Ohio State University Press, 1971); Cathy D. Knepper, *Greenbelt, Maryland: A Living Legacy of the New Deal* (Baltimore: Johns Hopkins University Press, 2001).

26. Clarence S. Stein, *Toward New Towns for America* (Cambridge: MIT Press, 1966), 130, 37.

27. Post, "Company Town on the Plains."

28. "Housing Units at Sunflower Filled," *Lawrence (Kansas) Journal-World* (hereafter LJW), November 24, 1943.

29. Allen, *Company Town*; "'Dynamite Junction' Slowly Loses Boom," LJW, March 27, 1957.

30. "Housing Units at Sunflower Filled."

31. Gertrude Pearson, "Introducing Sunflower Village," *Kansas Magazine* (1946).

32. "Housing Units at Sunflower Filled."

33. "'Dynamite Junction' Slowly Loses Boom."

34. Alexander, "Village Born in War Years."

35. E. Cross, personal communication with author, August 9, 2002.

36. M. Freeman, personal communication with author, December 3, 2002; I. Travis, personal communication with author, November 5, 2002.

37. Pearson, "Introducing Sunflower Village."

38. Francis Hess, "The People of the Village," *Sunflower Villager*, January 7, 1944.

39. Loren O. Wetzel, "Greetings from Sunflower Manager," *Sunflower Villager*, November 24, 1943.

40. Post, "Company Town Culture"; Post, "Modifying Sense of Place."

41. Andrew J. Dunar and Dennis McBride, *Building Hoover Dam: An Oral History of the Great Depression* (New York: Twayne, 1993).

42. Michael J. McDonald and John Muldowny, *TVA and the Dispossessed: The Resettlement of Population in the Norris Dam Area* (Knoxville: University of Tennessee Press, 1982), 228, 232.

43. Robertson, *Hard as the Rock Itself.*

44. Marsh, "Continuity and Decline."

45. David H. Mould, "The Company Town That Outlived the Company: Haydenville, Ohio," *Journal of Cultural Geography* 5, no. 2 (1985): 71–86.

46. Buckley, *Extracting Appalachia.*

47. Robertson, *Hard as the Rock Itself.*

48. Elliot, *Growing Up.*

49. Clyne, *Coal People.*

50. J. B. Jackson, *A Sense of Place, A Sense of Time* (New Haven: Yale University Press, 1994), 151, emphasis in original.

51. Yi-Fu Tuan, "Rootedness versus Sense of Place," *Landscape* 24 (1980): 3–8.

52. Barry Lopez, *The Rediscovery of North America* (New York: Vintage Press, 1990).

53. Lee Ann Rohrer, "Dynamite Junction Slowly Loses Boom," LJW, March 3, 1957.

54. Mildred Norris, personal communication with author, December 3, 2002.

55. Yi-Fu Tuan, *Space and Place: The Perspective of Experience* (Minneapolis: University of Minnesota Press, 1977), 33; see also David Lowenthal, "The American Scene," *Geographical Review* 58, no. 1 (1968): 61–88.

56. L. Moon, personal communication with author, September 9, 2002.

57. E. Cross, personal communication with author, August 9, 2002.

58. L. Moon, personal communication with author, September 9, 2002.

59. Ibid.

60. I. Travis, personal communication with author, November 5, 2002.

61. M. Freeman, personal communication with author, December 3, 2002.

62. Tuan, *Space and Place*, 185.

63. Mitchell, *Cultural Geography*.

64. Robertson, *Hard as the Rock Itself*.

65. Dunar and McBride, *Building Hoover Dam*; Marc Reisner, *Cadillac Desert: The American West and Its Disappearing Water* (New York: Penguin, 2003).

CHAPTER SIX

Glory Days No More

Catholic Paternalism and Labor Relations in Brazil's Steel City

OLIVER J. DINIUS

Volta Redonda should be known in the world. The work that is done here
is above all educational because it is a true example that our society moves
towards the exercise of the common good, something very precious to our
church. Therefore, we also feel responsible for this work.
—*Letter from Dom Agnelo Rossi, bishop of Barra do Piraí (1956–62),
to Edmundo de Macedo Soares e Silva, president of the* CSN *(1954–59)*

Dom Agnelo's letter refers to the "work" of constructing a steel mill and a
company town in Volta Redonda in the interior of Rio de Janeiro state. The
Companhia Siderúrgica Nacional (CSN; National Steel Company), a state-
administered enterprise created by Getulio Vargas's Estado Novo government
in 1941, chose the site for the country's first integrated mill and thus transformed
it into a center of the postwar industrialization drive. But Volta Redonda was
to be more than the engine of the nation's industrial economy. The government wanted the city to serve as an example for the industrial modernity and
social progress that it envisioned for the Brazil of the future. The CSN designed
a company town that offered its inhabitants far better accommodations, urban services, and leisure options than industrial workers enjoyed elsewhere
in Brazil — or anywhere else in Latin America for that matter. Already during construction, the company commissioned films and cinematic newsreels to
document the work and project an image of Volta Redonda as a site of national
destiny.

The construction of the company town progressed more slowly than anticipated and never quite matched the ambition of the original plan, but Volta Redonda nevertheless set a new standard. Rather than residing in overcrowded and unsanitary tenement housing so common in large cities, workers lived in single-family units whose size and level of comfort depended on the employee's rank in the company's occupational hierarchy. The houses all had running water, sewage, and electricity. Front lawns and cobble-stoned streets gave the residential neighborhoods a suburban quality reminiscent of the garden city design common in Anglo-American company towns of the late nineteenth and early twentieth centuries. In addition to a hospital and schools for all ages, the original urban design included parks, athletic facilities, cinemas, and a commercial center to meet the population's basic shopping needs.[1] In the first decade of its existence, the CSN sponsored the creation of social clubs for the employees, the construction of professional sports facilities, and the founding of numerous cultural and religious associations. The infrastructure enabled the city to host national sports events and large congresses. Many older residents still remember the day in the mid-1950s when the world-famous Harlem Globetrotters came to town.[2]

At the same time, the CSN exercised far-reaching control over the lives of all company town inhabitants. It took the monthly rent, debts owed to the

Figure 6.1 Volta Redonda's main workers' neighborhood, the Vila Santa Cecília. Note the grid pattern of the roads and the prominent place of Santa Cecília Church and the technical school (far left) in the town layout. Late 1940s. CSN Photographic Archive.

company store, repayments of advances, and charges for water, sewage, and electricity directly out of the paycheck, which on occasion reduced employees' take-home pay so much that they had difficulty meeting other expenses. The CSN also restricted the inhabitants' freedoms on company lands. Anybody who wanted to form an association, hold a meeting, or stage a rally had to receive written permission from the company. The CSN forbade any political demonstrations on company grounds and used its police force to disperse protestors in collaboration with state law enforcement. The company exercised tight control over the movement of people in the company town by imposing a nightly curfew for most of the 1940s and setting up road blocks to control the entry and exit of vehicles. Most invasive was the close cooperation with the federal political police against organizations that might challenge the CSN's control, such as the incipient metalworkers union.[3]

The company town thus stood for both rapid social progress and rigid social order. The ideological fabric that united those seemingly contradictory objectives was a paternalism that drew on developmentalist nationalism and Catholic social doctrine. The CSN's first technical director, Edmundo de Macedo Soares e Silva, who shaped that paternalist culture, instructed the employees to think of themselves as soldiers building a better Brazil and assured them that their sacrifice would be rewarded with economic security and a comfortable life in a modern town.[4] As a devout Catholic, Macedo Soares believed that the church's teachings should guide his administration and would help the workers to find their proper place in society. His travels to Europe in the 1920s and 1930s had left him with deep impressions of the social, economic, and political conflict triggered by rapid industrialization, and he hoped to avoid similar tensions in Volta Redonda by applying the teachings of the Catholic social encyclicals. Like many of the champions of Brazil's rapid industrialization, Macedo Soares believed that economic growth and the betterment of living conditions required an element of social stability, which a revitalized Catholic culture could provide. Volta Redonda became the real-world experiment of this vision.

The history of Catholic paternalism in Volta Redonda thus serves as a window into the particular social dynamics of a company town in the context of broader economic and political change.[5] Under Macedo Soares's leadership, the CSN established close relations with the local church in the 1940s and deepened them in the 1950s. Volta Redonda also became a testing ground for church strategies to use the laity and employ new organizational forms to strengthen the interaction with the faithful at a time when it lacked the priests to tend to all its parishioners. Ironically, the strengthening of the Catholic Church in the late 1950s and early 1960s coincided with a weakening of the CSN's paternalism, although the company maintained its financial support of religious associations and the church itself. By the late 1960s, the local church was as vibrant as ever but had positioned itself in firm opposition to the csn. Under bishop Dom Waldyr Calheiros (1966–99), the diocese received national attention as a center of progressive Catholicism. In little more than ten years, the local church had morphed from a reliable ally of the csn's paternalist regime into a stalwart opponent of the company.

How to explain such a rapid and profound transformation in the relations between the local church and the csn? The political, economic, and religious context of the late 1960s was very different from that of the late 1950s, which conditioned the transformations observed in Volta Redonda. In the early 1960s, Brazil experienced a major economic crisis accompanied by a political polarization that culminated in the military coup against President João Goulart (1961–64). Troops occupied Volta Redonda on the first day of the coup, removed the csn president, and launched a campaign of repression against political opponents. Both the city and the union remained under intervention for several years to protect the csn, a strategically important industry, from any subversive activity. The Catholic Church underwent profound change in the wake of the Second Vatican Council (1962–65), which modernized the liturgy and instructed priests and lay activists to work with social groups that had been neglected in the pastoral work: workers and the poor.

Brazil's new political reality and the new understanding of the Catholic faith set the context for the change in company-church relations in Volta Redonda, but the question remains why the transformation was so radical. Did the particularities of the company town and, more specifically, the close link between company policies and local religious culture favor radical over moderate change? Any change in church attitude toward the csn had not just local but national significance because of the company's strategic importance for the Brazilian economy. In defining its relationship with the csn, the church took a political position vis-à-vis the Brazilian state and its development model. Initially it endorsed the csn's vision of national development and sustained a paternalism that saw the company use its power to control labor relations and shape Volta Redonda to its image. As economic and social realities cast an ever longer shadow over the prevailing development model, the church asserted greater independence and offered the people of Volta Redonda a social ideology that defined the goals of development differently from the csn.

The csn assumed full responsibility only for those who lived on its property, offering access to subsidized housing, urban services, and education. The workers, however, saw all of Volta Redonda as a company town, not just the company-owned neighborhoods. The CSN held ample economic and political control over the workers' lives, and they expected the company to look after their well-being. The church had to serve all Catholics, on CSN property and beyond, thus sharing the workers' view of a city and community that included the peripheral areas. The difference between these two conceptions of the reach of the company's social responsibility mattered ever more as the inhabited area expanded beyond the limits of the original company town, with important ramifications for community culture, local politics, and industrial relations. For the CSN, these changes raised the question whether it would expand its social programs to the entire city, live with an increasing differentiation between insiders and outsiders, or gradually withdraw as town administrator. The history of relations between CSN, the local church, and the working-class community in Volta Redonda thus illuminates the challenges faced by company towns as urban growth developed a dynamic of its own and speaks to the changing nature of Brazil's state capitalism.

THE ORIGINS OF CATHOLIC PATERNALISM IN THE "CITY OF STEEL"

When the CSN built Volta Redonda in the early 1940s, the Brazilian Catholic Church enjoyed a strong resurgence centered on an ambitious program of social action. Throughout the 1930s, Rio de Janeiro's archbishop Dom Sebastião Leme had orchestrated public displays of faith to demonstrate the power of organized Catholicism in a campaign to increase the church's political influence.[6] He presented President Getúlio Vargas with a list of political demands that called for a new order based on Catholic social doctrine as spelled out in Pope Leo XIII's encyclical *Rerum Novarum* (1891) and Pius XI's *Quadragesimo Anno* (1931).[7] This included a "Christian reconstruction of human society," a "reform of . . . the state," and the creation of a "juridical and social order which [would] . . . give form and shape to all economic life."[8] Candidates endorsed by the Liga Eleitoral Católica (LEC; Catholic Electoral League) in the 1934 election for the Constituent Assembly had to support "labor legislation inspired by social justice and the principles of the Christian order."[9] The new constitution empowered the state to implement interventionist social welfare policies. Vargas's labor ministers, all devout Catholics, created a system of *sindicatos* to represent workers and employers, respectively, as well as government organs to mediate labor disputes.[10] The 1934 constitution also legalized state subsidies to Catholic associations, which helped build a strong lay movement.[11]

The church cemented its political gains under the Estado Novo (1937–45). Its corporatist constitution reflected the influence of neo-Thomist social doctrine, which conceived of society and state as an organic whole that united all Brazilians in a nation with a profoundly moral purpose — just like mankind was united in the mystical body of Christ.[12] The Estado Novo further strengthened the social welfare system and supported Catholic associations that aimed to engender a sense of social belonging in order to transcend class conflict.[13] The new federal labor law, the 1943 Consolidação das Leis do Trabalho (CLT; Consolidation of Labor Laws), reaffirmed the *sindicato* system, established a labor judiciary, and incorporated a range of welfare provisions for workers, creating a framework for industrial relations that would remain intact throughout the postwar Republic (1946–64) and beyond. Financial and political support for the church allowed for the creation of an increasingly powerful network of Catholic lay associations that promoted the Christian renovation of the social order. The government declared the celebrations for the fiftieth anniversary of *Rerum Novarum* in May 1941 a "national and civic hallmark," because "this directive — conducive to social peace — agrees with the policy for the protection of the worker that the national government adopted."[14]

Macedo Soares directed the construction of Volta Redonda, hoping to make the city into a model of this revitalized Catholicism. He imagined a close-knit community, the "family of steel" (*família siderúrgica*), built on the Catholic faith and loyal to the CSN and its mission for Brazil. The company supported the church from the very beginning: in the early 1940s, father Geraldo Fernandes read mass every Sunday in a room otherwise used as a leisure space for workers.[15] The construction of the parish church, Igreja Santa Cecília, was completed before any other building. Reverend Alfredo Piquet returned the favor with a call for spiritual support. "He ended his sermon advising his parishioners to always frequent this place of worship in large numbers, just as he had witnessed on that very day, and he invited them all to join in his prayers to the Divine Providence to support those who watched over the fate of Brazil, our state and the great mill in Volta Redonda."[16] Macedo Soares funded the promotion of the faith so generously that the bishop of Niterói nominated him for an ecclesiastical benefice. His letter to Pope Pius XII described Macedo Soares as "a grand benefactor of the Holy Church" who "had built a beautiful parish church and a house for the priest in Volta Redonda, in the value of 1.5 million *cruzeiros*." The letter highlighted Macedo Soares's reputation as a "sharp and biting enemy of atheist communism" and suggested that the award would set a good example "for other men to come to assist in the Catholic social work that Your Excellency propels so fervently."[17]

As part of its paternalist strategy, the CSN included a Catholic service in every official celebration in Volta Redonda. It invited the bishop for the Sul

Fluminense, Dom José André Coimbra, to hold an open-air mass for major religious or civic holidays and for the CSN's annual anniversary festivities.[18] The bishop also blessed new buildings and new equipment as part of the inauguration. Even the Lojas Americanas, the city's first commercial store, received an inaugural sprinkling with holy water followed by a mass at the Brotherhood of St. Christopher.[19] For most of the CSN's workers such a strong institutional presence of the church was a new experience. They came from rural areas of Minas Gerais, Rio de Janeiro, and Espírito Santo, regions where the church's endemic shortage of priests made it impossible to offer weekly Sunday mass and administer the sacraments on a regular basis. These regions had remained firmly Catholic nevertheless, and the migrants' traditional understanding of the faith shaped the church in Volta Redonda.

Under its paternalist strategy for labor relations, the CSN subsidized lay associations targeting workers. The founding of a Círculo Operário Católico (COC; Catholic Workers' Circle) in 1946 greatly strengthened the church's outreach to the workers and countered perceived Communist influence. Padre Brentano, founder of the national *circulista* movement, came to Volta Redonda to inaugurate the COC's facilities. The CSN administration expected the Workers' Circle to "spiritualize class relations" and donated a building to serve as its seat and classroom.[20] The *circulista* movement's national program included principles that appealed to workers and employers, respectively. On the one hand, it called for the "founding of factory councils with elected worker representatives" and spelled out a "right to education, hygiene, food, housing, health" for the "Christian proletariat." On the other hand, it stressed the "conscious learning of [the workers'] duties." Its corporatist character was most evident in the call for compliance with the CLT, for "legal equality between employers and employees," and for the "political, administrative, and legislative representation of the different organized professions in national councils for economy and work."[21]

With generous CSN subsidies the COC tried to emulate the national church's Fourth Week of Social Action, held in São Paulo in 1940, which had demonstrated how a combination of fairs, religious celebrations, theater, films, and even soccer games could advance the faith.[22] The COC organized a range of leisure activities for workers and their families, such as Boy Scout groups, a favorite in the Catholic arsenal.[23] On weekends the *círculo* invited workers to gather and discuss labor questions under the spiritual guidance of an ecclesiastical assistant as an alternative to indulging in sins such as drinking or being indoctrinated by "Communist elements."[24] Volta Redonda's parish priest relied on the *circulistas* to serve as lay leaders in the congregation. When Padre Brentano returned for a special communion in 1948, they led a procession of more than three thou-

Figure 6.2 Open-air mass celebrated on the front steps of csn's first Escritório Central (Central Administration Building). September 1945, Volta Redonda. csn Photographic Archive.

sand faithful through the streets of Volta Redonda carrying an iron cross cast in the very first tapping of the csn's blast furnace.[25] The coc brought employers and employees together by making the csn's directors honorary members. Macedo Soares (technical director, 1941–46; president, 1954–59), Silvio Raulino de Oliveira (president, 1946–54), Paulo C. Gomes Martins (technical director, 1946–50; vice president, 1950–54), and Paulo Monteiro Mendes (administrative director, 1954–59) regularly attended *circulista* events.

The church helped to identify suitable *circulista* leaders, and the csn employed them in positions where they exercised influence over workers. Both the company and church wanted *circulista* leaders to be "honest and hard-working elements, who had no political passions harmful to the ideals and the well-being of the Circle."[26] Valentim Marques dos Santos was one such exemplary leader. He had studied at a seminary but never took the priestly vow and worked instead as a reform school teacher in Valença, not far from Volta Redonda. The head of the csn's General Services Department, Captain Edgard Magalhães da Silva, recognized Valentim's commitment to social Catholicism and invited him to join the company in 1943. Before long he worked on Macedo Soares's personal staff. He served as the *círculo*'s secretary from its founding until the late

1950s and also twice as president in those years. The CSN assigned him to the Department of Social Services, where he worked until his retirement in 1967.[27] Valentim's appointment created a symbiotic relationship between the COC and the CSN's social services, both working toward social peace within the framework of Catholic paternalism.

The CSN created the Departamento de Assistência Social (DAS; Department for Social Assistance) to implement programs in the spirit of the Catholic social doctrine. Its stated goal was to foster collaboration between employer and employees, to provide means to appreciate (*valorizar*) the workers and their families, and to promote their "associative and communitarian spirit."[28] DAS was the CSN's version of the Serviço Social de Indústria (SESI; Social Service for Industry), which national employers' federations and the federal government had founded in 1946 to "provide a Christian and Brazilian face to the cultural formation of our workers, to let them participate at the side of the other social classes in the enjoyment of the riches of the spirit."[29] Macedo Soares had even more ambitious goals. He wanted the CSN's social services to foster the social well-being and "physical, moral and intellectual perfection" of its employees and intended to make Volta Redonda into the "capital of Brazilian social legislation."[30] The CSN spent an amount equivalent to 1 percent of its payroll to fund DAS, which employed no fewer than 335 people by 1949.[31]

DAS's Division for Study, Diagnosis, and Social Treatment addressed the "maladjustments" of employees who experienced difficulties "adapting to the social order the CSN established in Volta Redonda."[32] It channeled company subsidies to organizations that it expected to help with the adjustment: social clubs, a sports league, a cultural association, and, of course, the Catholic Workers' Circle.[33] The Clube dos Funcionários da CSN served as a model. It organized the annual Carnival ball and the Festa Junina, a traditional folk feast to celebrate Saint John, and managed recreational spaces such as the Ginásio Macedo Soares, the first athletic facility in Volta Redonda.[34] To shape the workers' leisure habits, DAS operated a cinema and maintained spaces where workers could meet, write letters, play games, and watch educational films. DAS encouraged board games but prohibited playing cards, presumably to prevent gambling. Groups could use the DAS leisure spaces for official business and events, but they had to register the meeting at least twenty-four hours in advance.[35]

The CSN exercised tight social control and aimed to resolve all grievances internally. The DAS's Division of Rights, Obligations, and Information cooperated closely with the Department of Industrial Relations on programs intended to discourage workers from taking recourse to the labor courts. It organized talks on labor rights and duties under the CLT to "enlighten" the employees and maintained a library with copies of the csn's daily Service Bulletin for Volta Redonda that published court decisions concerning work rules and benefits.[36] Any association had to receive permission from the csn before it could hold an event on company property.[37] Subsidized associations that violated company rules risked losing the funding in a periodic reassessment of the benefits that DAS subsidies brought for its broader social agenda.[38] The csn prohibited the establishment of bars to prevent alcohol abuse and restrict gatherings in spaces that were inherently difficult to monitor. To get a drink the workers had to leave company territory and head to "old" Volta Redonda, the former village, which had seen some commercial development since the early 1940s.[39] The strategy to impose strict social controls in the company town appears to have worked: a police spy reported in 1943 that he could not find any "particular spots [in the town] where workers met, played games, or hung out."[40]

GLORY DAYS: CATHOLIC PATERNALISM IN THE 1950S

The relationship between the csn and the local church changed little from the mid-1940s to the mid-1950s. Steel production began in 1946, and subsequent years saw a rapid growth in profits as the csn produced at capacity for a booming domestic market. It carried out two major mill expansions that had been part of the original design. The rhythm of inaugurations only slowed in the mid-1950s. The population of Volta Redonda grew rapidly as the csn hired both temporary workers for the construction of new facilities and permanent employees for the operation of the mill. The increasing profits raised the general level of prosperity, especially after a government-mediated labor agreement in 1952 that initiated a cycle of substantial annual salary increases and greatly expanded worker benefits.[41] The local church thus had an ever larger flock to tend to and the Catholic Workers Circle an ever larger number of workers to reach out to. Both continued to thrive with the help of generous csn subsidies. The early 1950s were the glory days of Catholic paternalism in Volta Redonda.

A change in leadership at the csn further strengthened the company's commitment to the church. After Vargas's suicide in August 1954, the more conservative government of former vice president João Café Filho asked Macedo Soares to take over from Raulino de Oliveira as csn president. In contrast to his predecessor, Macedo Soares took great personal interest in the development of the city of Volta Redonda, although he worked and lived in Rio de Janeiro. He expanded the company's institutional and material support for the church in a reaffirmation of the paternalist partnership. His right-hand man was the new *diretor secretário*, Paulo Monteiro Mendes, formerly a physician in the csn hospital, who like Macedo Soares aimed to reinvigorate traditional Catholicism in the spirit of Pope Pius XII. Both men saw anticommunism, the Christian family, moral behavior, and an acceptance of the social order as the bedrock of the Brazilian nation. They shared the vision of Catholic hegemony celebrated at the 1955 International Eucharistic Congress in Rio de Janeiro, which the CSN supported with a donation of eighty thousand cruzeiros.[42]

Nothing demonstrated Macedo Soares's commitment to a Christian society better than the decision to hand the administration of CSN-owned primary and secondary schools over to religious orders.[43] The nuns of the Congregação das Escravas Concepcionistas do Divino Coração ran the major girls school, and in December 1955 the Augustinian order took over the largest school for boys, the Colégio Macedo Soares.[44] Ten sisters of the Instituto das Missionárias de Jesus Crucificado received a CSN salary to perform educational and social services in close cooperation with the company's Department for Education and Social Studies.[45] An August 1957 article in the CSN newspaper *O Lingote* highlighted the presence of the Catholic Church in local education. The caption for a photograph showing one Brother Hilton in conversation with a young boy highlighted the brother's dedication and cordiality in accompanying the "psychological development" of the children. In another photo a teacher sings a hymn with her students, "partaking," in *O Lingote*'s words, "in the religious education of the children." Quotes by Catholic luminaries garnish the article, including by both the conservative pope Pius XI (1922–39) and the philosopher Jacques Maritain, who by the late 1950s became a hero of progressive Catholics clamoring for a more activist church.[46]

Traditional Catholic celebrations remained a central part of public life in Volta Redonda. In October 1956, the wandering image (*imagem peregrina*) of Our Lady of Fatima "visited" the city accompanied by five missionaries. The CSN's newspaper described the occasion as a "glorious event" that showed "once again the profound Catholic sentiments of the majority of the population of the City of Steel." A "great human mass" of faithful received the image in Volta Redonda's main square, where the CSN's industrial director Renato Frota de Azevedo welcomed both the image and the white doves that traveled with the image. After three days in the parishes, the image "visited" the mill. The industrial director and several other high-ranking CSN administrators accompanied the image in a motorized caravan around the mill, before the employees of the Transportation Department carried it through the department grounds on their shoulders. On the last day of the visit, one of the missionaries led a prayer over the airwaves on the company-owned radio ZYP-26.[47]

Other events of the mid-1950s had a more ambiguous impact on Catholic paternalism. In 1954, Volta Redonda became a municipality as the result of an emancipation movement supported by the majority of the inhabitants. They hoped that the newly created municipality would retain more of the wealth created by the CSN. Political autonomy meant that Volta Redonda elected its own city council and mayor, which appealed to the metalworkers union because of its membership's electoral clout. For the CSN, the change appeared to make little difference, as it retained territorial and administrative control over the company town, although the change accentuated the contrast with other parts of the new municipality that did not enjoy the same level of urban development. That difference became politically significant in the second half of the 1950s, when Sávio Gama, the first mayor of Volta Redonda, opened up lands outside the company town for residential construction as a measure to address the perennial housing shortage. The new neighborhoods needed infrastructure, which increased the political pressure to collect local taxes from the CSN. Residents called for a greater contribution by the company to alleviate the gap in living standards between those living on and those living off company property.

Relations between the CSN and the local metalworkers union began to deteriorate. In 1955 the Café Filho government had intervened in the union, declaring its regular election invalid and trying to impose a state-appointed president with the help of the political police. The union defied the police and did not allow the intervener to take power, but the episode created deep distrust between the workers, on the one hand, and the federal government and the CSN directorate, on the other.[48] The company could no longer count on the union directorates to share its vision of Catholic paternalism as the best approach to managing the company town and labor relations. Members who lived off company property pressured the union to demand that the CSN expand social services that had been available only to employees living in company housing.

Two changes within the Catholic Church affected its relations with the CSN. Volta Redonda became a co-seat of the diocese of Barra do Piraí soon after it had become a municipality.[49] The decision reflected the demographic and economic weight of the "City of Steel" as the regional center of the Sul Fluminense. In 1961, the CSN donated the land and materials for the construction of a co-cathedral, a seat for the diocese, an Episcopal residence, and headquarters for the local Catholic Action — further strengthening the church's physical presence.[50] The ordination of a new bishop in 1956 to replace Dom José André Coimbra sharpened the pastoral profile. Coimbra had been a loyal partner for the CSN's Catholic paternalism, a fixture at official functions, inaugurations, and company anniversaries, but he left no record of remarkable accomplishments or pastoral priorities in his twenty years at the helm of the diocese. The new bishop, Dom

Agnelo Rossi, was nationally recognized as a leading Catholic intellectual and powerful defender of the faith.[51] He asserted more independence from the csn, at least in public, often sending priests to represent the church at company functions. Father Oswaldo Greener, parish priest for Santa Cecília, administered the traditional congratulatory mass at the csn's first anniversary celebration after Dom Angelo's ordination. The new bishop remained on friendly terms with the csn, however, and welcomed its material support for the diocese.[52]

Dom Agnelo's foremost concern was the spread of Protestantism in Brazil, the subject of his theological studies in Rome (1933–37). After his return, in 1938, he published extensively on the "protestant question in Brazil" and fought against the Protestant threat as the founding organizer of the National Secretariat in Defense of the Faith. He also taught on "protestant heresy" at the seminary in Ipiranga and at the Catholic University in Campinas.[53] Dom Agnelo believed that a Catholic lay movement had a key role to play in the defense of the faith and the fight against communism.[54] Continuing the work of archbishop Dom Sebastião Leme (1882–1942), he helped train volunteer teachers for the Ação Católica Brasileira (acb; Brazilian Catholic Action), the umbrella organization of the national lay movement.[55] Dom Agnelo practiced a conservative Catholicism with a social conscience, in line with the neo-Thomist tradition of *Rerum Novarum* and *Quadrogesimo Ano*. He opposed the idea of a church for the poor but defended the alliance with the national development state. His lack of sensitivity for the issue of poverty might have been due to his background. In contrast to Dom Helder Câmara and Dom Waldyr Calheiros (his successor in Volta Redonda), who worked with shantytown populations and assumed more reformist positions, Dom Agnelo had served only in affluent cities.[56]

Dom Agnelo's most significant pastoral innovation in Volta Redonda was the popular catechism. To counter the effects of the shortage of priests, the church trained volunteers to read the Bible to a group of parishioners as a form of lay-administered service. The purpose was — in the spirit of Catholic Action — to involve the laity in support of the institutional church, but it also taught communities to organize. The church had always been strong in the company town, but the popular catechism strengthened its presence in the periphery, linking its reform agenda with the needs of the less privileged population. Inadvertently, then, Rossi's successful experiment with popular catechism prepared the ground for the more profound transformation of the local church in the 1960s, when activist members of Catholic lay organizations became the backbone of the local opposition to the military regime.[57] Upon his arrival in 1966, Dom Waldyr found a well-organized church, which he attributed to Dom Agnelo's work and the seeds it created for the formation of Comunidades Eclesiais de Base (CEBS; Ecclesiastical Base Communities).[58]

PATERNALISM CHALLENGED

Events of the late 1950s and early 1960s undermined the paternalist partnership. The CSN faced fundamentally new political and financial challenges that led it to rethink its obligations to the city and its people. By the late 1950s, the federal government no longer thought of the CSN as the lone locomotive of Brazil's industrial development. Juscelino Kubitschek, elected president in 1955 on a developmentalist platform, pursued a less nationalist agenda than his conservative opponents had feared and most of his labor allies had expected. Most importantly, he opened up the country to a rapid, if controlled, expansion of foreign capital in the automobile sector, which redefined the CSN's role in the national economy. It supplied the domestic market with rails, construction steel, and tin sheet for cans, to name just the most important products, but to meet the expectations of the auto industry the government needed a domestic supplier of large quantities of steel plate. The CSN could not meet the quality standards, however, and the auto manufacturers turned instead to imports and to COSIPA and USIMINAS, two state-owned domestic companies that began production in the early 1960s.[59]

At the same time, the CSN had difficulty controlling its prices. As effective monopoly producer, the company had been able to set prices that allowed it to meet the rising cost of inputs and labor, but the Kubitschek government tried to restrict that pricing power to help industries that consumed domestic steel. The new policy encountered resistance both from the company and the union. CSN president Macedo Soares resigned in 1959 after the federal government named João Kubitschek, the president's cousin, as financial director and tried to restrict the company's autonomy to set product prices. Macedo Soares's successors, who faced ever greater financial pressure because of fast-rising inflation, encountered firm resistance from the union as they looked at ways to reduce expenditure by controlling labor costs or relinquishing responsibility for the company town. In 1960, for example, a commission recommended that the CSN sell the company-owned houses and apartments to the employees.[60] However, the leaders of the powerful metalworkers union, the Sindicato dos Trabalhadores nas Indústrias Metalúrgicas, Mecânicas e de Material Elétrico de Barra Mansa (STIMMMEBM), pushed the CSN to assume greater social responsibility, especially for workers who did not enjoy the benefits of living in the company town.

The financial crisis thus accentuated the differences between the visions of the company and the workers with respect to the future of the company town and the social order in Volta Redonda. Under Macedo Soares and his immediate successors, the CSN publicly maintained its commitment to Catholic paternalism, although it explored avenues to reduce the cost of its social obligations. The union demanded that the CSN opt for a more expansive (and more costly) commitment to the city by extending the social benefits granted to the inhabitants of the company town to all of its workers. The union couched its demand in the CSN's paternalist language, but it had no intention of relying on the CSN's generosity. It counted on its bargaining power to advance an agenda that extended beyond the shop floor. The company wanted to retain its paternalist authority but shed the cost; the union wanted to retain the social benefits of paternalism but without extensive company control. The CSN wanted *less* company town in the sense of fewer responsibilities for the people it had always served; the union wanted *more* company town in the sense of expanding existing benefits to workers that did not yet enjoy them. The CSN's efforts to redefine its responsibilities for the company town in the early 1960s had an ambiguous outcome. The company transferred control of utilities such as water and electricity to the municipality and private companies, and it placed the housing assets into a holding company to prepare for a future sale. On the other hand, the union successfully pressured the CSN to assume greater financial responsibilities for the city's schools and medical services.[61]

The conflict over the CSN's social commitment to Volta Redonda mirrored a national conflict about development strategy at a time of economic stagnation and high inflation. Policy makers disagreed whether it was more promising to strengthen the position of large national (especially state-owned) companies and their workers, or whether it was preferable to reallocate their resources in order to fund development projects that reached more Brazilians, even if that required, as some advocated, an opening to foreign capital or, as others suggested, an increase in social spending and its more equitable distribution. Political divisions over this issue did not follow institutional, class, or party lines. They split the Brazilian army into ideological camps; they undermined the unity of the industrial working class and industrial capitalists, respectively; and they fragmented Brazil's preeminent labor party, the Partido Trabalhista Brasileiro (PTB; Brazilian Labor Party). These divisions reverberated in Volta Redonda. The population had grown much faster than the CSN's workforce, and an ever smaller share of those employed at the CSN enjoyed the benefits of living in the company town. Longtime employees with a high skill level lived in subsidized housing close to the workplace, sent their children to CSN schools, and took full advantage of the leisure programming. Less skilled workers, often more recent arrivals, had to buy or build a home in neighborhoods with heavier air pollution, a longer commute, and few urban conveniences. Ironically, the divide between the privileged and underprivileged — those that had benefited from development and those that had not — was more readily apparent in Volta Redonda than in less affluent cities because of its origin as a company town.

By the late 1950s, the church began to question its commitment to state-led development as the most promising path toward achieving social justice and lifting the poor out of misery. As long as state-led development appeared to be a success, the church hierarchy could reconcile its fundamental social conservatism with a commitment to social and economic development. Once it became apparent, however, that this development policy did not relieve poverty for shanty-town dwellers and the population outside the urban centers of the Southeast, parts of the lay movement and progressive clergy began to diverge from the hierarchy's interpretation of the Catholic social doctrine. The more radical members of the Catholic Workers Youth, the Catholic University Youth, and the Catholic Student Youth read the doctrine as a call for decisive intervention in the world to address pressing social problems. The encyclical *Mater et Magistra* (1961), in particular, appeared to justify an activist agenda for social change. Moderate segments of the ACB and the Catholic Workers Circles, on the other hand, subscribed to the neo-Thomist reading of social doctrine and aligned with the strongly anti-Communist Movement for Union Renovation to oppose any sweeping reforms such as those proposed by the government of João Goulart (1961–64).[62] By the time Dom Agnelo left, in 1962, the diocese had a vibrant lay movement whose members — emboldened by the reforms adopted by the Second Vatican Council (1962–65) — often took more radical positions on pressing social questions than the institutional church.

Socially progressive Catholicism played a central role in Volta Redonda politics, where various nominally socialist or laborist parties competed for the working-class vote. The PTB had emerged as the dominant party, but it was split between allies of Goulart and a faction that called for a return to the PTB's socially progressive Catholic roots. Its leader was Fernando Ferrari, former national party president and founder of the Labor Renovation Movement. Expelled from the PTB by Goulart and his allies, Ferrari ran in the 1960 election as the vice presidential candidate for the Christian Democratic Party and carried enough of the labor vote to push Goulart to the brink of defeat against Milton Campos, the vice presidential candidate of the conservative União Democrática Nacional (UDN; National Democratic Union).[63] Ferrari had a strong showing in Volta Redonda, where 38 percent of the voters preferred him as vice president compared to 39 percent for Goulart. The contrast with neighboring Barra Mansa, where Ferrari (22 percent) fell far short of Goulart's vote total (41 percent), suggests that socially progressive Catholicism resonated strongly with the workers of Volta Redonda.[64]

THE END OF CATHOLIC PATERNALISM

As for the nation as a whole, the early 1960s in Volta Redonda were a period of political conflicts and realignments as different social actors searched for a new path to combine economic and social development. The disagreement over the future of the company town mirrored the larger uncertainty about the future of Brazilian state capitalism during a crisis that called its economic and ideological foundation in question. The CSN, although still officially committed to a model that combined economic growth with social development, could no longer afford to preempt conflict over salaries, social welfare, and coadministration with lavish spending. The metalworkers union aggressively demanded improvements in all three areas, emboldened by the political support it received from the government when Goulart appointed former STIMMMEBM president Othon Reis Fernandes as the CSN's director for social services to represent the workers' interest. He promoted an agenda of social justice, but the close association with the company became a liability when he tried to win another mandate as union president. Reis Fernandes lost the election to a slate of candidates associated with a more radical labor confederation, the Central Geral dos Trabalhadores.[65]

The military coup on March 31, 1964, sealed the fate of Catholic paternalism in Volta Redonda. The coup had the support of several CSN directors, and the military purged the union directorate and other labor militants to deflate worker resistance and appointed a new directorate that would not challenge the CSN. The church hierarchy had good relations with the military and supported the coup, but the military purges targeted many Catholic lay activists organized in the *Ação Popular* and the ACB.[66] In Volta Redonda, the crackdown against the Juventude Operária Católica (JOC; Catholic Workers Youth) was swift and so unforgiving that it triggered protests by the national church. The CSN directorate also moved to end the cooperation agreement with religious orders that had been a mainstay of Catholic paternalism under Macedo Soares. In November 1964, for example, it canceled the contract with the Congregação das Irmas de São Carlos, whose sisters had assisted in the administration of the company hospital.[67]

The military regime charted an economic course that undermined the basis of the CSN's Catholic paternalism. It permitted state-owned companies such as the CSN to sell to international customers and abolished the obligation for national manufacturers to purchase basic industrial goods domestically, forcing the CSN to be more competitive and to control costs.[68] The new CSN directorate looked to reduce spending on social services and the company town. It accelerated the sale of the houses, first contemplated in 1960, to shed the obligation to subsidize rent and maintain the properties in working order.[69] In the meantime, the CSN raised rents to compensate for losses that had been caused by rent freezes in the early 1960s and by the failure to collect the rents since early 1964.[70] A proposal to charge the residents for fire insurance made the company's motives explicit: "it [the CSN] must *free itself as much as possible of its paternalist obligations.*"[71] In another, highly symbolic measure, the company ended the free supply of milk to all workers. Nurturing healthy workers had been a cornerstone of Catholic paternalism as the CSN tried to combine social and economic development, but the benefit appeared expendable under the new economic regime.[72] The CSN's gradual withdrawal from the company town signaled the end of the *mãe* CSN, the role of the caring mother it had assumed under the paternalist regime.

The local church mutated from legitimizing agent for the CSN's paternalism into the company's most visible and powerful opposition. The new bishop, Dom Waldyr Calheiros, cited Catholic social doctrine as his guide, but he understood it in light of Pope John XXIII's encyclicals *Mater et Magistra* and *Pacem in Terris* (1963) and in light of the Second Vatican Council.[73] Under Dom Waldyr's leadership, the local church further strengthened the role of lay communities — similar to Ecclesiastical Base Communities — in the periphery of the municipality. The church and its lay communities opposed the new military regime's development policies, which prioritized economic growth over social development and failed to address existing inequities.[74] The Workers' Circle, which had been instrumental to Catholic paternalism in Volta Redonda, lost its position as interlocutor. Brazil's National Conference of Workers Circles had been discredited because it accepted funding from anti-Goulart forces and ignored a call by the International Federation of Christian Trade Unions (IFCTU) to oppose the military government. As a result, the circles lost face and the IFCTU's financial backing.[75]

The local Catholic Church's opposition to the military regime received national attention in the late 1960s. In November 1967, two officers of the Catholic youth organization *Judica*, a young deacon and a student of theology, dispersed pamphlets in the streets of Volta Redonda that criticized the regime's social record and the restrictions on political freedoms. Soldiers of the 1. Batalhão da Infanteria Blindada promptly arrested them.[76] Dom Waldyr's principled and courageous response as he stood up for his parishioners during the most repressive phase of the military dictatorship (1968–73) established a public perception of Volta Redonda as a hotbed of Liberation Theology. The church's struggle in Volta Redonda was not, however, one to *liberate* those who had been oppressed for decades or even centuries, as in the cane fields of the Northeast. Rather, it was a struggle by workers against a loss of social services and for a more even distribution of benefits; it was a struggle to realize the benefits that the CSN's Catholic paternalism had promised but never delivered for many of its employees. The workers wanted all of Volta Redonda to become a company town on their terms, with the CSN assuming responsibility for the social well-being of the population without exercising social or political control. Activists guided by the Catholic social thought of the 1960s wanted the CSN to install a localized welfare state rather than a paternalist regime sustained by a neo-Thomist understanding of the employer's responsibility for moral and material well-being of the workers.

The events of the 1960s indicate a direct link between the changes in labor relations, changes in Volta Redonda's urban profile, and changes in the culture of Catholicism. In the late 1960s, the church played an important role for relations between the CSN and its employees, but in contrast to the glory days of Catholic paternalism in the 1940s and 1950s, it no longer sustained the CSN's managerial vision. Whereas earlier bishops had blessed the CSN's social assistance programs with their cooperation and presence, publicly endorsing company policies, Dom Waldyr challenged the company to assume greater social responsibility. The church had initially shared a vision of the company town as a space to realize a Catholic order for the industrial age. When changes in the state capitalist development model — triggered by changes in global industrial capitalism — made the CSN cut down on the social programs offered in the company town, however, Catholics in Volta Redonda endorsed a broader vision of social justice.

The history of relations between the CSN, its workers, and the Catholic Church in Volta Redonda thus serves as example for the effect the transition to a new cycle of capitalism has on a company town. What an economically diversified urban center would have experienced as gradual social change, a small tremor caused by the cycles of industrial capitalism, the single-industry town experienced as a shock to its social and cultural fabric. Volta Redonda, which owed its existence to Brazil's industrial expansion, was a seismograph for change caused by the advent of the next capitalist cycle. As a manufacturing town planned for a particular production regime, it struggled to adjust to the next cycle of industrial capitalism. Designed as a transformative experiment, driven by a powerful ideology of social change and social order, Volta Redonda succumbed to the forces of economic and demographic change as it became more and more similar to other industrial cities. The social order built around Catholic paternalism lasted less than twenty years before it was undermined by the crisis of state capitalism.

NOTES

The author would like to thank Wilson Menegele of the Usina Gráfica in Volta Redonda, who scanned the photographs for this essay on short notice and at no cost. José Vieira, Helton Fraga, and Solange Whehaibe helped get the photos into Wilson's hand, with the author thousands of miles away.

1. For details on the urban design of Volta Redonda, see Oliver Dinius, "From State Paternalism to Industrial Relations: The Workers of the National Steel Company and the Rationalization of Its Labor Regime," in *Space, Labor, and Culture: Brazilian Urban Workers in the Twentieth Century*, ed. Paulo Fontes and Michael Hall (Gainesville: University Press of Florida, forthcoming).

2. Eng. Ervin Michelstaedter, interviewed by author, July 22, 1998, Volta Redonda.

3. See Oliver Dinius, "Defending Ordem against Progresso: The Brazilian Political Police and Industrial Labor Control," in *Vargas and Brazil: New Perspectives*, ed. Jens Hentschke (New York: Palgrave Macmillan, 2006), 173–205.

4. "Aniversario do Snr. Presidente Getúlio Vargas," *Boletim de serviço de Volta Redonda* (hereafter *BSVR*), no. 065 (April 20, 1943): 443–44.

5. Sources on the religious history of Volta Redonda are surprisingly scarce, despite the Catholic Church's significance. The archive of the diocese is very incomplete, and religious history has not been a focus of oral history projects on Volta Redonda.

6. Margaret Todaro Williams, "The Politicization of the Brazilian Catholic Church: The Catholic Electoral League," *Journal of Inter-American Studies and World Affairs* 16, no. 3 (August 1974): 303.

7. *Rerum Novarum — Encyclical of Pope Leo XIII on Capital and Labor* (May 15, 1891). Official Vatican translation at http://www.vatican.va/holy_father/leo_xiii/encyclicals; *Quadragesimo Anno — Encyclical of Pope Pius XI on Reconstruction of the Social Order* (May 15, 1931). Official Vatican translation at http://www.vatican.va/holy_father/pius_xi/encyclicals (accessed January 21, 2010).

8. *Quadragesimo Anno*, Articles 78, 88, and 147.

9. On Cardinal Leme's role in the LEC, see Laurita Pessoa Raja Gabaglia, *O cardeal Leme (1882–1942)* (Rio de Janeiro: José Olympio, 1962), 319–22. On the Catholic influence on the Constituent Assembly, see Margaret Patrice Todaro, "Pastors, Prophets and Politicians: A Study of the Brazilian Catholic Church, 1916–1945" (PhD diss., Columbia University, 1971), 324.

10. The labor laws bore the intellectual imprint of the jurist Francisco José de Oliveira Vianna, who served as the Labor Ministry's adviser on "social economy" from 1931 to 1940. Luiz Werneck Vianna, *Liberalismo e sindicato no Brasil* (São Paulo: Paz e Terra, 1978), 155–64.

11. Kenneth P. Serbin, "Church-State Reciprocity in Contemporary Brazil: The Convening of the International Eucharistic Congress of 1955 in Rio de Janeiro," *Hispanic American Historical Review* 76, no. 4 (November 1996): 729.

12. For an emphatic statement of this interpretation of Ibero-American corporatism, see Howard J. Wiarda, *Corporatism and Development: The Portuguese Experience* (Amherst: University of Massachusetts Press, 1977), 20–21.

13. On the influence of Catholic social doctrine on Brazilian *trabalhismo*, see Jessie Jane Vieira de Sousa, *Círculos Operários: a Igreja Católica e o mundo do trabalho no Brasil* (Rio de Janeiro: Editora UFRJ/FAPERJ, 2002).

14. *Decreto-Lei n.º 3.270, de 14 de maio de 1941*. Reprinted in *Boletim do MTIC*, no. 82 (June 1941): 26.

15. Alkindar Costa, *Volta Redonda: ontem e hoje — visão histórica e estética* (Volta Redonda: Sociedade Pró-Memória de Volta Redonda, 1991), 361.

16. "Dia do Trabalho," *BSVR*, no. 083 (May 5, 1944): 745–46.

17. Bishop Dom João de Matha Andrade e Amaral to Pope Pius XII; EMS f-publ 47.04.02, Pasta 3.

18. Photos from a *missa de campo* for the *Dia da Independência* on September 7, 1945. Photos A89-5 to A89-8, Religião, Arquivo Fotográfico da CSN.

19. "Direção Industrial," *BSVR*, no. 143 (July 29, 1947): 1293.

20. Jessie Jane Vieira de Sousa, "Valentim, o guardião da memória circulista (1947–1958)" (master's thesis, Universidade Estadual de Campinas, 1992), 52. The historian Angela Castro Gomes coined the expression "spiritualization of class relations" to describe the agenda of Catholic intellectuals on labor. Angela M. de Castro Gomes, *Burguêsia e trabalho: política e legislação social no Brasil, 1917–1937* (Rio de Janeiro: Campus, 1979), 209.

21. The Confederação Nacional dos Operários Católicos (CNOC) served as official consultative organ to the *trabalhista* Labor Ministry under Alexandre Marcondes Filho (1941–45). Sousa, "Valentim," 60–61.

22. Jessie Jane Vieira de Sousa, "Da transcendência à disciplina: os círculos operários e a intervenção da Igreja Católica no mundo do trabalho (1930/1964)" (PhD diss., Universidade Federal Fluminense, 1999), 197–98.

23. "Fundo de Assistência Social — Aplicação durante o mês de outubro de 1950," *BSVR*, no. 008 (11 January 1951): 71, appendix.

24. Jessie Jane Vieira de Sousa, "Igreja e movimento operário: uma visão preliminaria," in *Arigó — O pássaro que veio de longe: a construção do sindicato dos metalúrgicos: a chegada da CSN e seu aparato de dominação* (Volta Redonda: Centro de Memória Sindical, 1989), 67.

25. Sousa, "Valentim," 89–91.

26. Quote from "Ata da reunião da Diretoria do Círculo Operário de Volta Redonda, 04/07/1946," in Sousa, "Valentim," 74.

27. Sousa, "Valentim," 69–73.

28. "Regulamento do Departamento de Assistência Social: da finalidade e atribuições," *BSVR*, no. 194 (October 16, 1951). It existed since the early 1940s, if under a different name.

29. Roberto C. Simonsen, "O problema social no Brasil," reprinted in Simonsen, *Evolução industrial do Brasil (e outros estudos)* (São Paulo: Editora Nacional, 1973), 441–54; quote on 443. For an institutional history of SESI in São Paulo, see Barbara Weinstein, *For Social Peace in Brazil: Industrialists and the Remaking of the Working Class in São Paulo, 1920–1964* (Chapel Hill: University of North Carolina Press, 1996), 140–65.

30. Labor Minister Marcondes Filho used these words to describe the CSN's goals during a visit to Volta Redonda in 1944. "Ministro Marcondes Filho," *BSVR*, no. 073 (April 19, 1944): 634–36.

31. CSN, *Resolução da Diretoria (RD)* 2250, Rio de Janeiro, December 8, 1950; "Efetivo de Pessoal em 30/06/49," *BSVR*, no. 132 (July 12, 1949).

32. "Regulamento do Departamento de Assistência Social."

33. "Fundo de Assistência Social — Aplicação durante o mês de outubro de 1950," *BSVR*, no. 008 (January 11, 1951). On the sports leagues, see "Liga de Desportes de Volta Redonda," *BSVR*, no. 216 (November 11, 1945): 1994; and Report by Livio Fleury Curado to DPS/DF, April 10, 1943, DOPS/DGIE, Geral 21, Dossier 1, 142.

34. "Expediente durante o Carnaval," *BSVR*, no. 036 (March 4, 1943): 263; "Expediente de Carnaval," *BSVR*, no. 040 (February 27, 1946): 343; "Ginásio Macedo Soares," *BSVR*, no. 054 (March 3, 1946): 437.

35. "Cinema no Galpão de Diversões," *BSVR*, no. 191 (October 5, 1944): 1651, "Recreio dos operários," *BSVR*, no. 217 (November 12, 1944): 1889; "Galpão de Diversões," *BSVR*, no. 174 (September 12, 1944): 1501–2.

36. "Regulamento do Departamento de Assistência Social: da finalidade e atribuições," *BSVR*, no. 194 (October 16, 1951).

37. "Organização," *BSVR*, no. 86 (May 7, 1946): 655.

38. CSN, *RD* 565, Rio de Janeiro, September 29, 1947; CSN, *RD* 1.957, Rio de Janeiro, February 13, 1950.

39. Tomke Christiane Lask, "Ordem e progresso: a estrutura de poder na cidade operária da CSN em Volta Redonda, 1941–1964" (master's thesis, Universidade Federal do Rio de Janeiro, 1991), 162, 166.

40. Report by Livio Fleury Curado to DPS/DF, April 10, 1943, DOPS/DGIE, Geral 21, Dossier 1, 142.

41. For details, see Oliver J. Dinius, "Work in Brazil's City: A History of Industrial Relations in Volta Redonda, 1941–1968" (PhD diss., Harvard University, 2004), 444–59.

42. Serbin, "Church-State Reciprocity," 735, 749–51; CSN, RD 6.644, Rio de Janeiro, December 2, 1954.

43. Memo by Dom Agnelo Rossi, October 6, 1961, archived at the Curia Diocesana de Volta Redonda. Dom Agnelo expressed his enthusiasm about the development and noted that it had helped the Catholic Church gain ground.

44. O Lingote 2, no. 48 (March 10, 1955), 7; O Lingote 3, no. 56 (July 10, 1955), 10; O Lingote 3, no. 66 (December 10, 1955), 1.

45. CSN, RD 10.776, Rio de Janeiro, April 6, 1960.

46. "Junto com a usina construiram-se escolas," O Lingote 5, no. 104 (August 1957), n.p.

47. "Apoteótica recepção em Volta Redonda à imagem peregrina de N. Senhora de Fátima," O Lingote 6, no. 87 (October 25, 1956), 9.

48. See Dinius, "Work in Brazil's Steel City," 473–84.

49. Costa, Volta Redonda: ontem e hoje, 361.

50. Diocese de Barra do Piraí, 2.° Livro de Tombo (1961–), 5-2 and 6-1. CSN, RD 10.922, Rio de Janeiro, June 9, 1960.

51. A source that unites scarce and dispersed information on Dom Agnelo Rossi's biography is Salvador Miranda, The Cardinals of the Holy Roman Church, digital resource at http://www.fiu.edu/~mirandas/bios-r.htm (accessed August 20, 2009). Miranda uses an impressive array of primary and secondary sources, although he does not footnote the individual biographical sketches.

52. "Reafirmada, mais uma vez, a unidade da família siderúrgica," O Lingote 5, no. 99 (April 1955), 4–5.

53. Riolando Azzi, Presença da Igreja Católica na sociedade brasileira, 1921–1979 (Rio de Janeiro: Tempo e Presença, 1981), 62.

54. Agnelo Rossi, A filosofia do comunismo (Petrópolis: Editora Vozes, 1958).

55. Agnelo Rossi, A formação de estagiários para a Ação Católica (Petrópolis: Editora Vozes, 1949).

56. Dom Agnelo left Volta Redonda in 1962 to become bishop of Riberão Preto (São Paulo state). He headed the National Bishop's Conference of Brazil (CNBB) starting in 1964. In 1965, he became archbishop of São Paulo and a cardinal.

57. Scholars disagree about the significance of the popular catechism for the growth of the Ecclesiastical Base Communities. Scott Mainwaring rejects the interpretation of Brazilian scholars who see a direct link between the two. He points to the central role of clerics in the practice of the popular catechism and cites the lack of evidence for CEBs tracing their origin to the late 1950s. Scott Mainwaring, The Catholic Church and Politics in Brazil, 1916–1985 (Stanford: Stanford University Press, 1986).

58. O bispo de Volta Redonda: memórias de Dom Waldyr Calheiros, organizado por Celia Maria Leite Costa, Dulce Chavez Pandolfi, and Kenneth Serbin (Rio de Janeiro: FGV Editora, 2001), 83.

59. On Kubitschek's economic policy, see Kathryn Sikkink, *Ideas and Institutions: Developmentalism in Brazil and Argentina* (Ithaca: Cornell University Press, 1991).

60. CSN, *GT para estudo de venda das casas: relatório* (Volta Redonda: CSN, 1960).

61. Symbolically the most important result of this push was a union-mediated agreement between the CSN, the municipality of Volta Redonda, and the state of Rio de Janeiro to improve primary and secondary education in all city schools. CSN, *RD* 12.154, Rio de Janeiro, February 6, 1961.

62. Sousa, "Valentim," 39.

63. Fernando Ferrari, *Minha campanha* (Rio de Janeiro: Editora Globo, 1961); "Fernando Ferrari," *Dicionario histórico-biográfico brasileiro, Pós-1930,* ed. Alzira Alves de Abreu, Israel Beloch, Fernando Lattman-Weltman, and Sérgio Tadeu de Niemeyer Lamarão (Rio de Janeiro: Editora FGV/CPDOC, 2001), 2151–53.

64. Brasil Tribunal Superior Eleitoral, *Dados estatísticos,* vol. 5: *Eleições federais, estaduais realizadas no Brasil em 1960, e em confronto com anteriores* (Rio de Janeiro: Departamento de Imprensa Nacional, 1963), 63/64.

65. Waldir Amaral Bedê, interviewed by author, Volta Redonda, January 20, 1998. For an account of the 1963 union elections, see Regina Lúcia de Moraes Morel, "A ferro e fogo: construção e crise da 'família siderúrgica': o caso de Volta Redonda (1941–1968)" (PhD diss., Universidade de São Paulo, 1989), 392–94.

66. On military-church cooperation in the organization of the 1955 International Eucharistic Congress, see Serbin, "Church-State Reciprocity," 752–53.

67. CSN, *RD* 13.473, Rio de Janeiro, November 26, 1964.

68. *O Lingote* 12, no. 166 (August 1964), 1.

69. CSN, *RD* 13.631, Rio de Janeiro, February 25, 1965.

70. Ibid., 13.182, Rio de Janeiro, June 4, 1964.

71. Ibid., 13.235, Rio de Janeiro, July 2, 1964 (my emphasis).

72. Ibid., 13.317, Rio de Janeiro, August 13, 1964. Ervin Michelstaedter, former head of the industrial relations department, remembered that the distribution no longer served its purpose because workers used it to make sweets for sale rather than drink it. Eng. Ervin Michelstaedter, interviewed by author, July 22, 1998, Volta Redonda.

73. My interpretation highlights the pre–Vatican II roots of the reforms in the 1960s. It is all too easy to overstate the novelty of Vatican II, as if liberation theology had been its intended outcome.

74. *O bispo de Volta Redonda*, 83–85.

75. Sousa, "Valentim," 39.

76. *O bispo de Volta Redonda*, 93–98.

CHAPTER SEVEN

Borders, Gender, and Labor

Canadian and U.S. Mining Towns during the Cold War Era

LAURIE MERCIER

The isolated and scattered mining communities that stretch from the U.S. Rockies across Canada may not meet the standard definition of "company towns" — because since the 1940s individuals, not the mining companies, have largely owned local housing and businesses. But the underlying aspect of corporate control links company, single-industry, resource, or company-dominated towns in the mining world. Companies controlled the workforce through a combination of paternalism and intimidation, which often included spatially arranging worker housing near mines or the smelter, maintaining political power, creating corporate welfare programs, sustaining local institutions, and busting unions, as well as controlling jobs.[1] However, despite these designs, mining communities throughout North America have exhibited surprising militancy against the main employer. Women have often been at the forefront of that militancy, at times welcomed and at other times resisted by their male kin and comrades. Just as the free movement of capital and globalized mining link these communities, so too do ideas about labor rights and gender roles, which also cross national borders. The domination of powerful mining companies is but one feature of mining towns; the militancy of miners and their families and the persistence of rigid gender roles are two other central characteristics that deserve examination.

Gender — the socially constructed sex roles for women and men — has seemed an almost exaggerated component of the mining world. In our anthology project about women and mining, Jaci Gier and I discovered that what many believe to be the most "masculine" of industries has not uniformly banned women across time and space but rather erected gender exclusions at particular historical moments. Whether in Asia, the Pacific, Europe, the Americas, or Africa, mining became more fully associated with men as it became more capitalized and centralized. Societies and employers normalized women's exclusion from working underground through an elaborate set of beliefs, traditions, sexual metaphors, and seemingly "rational" and "natural" justifications, which were enforced through legislation or cultural taboos.[2]

In North America as women were removed from the mining process, capital alternately viewed women as assets or liabilities in its efforts to control labor. Companies often encouraged marriage and constructed family housing in order to secure a more docile workforce; at other times, they tried to limit the number of women in a mining camp. This illustrates the vacillation of employers and the state in either embracing or rejecting mining women, almost always tied to structural conditions. Companies saw their own interests tied with patriarchal male miners and reinforced gendered practices, depending on women's reproductive and domestic work. As a U.S. Women's Bureau study concluded in the 1920s, miners' wives were of "peculiar industrial and economic importance" to keep miners rooted.[3] Women created economic niches through direct relationships to mining in surface operations that admitted them — and in the brothels, taverns and cafes, households, and other businesses that male miners frequented.

Much research has focused on ways that women through their reproductive labor supported the industry and in their militancy as wives helped male miners through strikes and other labor actions.[4] Women often manipulated gender assumptions to more effectively and physically assert strike goals when men were enjoined from more public demonstrations through injunctions, or military and police violence. Labor movements preserved the ideals of female domesticity and the male worker as head of household, but women creatively exploited these assigned roles to pursue their own interests and their own forms of protests.[5] Abundant examples from the hemisphere's mining communities reveal how women exaggerated gender claims in solidarity for what they viewed as family and community, not just union, efforts.[6]

In the process of supporting men's labor rights, women often came to contest the gendered rules for protest and question their own roles in unions, families, and communities. Because these moments of protest often appeared as much about challenging patriarchy as capitalism, male miners and unions were not always as supportive of women's independent militancy as they were when women performed more traditional support roles during strikes.[7] Women and men repeatedly struggled over and renegotiated those gender roles.

Women in Canadian and U.S. mining communities asserted their importance to the mining economy and union through their domestic labor and by participating in women's auxiliaries and becoming miners and smelter workers. Yet their roles remained limited even as in the two nations married women entered the paid workforce in ever increasing numbers, and as feminist movements challenged patriarchal traditions. This essay explores why the International Union of Mine, Mill and Smelter Workers (and later the United Steelworkers of America) in mining towns on both sides of the border remained so resistant to female employment and activism from 1940 to 1980. By looking closely at the cross-border relationships and experiences within one international union and how ideas about gender influenced union politics, we see how working-class women and men in mining communities both embraced and contested these ideologies.

Metal mining is an industry that is associated with the American and Canadian Wests, although what constitutes the "West" is often debated. In Canada, significant ore reserves and mining communities in Ontario undermine the regional characterization. Many British Columbians distinguish their province as a geographic region of its own, known as the "West Coast" or the "Pacific." At the same time, many in British Columbia and Alberta do not consider Manitoba part of the West because it is located in the center of Canada. Manitobans, however, consider themselves to be Western Canadians, and the province's economy and history mirror its western neighbors far more than Eastern Canada. In fact, resource extraction and accompanying company towns are often associated with the Canadian "North." South of the border, too, region is contested. Smelter workers and their families in urban Tacoma felt more kinship with the logging and mining towns further east than neighboring metropolitan Seattle. And some western mining communities have shunned an association with their region, feeling more linked to industrial communities nationwide. For example, in the 1970s Butte, Montana, promoted itself as "Butte, USA," to distinguish itself from its "western" and more parochial state. Former Anaconda smelter worker Andy Kovacich described his community "like a piece of the industrial East among the farms and ranches of the pristine West."[8] These debates about the notion of region reveal that spatially workers saw themselves connected by industry and class rather than popular perceptions of place, even as they often invoked region to strengthen labor's causes, especially those linked to gender.

Mining has been part of a larger culture of masculinity that infused industrial work in the North American Wests. From the late nineteenth through the late twentieth centuries, resource-based industries — logging, mining, agriculture, fishing — distinguished the gendered and racialized character of work, eliciting images of tough, masculine outdoor labor and independence.[9] They have also resisted hiring women and racialized ethnic groups except when labor demands have overwhelmed the exclusionary rigid boundaries they erected. The white male breadwinner ideal and the reputed toughness of the work that supposedly discouraged women from employment often disintegrated when labor markets expanded, when families required multiple breadwinners, or when these "rugged" jobs became seasonal and low paid, which then made women and people of color ideally suited for the work.[10]

Despite union gains after the 1930s, many mining union leaders and rank-and-file workers continued to believe that the association of masculinity with militancy aided their cause. The western-based International Union of Mine, Mill, and Smelter Workers (or Mine Mill), which represented U.S. and Canadian nonferrous miners and refiners, celebrated masculinity in its iconography and rhetorical traditions to assert its fierce independence and militancy. It often acted autonomously from the rest of the North American labor movement.[11]

Mine Mill's internationalism went far beyond most "international" unions dominated by the United States.[12] Aside from the international causes that Mine Mill advocated, whether supporting republicans fighting Franco's fascists or peaceful relations with the Soviet Union, the union encouraged cross-border exchanges between Canadian and U.S. locals, even as the cold war limited travel of labor activists. Mine Mill workers recognized their common interests with other union workers and communities whether in Ontario, Montana, Manitoba, or New Mexico.

However, immediately following World War II, charges of Communist influence began to plague the union on both sides of the border even as it enjoyed organizing successes. Responding to government, business, media, and trade union anticommunism, the Canadian Congress of Labour expelled Mine Mill in 1949; the U.S. Congress of Industrial Organizations (cio) expelled it in 1950. In the postwar period Mine Mill capitalized on a masculine regional identity to resist anti-Communist attacks and raids by the United Steelworkers of America (uswa), Canadian and U.S. labor federations, governments, corporations, and the media. Despite intense raiding by uswa through the 1950s and early 1960s, Mine Mill remarkably held on to most of its western Canadian and U.S. locals.[13] If union membership seemed more important than region in shaping one's identification with work and community, Mine Mill tapped into some kind of regional allegiance in response to cold war attacks. uswa organizers, in fact, contended that geography, the nature of the mining industry, and Mine Mill's "masculine, militant heritage" had made its locals more independent and less susceptible to red-baiting.[14]

To protest the Canadian and U.S. cold wars, in 1952 Mine Mill invited the great African American singer and leftist critic Paul Robeson to sing at its international convention in Vancouver. The U.S. State Department intervened and refused to allow Robeson to leave the country, stopping him at the Washington State border. Outraged union delegates protested before the American consulate in Vancouver and began planning a concert at the border to protest the State Department's actions as an infringement of civil liberties. During Robeson's next two-month tour, where in the cold war climate small audiences met harassment for attending the concerts, he had his most successful performance at the Peace Arch on the Canada/U.S. border in Blaine, Washington. Thanks to organization and publicity by Mine Mill locals and women's auxiliaries, forty thousand people came to hear the famous singer, inaugurating the first of four annual concerts with Robeson to advocate for civil liberties and the right of free movement for Robeson, trade unionists, and progressives across the border.[15]

The border concerts with Robeson epitomized Mine Mill's efforts to press its members to move beyond bread-and-butter issues to pursue broader social and political concerns. To help members counter the powerful grip of mining companies, which often controlled the towns in which its workers lived, the union helped communities forge alliances with other unions, create labor-oriented cultural institutions and activities, develop political clout within the province or state, and obtain better housing, education, and recreation. Mine Mill was often "the heart" of mining, smelting, and refining communities.[16]

Mine Mill also had one of the largest union auxiliaries, officially encouraging women's involvement in community and labor affairs. Gender appeals became important to Mine Mill supporters and detractors during the cold war, as women, like men, divided over ideological and other issues. Corporations, churches, the media, and rival unions all played roles in undermining Mine Mill's capacity to organize and retain support as it beat back anti-Communist attacks. But the union's position on gender roles as actually practiced vis-à-vis the auxiliaries, and the degree to which it involved women in its mission, also affected its survival, regardless of borders and region.

Women's auxiliaries thrived from the 1930s through the 1950s, especially in single-industry communities that excluded women from the workforce.[17] Prohibited from the mining, smelting, and refining workplace, women found other ways to supplement family earnings, and auxiliaries offered a way for them to participate in class politics and work for their economic interests and communities outside the home. Unlike many international unions that were ambivalent about women's potential clout, Mine Mill recognized the broader political and economic value of women's participation and actively encouraged women's auxiliary membership, often pronouncing, "A union without the women is only half organized."[18]

Despite its lofty rhetoric, however, within local unions and mining communities women's roles were more constricted. Auxiliaries were especially active during strikes, when their labor was particularly critical. Yet even then women were usually funneled into domestic roles — cooking in strike kitchens, distributing clothing to families, organizing other wives — rather than utilized in policymaking or public roles. Alexander Sokalski recalled gender and generational paternalism in the 1947 strike in Sherridon, Manitoba, at the Sherritt Gordon mine. Strikers and families marched from the town of Kississing to Sherridon, with Mine Mill Local 695 union executives leading the way, followed by the children, members of the women's auxiliary, and finally the mass of male strikers. Sokalski recalled that his own mother, along with many other women, remained behind at the hall, preparing food for the marching strikers.[19]

Despite Mine Mill's enthusiasm for organizing auxiliaries across borders, by the late 1940s the cold war intervened to heighten gender and ideological divisions within the international. In January 1947, Mine Mill International Auxiliary president Mary Orlich of Butte, tireless advocate for the auxiliary movement, became alarmed by CIO claims that domestic Communists, many of whom were in the labor movement, threatened American security. In the conservative *Saturday Evening Post* Orlich publicly charged her own brother union as being a tool of Communist subversion and called for women to mobilize to defeat it: "I want to organize all the housewives in America to fight this scourge; I want to inform the women of America how their way of living is threatened. The commies are a common enemy, and the people don't know it."[20]

While women may have divided ideologically over the indictment or questioned the tactics of Orlich or her opponents in damaging the auxiliary movement, male Mine Mill members widely condemned Orlich for "meddling in men's union affairs." Moreover, men questioned the efficacy of the auxiliary movement and marginalized its potential strength.[21] The Mine Mill executive board forced Orlich to resign and organized a new Ladies Auxiliary.[22] Although men's "meddling" dampened enthusiasm for the auxiliary in the United States, Canadian auxiliaries pushed for a stronger position within the recently autonomous Canadian Mine Mill Council.[23] Rachael Wood, financial secretary of the auxiliary in Trail, British Columbia, and a former wartime smelter worker, wrote a prize-winning essay featured in Mine Mill's newspaper, "What Being a

Member of a Mine-Mill Auxiliary Means to Me," to justify wives' increased participation in union affairs as she affirmed women's loyalty to Mine Mill political goals. She reminded her sisters that women needed to join men in "upholding our International Constitution" and "preserve the democratic rights of all workers," including "freedom to choose one's own . . . politics."[24]

Although the auxiliary seemed safely purged of Communist leadership, women still pushed for a more active role in union issues and often pursued their own agenda, which did not match men's goals. The *Mine-Mill Union* reported that at the 1951 Women's Auxiliary annual convention held in Nogales, Arizona, the women adopted an ambitious program of education and support for the union. But it failed to report what appeared in a banner headline in the auxiliary's own newsletter announcing that delegates to the convention had adopted a new women's rights resolution advocating equal opportunity for women in the workplace and public life. The women also vowed to seek joint activities with local unions to discuss the role of women. Mine Mill's silence on these goals indicates reluctance by the union to share with its locals the more independent interests of its auxiliary women.[25]

The newsletters and files of the Mine Mill Auxiliary reveal local women's persistent struggles, and frustrations, during the 1950s and early 1960s to gain acceptance in their communities and to win the respect of their union men while pushing for wider roles. The Mine Mill executive board and organizers repeatedly praised the potential roles for women in local unions. But resistance on the local level must have remained firm. International Auxiliary president Eva Pence, of Cobalt, Idaho, demanded to know why men hesitated in asking women to help in policing the health plan. Pence instructed auxiliary members to offer their help to the local union, and if refused, they should keep trying again until the union sees "that the women can do more than cook a good dinner, put on a banquet or help with that dance or picnic." Pence's irritation persisted, and in subsequent convention meetings she complained that local unions always depended on the auxiliaries in a crisis, such as strikes, election campaigns, or for "some food cooked and served . . . but when we need help we are forgotten and have no place in the labor movement."[26]

American women envied their sisters in Canada, who they believed wielded more influence with Mine Mill. There, women could attend local union meetings and make recommendations. "We had a voice, we could always express our views," noted auxiliary member Ruth Reid, "even if we couldn't always vote." Former Mine Mill organizer Clinton Jencks recalled his efforts in New Mexico to involve more women in the union, but men resisted because they feared losing some of their power and privilege. "I wondered why the Canadian women were so courageous . . . to say something on the floor and not just to be the auxiliary that serves the coffee and the cookies." He attributed their successful collaborations to male and female activists realizing that Mine Mill could be so much more effective by strengthening the auxiliary movement. After the Canadian auxiliary became autonomous in 1955, U.S. and Canadian sisters continued to exchange news and ideas, leading Eva Pence to grumble, "[The auxiliary in] Canada has advanced while we are just moving along." Pence concluded that this was "due to the [American] local union members" whose ambivalence or outright hostility turned away potential supporters.[27]

In some ways Canadian women may have had a greater voice in Mine Mill affairs, but gender and cold war divisions also hampered their union and auxiliary. During the critical 1958 Inco strike in northern Ontario, Sudbury merchants and politicians organized a "back-to-work" movement of union members' wives. Mercedes Steedman describes how gender tensions within the union provided fertile ground for an effective use of cold war propaganda among the women. Because Mine Mill had failed to allow a more inclusive political role for women auxiliary supporters, anti–Mine Mill forces gained momentum. In pursuit of their "manhood" in initiating the strike, the union failed to consider women's interests and found many women in the community pulled instead to an anti-Communist faction that had framed the strike as an assault on the family. Soon, workers and their families switched allegiances to a different union.[28]

Most of Mine Mill's western locals in Canada and in the United States more successfully resisted such cold war assaults, but two large and important locals in Kellogg (Idaho) and Anaconda (Montana) met similar fates by the early 1960s, signaling more trouble for Mine Mill's survival.[29] Katherine Aiken describes how Kellogg Local 18 had a tradition of involving its auxiliary women in significant ways. In addition to helping in strike kitchens, women participated in the union's meetings and radio broadcasts. But during the 1960 strike, and before an upcoming National Labor Relations Board (NLRB) election, the anti-Communist Northwest Metal Workers appealed to women by claiming that Mine Mill called unnecessary strikes, which hurt families and increased tensions. Although auxiliary support remained firm, in associating family values with anticommunism, the rival union peeled off enough votes from men to narrowly defeat Mine Mill.[30]

A similar catastrophe struck Mine Mill in Anaconda. Unlike in Sudbury and Kellogg, which had strong women's auxiliaries through the 1950s, the Anaconda auxiliary disintegrated after the Mary Orlich scandal and men's reluctance to support an autonomous women's group. In the next decade, a series of exhausting strikes, USWA raids, and gender divisions helped anti-Communist arguments take root. As in Sudbury and Kellogg, many Anaconda women and men came to believe anti–Mine Mill propaganda that linked the union to the strikes that created tremendous economic hardships and bargaining ineffectiveness. USWA explicitly linked family with patriotism and championed its "American program" that would improve the family wage; Mine Mill defended its bargaining gains that had made it possible for workers to "breathe easier" about taking care of families. Rhetoric about dependent women and male breadwinners celebrated restrictive gender roles. In discourse that excluded women from substantive matters, without connections to or space within Mine Mill to express themselves and their concerns, many women decided that they would be better off with USWA, which as a more powerful international union promised more support for families. In 1962 Anaconda men voted to support USWA as their new, and more virile, union.

Despite geographical differences, Sudbury, Kellogg, and Anaconda had much in common. The communities were ethnically diverse and were dominated by large multinational minerals corporations. In the postwar period they were transformed from company towns into union towns. Because of Mine Mill's influence, they created alternative politics and cultures, developing clout in local and state politics, a summer camp, an annual smelter workers' celebration, and union halls that served as community centers. Because they were among the largest Mine Mill locals, they were strategically important and were specific targets of USWA raids. With local unions ambivalent at best in supporting women's auxiliary work, Mine Mill lost a potential ally.[31]

By the early 1960s, almost all the women's auxiliaries of Mine Mill had become inactive or dissolved. The international made an effort to revive them, but its preoccupation with USWA raiders, trials of its officers, an empty treasury, a changing industry, an endless cycle of contract negotiations, and its persistent adherence to gender assumptions contributed to a lukewarm response. Ideologies about difference often sank deeply within many rank-and-file workers who resisted their own union's rhetoric of solidarity across skill, race, region, and gender. Mine Mill simultaneously advocated difference — the uniqueness of mining and smelting required rugged men — and equality.[32] Women, too, became less interested in joining auxiliaries. As more women entered the workforce and found other avenues for political participation and social expression in their own unions, political parties, and clubs, auxiliaries held little appeal.

But available jobs outside mines and smelters in these communities were limited, and women struggled for decades to gain access to these forbidden workplaces. In Canada and the United States, two decades, the 1940s and 1970s, offer exceptions in women's employment in mining and some insights on why these gender barriers were so difficult to dislodge. World War II presented a labor shortage that forced governments, companies, and unions to recognize that women could (in their minds temporarily) fill critical mining positions. Later, the feminist movements of North America compelled governments to open up former male bastions such as mining through equal employment opportunity (EEO) legislation. Much like in the auxiliary struggles to gain a voice in union affairs, women encountered resistance when they boldly asserted their economic and social rights to do "men's" work.

Even during World War II, when many North American industries opened jobs to women, company, government, and union officials sought to preserve men's claims to mining work. Montana's war manpower director, for example, claimed that the state needed "men for the hard, heavy and unpleasant jobs" in mines, mills, and woods, "where women cannot be used." Anaconda Copper Mining Company and Mine Mill union officials agreed that mines, mills, and smelters could not employ women because the work required strength and stamina. But physical prowess evidently was not the chief requisite because the company began recruiting retired and disabled men.[33] Nancy Forestell charts how gold mines in Ontario resisted hiring women even during the war labor shortages. In other mining centers companies supported hiring women with the understanding that they could free up large numbers of men on the surface to work underground. But gold-mining executives decided not to pursue female workers since the mines employed disabled male workers on the surface, maintaining the gender exclusivity of the industry.[34]

Although mines never accepted women underground, many of the region's smelters and refineries were compelled to employ some women to meet war labor needs. Since 1890, Ontario mining legislation had prohibited the employment of women in mines. But calling on the War Measures Act, the Canadian government issued an order on August 13, 1942, that allowed women to be employed to allay a labor shortage, but only in surface operations. At International Nickel's Sudbury operations, over fourteen hundred women were hired for production and maintenance jobs for the duration of the war. They performed a variety of jobs such as operating ore distributors, repairing cell flotation equipment, piloting ore trains, and working in the machine shop. At the end of the war, the government rescinded the order allowing the employment of women in the company's surface operations, and Inco returned the positions to servicemen.[35] Pearl Chytuk, who moved to Sudbury from Regina, Saskatchewan, in 1941, was able to get a job at the Inco smelter during the war, but she was surprised that people were fearful of talking about unions. While working at the smelter, Chytuk actively organized for Mine Mill Local 598. She remembered the hesitancy of some of her male coworkers, but many of the women activists were "from the West where we always felt more free." However, despite their activism, the union could not help them retain their jobs at the war's end.[36]

In Anaconda, Montana, the Anaconda Company manipulated perceptions of difference to convince union representatives to allow women into its smelter during the war. Appealing to racial prejudices, management threatened to import African Americans and Mexicans to fill the labor void, emphasizing that they would prefer Anaconda women "rather than Mexican boys," but the federal government could send "colored men" any time. Management and labor then agreed that they would preserve community values that championed white male and female breadwinners. The new employees had to be Anaconda residents, wives of former smelter workers in the service or recently deceased or disabled, and with children or parents to support.[37] Although the company never advertised the smelter openings in late 1943, word spread quickly, and many women eagerly applied, seizing the opportunity to earn men's wages. Ursula Jurcich, strapped to care for an invalid husband and young son, noted: "Everybody was talking about it . . . so I thought I might as well go and see if I can get on. . . . The money was big, that was important."[38] Nonetheless, company ambivalence and the firm community male breadwinner ideal led it to hire just over a hundred women at the smelter (compared to almost four hundred men over sixty years in age) during the war.

Why did urban wartime shipyards and aircraft plants actively recruit women, while mining communities resisted hiring them? Well-entrenched gender ideologies, accompanying lore about the work, and past union struggles for job security in a declining industry influenced practices. This helps explain why women never constituted more than 5 percent of the smelter workforce in Anaconda, for example, while they made up 28 percent of the Portland (Oregon) shipyard workers.[39] Even Mine Mill wavered from its expressed goals of gender equality given male rank-and-file resistance. In Anaconda, when the company tried to bypass union seniority rules to give women "soft" positions, union leaders, struggling to preserve a male breadwinner workplace while maintaining labor principles, alternated between insisting that women be excluded as a weaker sex and that they be treated equally. At the end of the war, Mine Mill Local 117 defended the women in a retroactive pay contractual issue and even sought to retain jobs for widows, who it believed merited continued employment because of their economic circumstances. But the union became caught in its own web of seniority rules, and the company insisted that the last woman hired would be the first laid off when a serviceman reclaimed his job. Within a few months no women were employed in production at the smelter, and old gender barriers were re-erected.[40]

If women received a frosty reception in the mining workplace during wartime labor demands, their efforts to re-enter mines and smelters several decades later following government and union mandates presented even more challenges in the light of a declining industry. In the United States and Canada, women won the legal right to enter male mining workplaces just as the industry began to mechanize, move operations out of the country, and lay off workers in the 1970s. Federal affirmative action orders opened coal and hard-rock production jobs to women for the first time since World War II.[41] For women in places like Arizona, Montana, Appalachia, and Ontario, despite male resistance and harassment, the good wages offered made competition stiff for the relatively few mining jobs available.

In the tight-knit copper-smelting community of Anaconda, women remembered their World War II predecessors and with EEO openings in the 1970s seized opportunities for higher pay. But community attitudes toward the new generation of women smelter workers were different in a climate of retrenchment. As former wartime smelter worker Katie Dewing recalled, the women who crossed gender boundaries "the second time around" in the 1970s "had hard jobs" because they "were taking men's jobs." Yet despite workforce reductions, Anaconda Copper Mining Company (ACM) personnel director Bob Vine insisted that the women "were readily accepted" by male workers. This may be because few women lasted. In March 1974 Carolyn Crisler left her position as a nurse's aide to work at the smelter. Since she weighed less than the required 130 pounds, she slipped weights into her pants to get the job because "we were trying to buy a house, and we needed the money, and I knew if I got up there, I could save a lot of money." Despite the hot, dirty, and dangerous work in the converters, she "liked the crew . . . and the men accepted me and I did my work." Nevertheless, she quit after two years because the physically exhausting work interfered with raising her young children.[42] Then in 1980, the Atlantic Richfield Corporation, which bought the Montana ACM mines and smelters in 1977, shut down the state's operations, ending many working-class women and men's opportunities to earn a family wage.

Jennifer Keck and Mary Powell outline how a hundred pioneering women took jobs at Inco in Sudbury, Ontario, in the mid-1970s after provincial legislation removed barriers to women's employment in surface jobs (1970) and later underground (1978). Motivated primarily by higher wages, the women Inco workers found that "men's" jobs offered a great deal of satisfaction as well as greater financial independence. They endured the physically hard work, sexual harassment, and difficulties finding child care to better support themselves and families. In adapting to masculine work culture, they had to prove they could "do the work of a man" in order to be treated the "same as a man." In the process, they could achieve "manhood" regardless of sex, breadwinner status based on family need, and respect for fighting back. During the strike of 1978–79 women workers saw themselves as workers first and declined to join wives in making sandwiches, instead joining their brothers on the picket line and in negotiating committees.[43]

Yet in other communities it was more difficult to dislodge firm gender segregation. In Flin Flon, Manitoba, mining jobs in the 1970s remained restricted to single women and then only on the surface, not underground. Meg Luxton found in her fieldwork that married women wanted to work outside the home, but because Flin Flon "was a man's town," it was difficult to find paid work.[44] And because the union local and its members resisted wives' involvement in union affairs, women became susceptible to management manipulation to take anti-union positions. Women resented that the union only welcomed their participation during strikes, when they were needed to walk picket lines and provide other assistance, although most seized the opportunity to help, since their own class interests made them anxious to support union goals for better wages and conditions.[45]

By the 1970s mineral companies and the USWA Union (which absorbed Mine Mill in 1967) officially opposed discrimination and harassment, but official pronouncements rarely squared with reality. By the 1980s, many women had formed an uneasy alliance with their male coworkers in mines and smelters. But automation and industrial decline forced layoffs, and women, having the least seniority, made up a larger proportion of those terminated. And evidence suggests that for those who remained, sexual harassment persisted and at times increased. Although men and women together faced uncertain futures, women had spent a decade proving themselves, only to see men hang on to the few remaining skilled mining jobs.

The Arizona copper mining strike of 1983–85, involving the large multinational Phelps Dodge and the Steelworkers Union, represented a watershed moment in North American labor and mining history. Once again, women assumed a dominant role in maintaining the strike, loyally and passionately picketing for the same reasons they had in years past — to improve their families' living conditions and to support striking men (and some women miners) who were legally enjoined from action. The strike ultimately failed, and the company successfully decertified the union with its permanent replacement workers, ushering in a new nonunion era in the American mining industry.[46] Women miners and miners' wives in Arizona joined thousands of women from other declining mining communities in North America to find other wage work, often in the expanding service sector, and sometimes becoming the main breadwinners in their families.

The Minnesota iron mines, positioned on the border just south of Canada and edging onto the American West, at the end of the twentieth century became the site of one of the last gender struggles over mining jobs. In the mid-1970s when federal pressures allowed women into this "man's world," at the Eveleth Mines men's resistance was reflected in the company's decision to hire only a few dozen women, who were identified as "hardship cases," without the support of a husband or father. The 2005 film *North Country*, a fictionalized account of the landmark 1984 *Jenson v. Eveleth Mines* case that made sexual harassment illegal in the American workplace, simplifies the historical episode but captures the depth of persecution that women miners experienced. They endeavored to ignore and take precautions to avoid harassment. Some gained weight, refused to smile, or dressed to make themselves less attractive, disguising their sexuality. Some carried weapons or worked in pairs for self-defense; some suffered posttraumatic stress disorder (PTSD); others never left their homes or quit. But the crude and physical abuse continued. As miner Jeannie Aho noted, "Nobody really knew what to do. We just thought, well, you had to take it because you were in a man's world."[47]

Patricia Kosmach, a union activist, repeatedly tried to get USWA leadership to come to the aid of the women workers. Finally, Lois Jenson, who had worked at the mine since 1975, brought a legal challenge against the USWA Local 6860 and mine operators. She and the other twenty female plaintiffs became pariahs in their mining communities as well as the workplace. As the mines slowed operations due to global competition, men and women blamed the miner plaintiffs for eliminating jobs. In the early 1980s the mine cut production and halved the workforce to just 723, eliciting anger at the women who had enough seniority to remain. The trial paraded degrading personal information about the women miners and took a heavy physical and psychological toll on them. Finally, in 1998, the remaining women won a multimillion-dollar settlement on appeal, but by then many of North America's mines, smelters, and refineries had shut down.[48]

As these examples from North America demonstrate, women have persistently sought access to mining jobs and expanded roles in the union that represented their family members. Women miners endured discrimination, harassment, and dangerous and demanding labor in order to gain more comfortable lives and in many cases the self-satisfaction that they could work a "man's" job.

Yet these challenges to the gender division of labor became muted as the minerals industry restructured, downsized, and deunionized in the 1980s; women and minority workers with the least seniority were laid off first. These cases remind us how masculine work culture, entrenched corporate practices, and social assumptions about gender, even in periods of labor expansion (such as World War II) or structural legislative changes (as in the EEO push of the 1970s), can impede the entry of and survival of women in the mining workplace.

The class militancy of mining communities and unions sharply contrasted with the conservative domestic ideology that pervaded work, home, and community life. Both Mine Mill and its successor USWA espoused inclusive labor goals but also embraced a masculinity that was exclusionary, in resistance to cold war anticommunism but also to expanded roles for women in union auxiliaries and the mining workplace. By the 1960s cold war fears and regional sentimentality gave way to pragmatic concerns about union survival. Most Mine Mill locals merged with the more powerful USWA in 1967, but in subsequent years labor militancy could not alter the downward slide of mining unionism. What did survive was resistance or ambivalence to women in the workplace and in union politics. The persistence of gender ideologies in both Canadian and U.S. mining towns indicates that differences based on geography, region, and borders were perhaps more perceived than real. And the inability to embrace the potential of working-class solidarity across gender lines, union rhetoric to the contrary, diminished labor internationalism's clout to match global capital.

NOTES

1. On mining company towns in Canada and the United States, see, for example, Robert Robson, "Manitoba's Resource Towns: The Twentieth Century Frontier," *Manitoba History*, no. 16 (Fall 1988): 2–6; Margaret Crawford, *Building the Workingman's Paradise: The Design of American Company Towns* (New York: Verso, 1995), 129–51.

2. Laurie Mercier and Jaclyn Gier, eds., *Mining Women: Gender in the Development of a Global Industry, 1670–2005* (New York: Palgrave Macmillan, 2006). Although focused on artisanal small-scale mining, Kuntala Lahiri-Dutt and Martha Macintyre reach similar conclusions in *Women Miners in Developing Countries: Pit Women and Others* (Hampshire, Eng.: Ashgate, 2006). For a description of the specific myths, traditions, movements, and legislation that forbade women from working underground, see Angela V. John, *By the Sweat of Their Brow: Women Workers at Victorian Coal Mines* (London: Croom Helm, 1980); Jane Mark-Lawson and Anne Witz, "From 'Family Labor' to 'Family

Wage'? The Case of Women's Labor in Nineteenth-Century Coalmining," *Social History*, no. 13 (1988): 151–74; Barbara Kingsolver, *Holding the Line: Women in the Great Arizona Mine Strike of 1983* (New York: ILR Press, 1989), 1–21; Richard V. Francaviglia, "In Her Image: Some Reflections on Gender and Power in the Mining Industry," *Mining History Journal*, no. 5 (January 1998): 118–26.

3. Quoted in Mildred Allen Beik, *The Miners of Windber: The Struggles of New Immigrants for Unionization, 1890s–1930s* (University Park: Pennsylvania State University Press, 1996), 94.

4. See, for example, Nancy M. Forestell, "The Miner's Wife: Working-Class Femininity in a Masculine Context, 1920–1950," in *Gendered Pasts: Historical Essays in Femininity and Masculinity in Canada*, ed. Kathryn McPherson, Cecilia Morgan, and Nancy M. Forestell (Don Mills, Ont.: Oxford, 1999), 139–57.

5. As Thomas M. Klubock found in Chile's El Teniente, for example, women used the "family wage" ideal to claim their rights to husbands' wages and benefits as well as work with men to extract economic and social concessions from Kennecott Corporation. Klubock, *Contested Communities: Class, Gender, and Politics in Chile's El Teniente Copper Mine, 1904–1951* (Durham, N.C.: Duke University Press, 1998).

6. Janet L. Finn documents in Chuquicamata, Chile, that when the company tried to crush a strike, groups of women hid lunch buckets and even seized and dressed strike-breakers in women's clothing to ridicule their lack of manhood in failing to support the strike. Finn, *Tracing the Veins: Of Copper, Culture, and Community from Butte to Chuquicamata* (Berkeley: University of California Press, 1998).

7. As June Nash discovered in her study of Bolivian tin-mining communities, despite women's proven critical role in labor actions, male miners often "ordered wives back to the kitchen." Nash, *We Eat the Mines and the Mines Eat Us: Dependency and Exploitation in Bolivian Tin Mines* (New York: Columbia University Press, 1979).

8. Quoted in Laurie Mercier, *Anaconda: Labor, Community and Culture in Montana's Smelter City* (Urbana: University of Illinois Press, 2001), 204–5. For a discussion of borders and the differences in the Canadian and U.S. Wests, see Elizabeth Jameson and Sheila McManus, *One Step over the Line: Toward a History of Women in the North American Wests* (Edmonton: University of Alberta Press), xvi–xxiii.

9. Carlos A. Schwantes has written extensively about the male worker's milieu. See, for example, *Radical Heritage: Labor, Socialism, and Reform in Washington and British Columbia, 1885–1917* (Seattle: University of Washington Press, 1979); "Protest in a Promised Land: Unemployment, Disinheritance, and the Origin of Labor Militancy in the Pacific Northwest, 1885–86," *Western Historical Quarterly* 13, no. 4 (October 1982): 373–90; "Images of the Wageworkers' Frontier," *Montana: The Magazine of Western History* 38, no. 4 (Autumn 1988): 38–49.

10. Laurie Mercier, "Reworking Race, Class, and Gender into Pacific Northwest History," *Frontiers: A Journal of Women Studies* 22, no. 3 (2001): 61–74.

11. The union had a profound influence on mining communities in Canada and the United States since its founding (as the Western Federation of Miners) in Butte,

Montana, in 1893. After moribund years from state repression in the early twentieth century, in 1934 successful strikes in Montana helped revitalize the union and the labor movement. The Kirkland Lake, Ontario, gold miners' strike in 1941, though unsuccessful, paved the way for Privy Council Order 1003, Canada's Wagner Act, and successful Mine Mill organizing. Laurel Sefton Macdowell, *"Remember Kirkland Lake": The History and Effects of the Kirkland Lake Gold Miners' Strike, 1941–42* (Toronto: University of Toronto Press, 1983).

12. In the North American context, labor "internationalism" has meant U.S. unions with affiliates in Canada.

13. After almost two decades of internal struggle, the Mine Mill membership in 1967 voted to formally merge with the USWA.

14. Laurie Mercier, "'Instead of Fighting the Common Enemy': Mine Mill versus the Steelworkers in Montana, 1950–1967," *Labor History*, no. 40 (1999): 459–80. The literature on the cold war and labor unions is extensive. See, for example, Reg Whitaker and Gary Marcuse, *Cold War Canada: The Making of a National Insecurity State, 1945–1957* (Toronto: University of Toronto Press, 1994); Al King with Kate Braid, *Red Bait! Struggles of a Mine Mill Local* (Vancouver: Kingbird, 1998); Harvey A. Levenstein, *Communism, Anticommunism, and the CIO* (Westport, Conn.: Greenwood Press, 1981); and Steve Rosswurm, ed., *The CIO's Left-Led Unions* (New Brunswick, N.J.: Rutgers University Press, 1992).

15. Laurel Sefton MacDowell, "Paul Robeson in Canada: A Border Story," *Labour/Le Travail* 51 (Spring 2003): 177–221, http://www.historycooperative.org/journals/llt/51/macdowell.html (accessed February 7, 2007).

16. Ruth Reid, quoted in "Panel Review," in *Hard Lessons: The Mine Mill Union in the Canadian Labour Movement*, ed. Mercedes Steedman, Peter Suschnigg, and Dieter K. Buse (Toronto: Dundurn Press, 1995), 151.

17. For discussions of union auxiliaries see Caroline Waldron Merithew, "'We Were Not Ladies': Gender, Class, and a Women's Auxiliary's Battle for Mining Unionism," *Journal of Women's History* 18, no. 2 (Summer 2006): 63–94; Melinda Chateauvert, *Marching Together: Women of the Brotherhood of Sleeping Car Porters* (Urbana: University of Illinois Press, 1998); Paula F. Pfeffer, "The Women behind the Union: Halena Wilson, Rosina Tucker, and the Ladies Auxiliary to the Brotherhood of Sleeping Car Porters," *Labor History* 36 (Fall 1995): 557–78; Susan Levine, "Workers' Wives: Gender, Class and Consumerism in the 1920s United States," *Gender and History* 3, no. 1 (Spring 1991): 45–64; Marjorie Penn Lasky, "Where I Was a Person: The Ladies' Auxiliary in the 1934 Minneapolis Teamsters' Strikes," in *Women, Work, and Protest: A Century of U.S. Women's Labor History*, ed. Ruth Milkman (Boston: Routledge, 1985), 181–206; Christiane Diehl-Taylor, "Partners in the Struggle: The Role of Women's Auxiliaries and Brigades in the 1934 Minneapolis Truck Drivers Strikes and the 1936/37 Flint General Motors Sit-Down Strike," unpublished research paper, University of Minnesota, 1990; Judy Aulette and Trudy Mills, "Something Old, Something New: Auxiliary Work in the 1983–1986 Copper Strike," *Feminist Studies* 14, no. 2 (1988): 251–68; Deborah Silverton

Rosenfelt, commentary on *Salt of the Earth* by Michael Wilson (New York: Feminist Press, 1978).

18. International Union of Mine, Mill, and Smelter Workers (hereafter IUMMSW), "Report of the Proceedings of the 38th Convention," Joplin, Mo., August 1941, 9–10, 84–85. As Cynthia Loch-Drake finds, Mine Mill was the only union willing to organize women workers in Alberta. But it accepted gender-based differences in wages and job opportunities in its Medicine Hat pottery factory, even as women demonstrated their militancy in the 1947 strike. The author finds that women, too, for the most part accepted a male breadwinner model, believing that women's wage work was temporary until marriage. Workers and Mine Mill sought to improve women's situation "within a patriarchal paradigm." Cynthia Loch-Drake, "Jailed Heroes and Kitchen Heroines: Class, Gender, and the Medalta Potteries Strike in Postwar Alberta," in Jameson and McManus, *One Step over the Line*, 341–80.

19. Alexander Sokalski, "The Sherritt-Gordon Mine Strike of 1947," *Manitoba History*, no. 46 (Autumn/Winter 2003–4): 21–26.

20. "Miner's Wife Fights Off Red Invasion of Union," *Saturday Evening Post*, January 18, 1947. For more on this controversy and the Mine Mill Auxiliary, see Laurie Mercier, "'A Union without Women Is Only Half Organized': Mine Mill, Women's Auxiliaries, and Cold War Politics in the North American Wests," in Jameson and McManus, *One Step over the Line*, 315–40.

21. Correspondence, Orlich collection; William Mason and Harry I. Baird, Butte, to Editors *Saturday Evening Post*, January 23, 1947.

22. M. E. Travis to all IUMMSW Ladies Auxiliaries, December 9, 1947, box 126, folder "Executive Board Action re Controversy," Western Federation of Miners/International Union of Mine, Mill and Smelter Workers Collection, University of Colorado, Boulder (hereafter IUMMSW).

23. Mercedes Steedman, "Godless Communists and Faithful Wives, Gender Relations and the Cold War: Mine Mill and the 1958 Strike against the International Nickel Company," in Mercier and Gier, *Mining Women*, 233–53. In 1955 Mine Mill became the first international union to grant autonomy to Canadians.

24. Rachael Wood, "What Being a Member of an MMSW Auxiliary Means to Me," *Mine-Mill Union*, April 24, 1950, 6.

25. *Mine-Mill Union*, October 8, 1951; "Women's Rights — New Plank in Auxiliary Program," Ladies' Auxiliary of the IUMMSW, *Newsletter* 1, no. 1 (October 1951), box 159, folder "Auxiliary Newsletter," IUMMSW.

26. *Mine-Mill Union*, April 1956; IUMMSW Auxiliary president Eva Pence, reports, ca. 1955 and 1956; Pence to IUMMSW and Ladies Auxiliary, n.d., box 159, folder "Auxiliary," IUMMSW.

27. Reid and Jencks quoted in Steedman, *Hard Lessons*, 8, 153, 171; Mine Mill *Auxiliary Newsletter*, July 21, 1955, and Eva Pence to members of the International Union of Mine Mill and Ladies Auxiliary, ca. 1957, Box 159, folder "Auxiliary Newsletter," IUMMSW. That the border and auxiliary separation remained fluid is represented by continued British

Columbian attendance at auxiliary meetings and conventions in Spokane, Salt Lake City, and other U.S. western cities.

28. Solski, 136–37; Steedman, "Godless Communists."

29. The case of Britannia Beach, British Columbia, is one interesting example of a workforce not only resisting cold war designs but also mobilizing against the reach of U.S. capitalist expansion. Katharine Rollwagen documents how the idea of "community" failed to successfully mobilize people in the copper-mining town to halt a shutdown in 1958, but in 1964 a more disperse commuter workforce came together to resist the Anaconda Company's plan to shut down the mine during a labor dispute. Workers and women supporters successfully mobilized labor across Canada to insist that the U.S. corporate giant keep the mine open. Katharine Rollwagen, "When Ghosts Hovered: Community and Crisis in a Company Town, Britannia Beach, British Columbia, 1957–1965," *Urban History Review* 35, no. 2 (Spring 2007): 25–36.

30. Katherine G. Aiken, "'When I Realized How Close Communism Was to Kellogg, I Was Willing to Devote Day and Night': Anti-communism, Women, Community Values, and the Bunker Hill Strike of 1960," *Labor History* 36, no. 2 (Spring 1995): 165–86.

31. For a full discussion of the role of gender, ideology, and regionalism in Mine Mill's decline in Anaconda, see Mercier, *Anaconda*, and Mercier, "Instead of Fighting the Common Enemy."

32. The union's film *Salt of the Earth* in many ways reflects its enlightened politics — while at the same time rendering its women's auxiliary powerless. The 1951 Empire Zinc strike in New Mexico pushed masculine assumptions aside as a court injunction prevented male strikers from picketing, and Mine Mill wives took over in physically holding back deputies and scabs. As Ellen Baker documents, the reactions to the women's picket revealed the tensions inherent in the two models of unionism that had coexisted in this, and in many other, mining communities: one model based on a brotherhood of men as breadwinners, and the other model based on a larger union family beyond the workplace. Ellen Baker, "'I Hate to Be Calling Her a Wife Now': Women and Men in the *Salt of the Earth* Strike, 1950–52," in Gier and Mercier, *Mining Women*, 213–32, and Ellen Baker, *On Strike and On Film: Mexican American Families and Blacklisted Filmmakers in Cold War America* (Chapel Hill: University of North Carolina Press, 2007).

33. Plant Manpower Analysis, November 18, 1943, ACM Collection, Box 62, Folder 3, Montana Historical Society Archives, Helena (hereafter MHSA).

34. Nancy M. Forestell, "'And I Feel Like I'm Dying from Mining for Gold': Disability, Gender, and the Mining Community, 1920–1950," *Labor: Studies in Working Class History of the Americas* 3, no. 3 (2006): 77–93. Forestell notes that despite the high disability rate among gold miners, male miners sought to retain male dominance in the home as well as the mines, burdening women with the care of injured husbands and kin.

35. Stan Sudol, "Inco's Sudbury Nickel Mines Were Critical during World War Two," *Republic of Mining*, http://www.republicofmining.com/category/women-in-mining/ (accessed October 4, 2008).

36. Mike Solski and John Smaller, *Mine Mill: The History of the IUMMSW in Canada since 1895* (Ottawa: Steel Rail, 1985), 124; Steedman et al., *Hard Lessons*, 162–65.

37. Mercier, *Anaconda*, 67–68.

38. Ursula Jurcich, interview by author, August 12, 1986, MHSA.

39. Amy Kessleman, *Fleeting Opportunities: Women Shipyard Workers in Portland and Vancouver during World War II and Reconversion* (Albany: State University of New York Press, 1990).

40. For an extended discussion of the women smelter workers and gendered debates about employment during and after the war, see Mercier, *Anaconda*, 64–77.

41. Although 1965 U.S. civil rights legislation was amended in 1967 to include gender as a basis for nondiscrimination, abolishing state prohibitions against women mining, social sanctions remained, as Carletta Savage notes, "in full force." A class-action lawsuit settled in 1978 forced Appalachian coal companies to open their tunnels to women. In 1977 women made up just 1 percent of the mining workforce; by 1979, they had increased to over 10 percent. Savage, "Re-gendering Coal: Female Miners and Male Supervisors," *Appalachian Journal* 27, no. 3 (2000): 232.

42. ACM, *Annual Report* (1975), 23; interviews by author with Kathryn Dewing (August 11, 1986), Bob Vine (May 27, 1986), and Carolyn Crisler (March 16, 1987), MHSA.

43. Jennifer Keck and Mary Powell, "Women into Mining Jobs at Inco: Challenging the Gender Division of Labor," in Gier and Mercier, *Mining Women*, 280–95.

44. Meg Luxton, *More Than a Labour of Love: Three Generations of Women's Work in the Home* (Toronto: Women's Press, 1980), 177. Luxton's interviews with Flin Flon women reveal their struggles to recognize long-term interests that required supporting union strikes and short-term interests to sustain families during the strike period with no wages coming into the household. She also explores how the women felt dependent on the husbands' wages and powerless to control their lives through the lack of wage work opportunities. The level of company control in Flin Flon is also explored in James D. Mochoruk, "Oral History in a Company Town: Flin Flon, 1926–1946," *Canadian Oral History Association Journal* 7 (1984): 5–12.

45. Luxton, *More Than a Labour*, 215.

46. Barbara Kingsolver, *Holding the Line: Women in the Great Arizona Mine Strike of 1983* (New York: ILR Press, 1989).

47. Kirstin Downey Grimsley, "A Hostile Workplace into an Abyss of Sex Harassment at Eveleth Mine," *Washington Post*, October 27 and 28, 1996, a1; Catherine Winter and Stephanie Hemphill, "No Place for a Woman," transcript, American RadioWorks, September 2005 http://americanradioworks.publicradio.org/features/ironrange/transcript.html (accessed April 1, 2009).

48. Ibid.

CHAPTER EIGHT

El Salvador

A Modern Company Town in the Chilean Andes

EUGENIO GARCÉS FELIÚ and
ANGELA VERGARA

This chapter analyzes the social, urban, and architectonical characteristics of El Salvador, a company town built by the Andes Mining Copper Company in the Chilean Andes in the late 1950s. A U.S. company subsidiary of the Anaconda Copper Company — one of the three largest copper producers at the time — Andes Copper launched in 1956 the El Salvador Project to replace the failing mine of Potrerillos. Inspired by modern ideas on copper production, labor management, and urban planning, Andes Copper built a new mine, industrial plants, roads, and a camp. The town became a unique experiment in urban planning and social engineering, integrating diverse — and sometimes contradictory — traditions such as previous Chilean experiences with company towns in nitrate and copper settlements, U.S. company town planning of the early twentieth century, and U.S. post–World War II urban practices.

Company towns were an integral component of the Chilean industrial landscape and played a central role in the establishment and growth of Chile's most important commodities: nitrate and copper. Built in the 1910s, copper camps such as Sewell, Chuquicamata, and Potrerillos became emblematic examples of the introduction of the company town model in the Chilean copper mines as well as of the success of U.S. capital in the industry. Located next to the mines, these camps grew isolated from the rest of the country, and U.S. businesses considered and ruled them as private properties. Following policies resembling those implemented in other U.S. operations in Latin America, U.S. copper companies strictly segregated Chilean workers from U.S. management, encouraged workers to settle with their families, and sponsored a wide range of social services and urban infrastructure such as schools, sports fields, health-care facilities, and special programs for housewives.[1] Company towns, however, were always highly contradictory institutions and the site of intense labor and social tensions. While many contemporaries applauded the housing and social benefits provided by management and their welfare departments, many others such as Chilean writer Ricardo Latcham described these camps as a "Yankee feud."[2]

In the late 1950s, the El Salvador Project became emblematic of the modernization of copper production and living arrangements for mine workers. It was part of an international trend to improve productivity in mining and achieve increasing degrees of influence and control over a labor force that management perceived as too radicalized and expensive. The separation of the El Salvador camp and plant, the semicircular layout, and the high quality of housing show the influence of new ideas in town and industrial planning. However, El Salvador did not completely break with its past. As a traditional mining camp, El Salvador was still attached to the old tradition of company towns in Chile as well as in the rest of the Americas. As in previous company towns, the company perceived housing, social services, and industrial plant infrastructures as forms of social and labor control, increasing workers' dependency toward the company. The intense conflicts and confrontations that characterized the history of El Salvador in the following decades suggest that this model town did not achieve the harmonic balance between capital and labor that its planners had in mind.

This chapter is organized in four sections. The first section places El Salvador in the history of company towns in Chile, demonstrating the influence of company towns in the country. The second part explains the genesis of the El Salvador Project and Anaconda's campaign to modernize the copper industry and its Chilean properties. The third section analyzes the architectural and social aspects of El Salvador, showing the influence of new urban and planning ideas on Chile. The chapter ends with a short discussion of the labor and social tensions in Salvador throughout the 1960s, suggesting the tensions that the implementation of a company town caused in this community.

COMPANY TOWNS IN CHILE

In Chile, the most important planning efforts preceding the copper towns were the nitrate camps. Following the War of the Pacific (1879–83), nitrate became Chile's most important export commodity. Controlled by British capital, nitrate fields were spread out throughout the Atacama Desert. Given the isolation and low demographic density of this northern region, labor recruiters (called *enganchadores*) traveled around the country, especially to small towns in rural areas in the Central Valley, offering "good" jobs and salaries in the nitrate plants. Once in the North, workers experienced a harsh working and living environment and few possibilities to return home.[3]

In the early nitrate towns, employers offered basic urban infrastructure but few social welfare services beyond the company-owned store. The company store itself was a controversial institution, and its recurrent abuses and the use of scrip tokens inspired constant grievances and strikes.[4] Although World War I and the discovery of chemical fertilizers reduced the world demand for Chilean natural nitrate, production continued in the following decades but was now controlled by U.S. capital. Along with technological innovation, U.S. companies such as the Guggenheim Brothers adopted some ideas of urban planning and emphasized the importance of providing better housing, social services, and urban infrastructure to its residents. For example, the carefully planned towns of María Elena (1925) and Pedro de Valdivia (1931) included services such as schools, hospitals, sport facilities, and social clubs and resembled the copper camps that were being built at the time.[5]

Paralleling the construction of the latest nitrate company towns, the copper industry offered unique opportunities for the development and expansion of the company town model in Chile. U.S. copper companies arrived in Chile in the early twentieth century, transforming a copper industry that was outdated and barely surviving since the 1880s. By investing large amounts of capital and introducing technology and new labor and social ideas, large-scale copper companies made possible the exploitation of low-grade copper deposits located in isolated regions of the country. The Guggenheim Brothers purchased the El Teniente mine, located in the southern province of Rancagua, in 1908, and in 1915 they formed the Kennecott Copper Company to control all of their investments in copper. Anaconda organized the Andes Copper Mining Company to exploit the mine of Potrerillos in 1916, and a year later it created a second operating subsidiary, the Santiago Mining Company, to exploit two small mines located near the capital city of Santiago: La Africana and Lo Aguirre. In 1923, Anaconda purchased from the Guggenheim Brothers its largest mine in Chile, Chuquicamata (called Chile Exploration Company). Both the Kennecott Corporation and the Anaconda Company adapted the model of company town. Early descriptions of Chuquicamata highlighted its novelty in the Chilean industrial landscape. "It can be said," explained a document issued by the regional government in Antofagasta, "that in this mine workers enjoy conditions that are far superior to the ones that workers enjoy in the *pampa* [northern desert, usually nitrate fields]. Because of its housing, schools, medical services, cultural, social, and sport centers, as well as because of the organization of work, Chuquicamata is not only an industrial plant but it is also a school of moral and material improvement for its personnel."[6]

U.S. mining companies in Chile were influenced by contemporary debates in the United States and the so-called new company town movement of the early twentieth century, but they also incorporated some traditional Chilean features. In the United States, new company towns were carefully designed by architects and emphasized a wide range of welfare and social programs.[7] These new settlements attempted to overcome their industrial image, replacing the traditional and rigid geometrical layout with some of the features of the garden city movement to promote social harmony and industrial peace. An important component of the U.S. new company town, which was also a response to the Pullman strike of 1894, was the companies' desire to limit its control over the town itself and thus to start encouraging workers' home ownership.[8] In early twentieth-century Chile, U.S. capital made little effort to challenge the traditional geometrical layout (which was also part of Chile's traditional urban design), and while copper companies did establish a wide range of social and welfare programs, they maintained a strict control over the space and the people.

The region of Atacama, a traditional mining center, shows the characteristics and impact of company towns in Chile, the existence of different models and experiences, and their evolution over time. In the 1920s, Andes Copper built the first company town in the region, Potrerillos. Potrerillos was located at the southern edge of the driest desert in the world, Atacama, and included buildings and facilities in a scale unknown in early twentieth-century Chile. Potrerillos was part of an interconnected system of five mining camps that supported the exploitation and transportation of the copper produced in the Potrerillos Mine. Distributed from coast to mine (west to east), the camps included Barquito (port facilities and electric power station), Llanta (machine shops and railway station), Potrerillos (main camp, management office, and plants), Las Vegas (repair shops and sawmill), and La Mina (underground mine). Among all the camps, Potrerillos best exemplified the ways Andes Copper adapted the company town model to the Chilean high-altitude desert. With a population of about six thousand people in the 1930s, Potrerillos was a populated, diverse, heterogeneous, and well-equipped camp. It had a traditional square grid plan or *plan damero*. The railway station was located at the end of the town, dividing — at least symbolically — the town's industrial and urban zone. Right next to the center was the "Chilean village" and further east the "American camp," representing the visible segregation between Chilean workers and foreign employees.[9]

The camp offered six types of housing alternatives according to national origin, marital status, and job position: U.S. single men's houses, U.S. family houses, staff bachelors' houses, Chilean single men's barracks (*camarotes*), Chilean boarding houses, and Chilean family houses. While housing for foreign employees was of excellent quality and built according to the California-bungalow style, Chilean houses were small, were made of calamine or adobe, and lacked private bathrooms. Chilean family houses had three or four rooms (one or two bedrooms, a living room, and a kitchen) and were arranged on blocks of twelve houses with collective toilets in the center. Some family houses were attached houses, each row containing four to seven houses with collective bathrooms at the end. The *camarotes*, where the majority of blue-collar workers lived, housed around fourteen workers in seven rooms and had collective bathroom facilities. The Chilean camp had a monotonous and unappealing appearance.

The company provided free housing for its employees and people who worked in the town, such as teachers and police officers. The company owned all houses in the camp, and unlike some companies in the United States at the time, it never encouraged home ownership within the town. Community and housing regulations were strict, and residents were responsible for maintaining their houses. The housing regulations prohibited renovations or changes to the buildings, construction of any kind inside or outside the house, running businesses or shops, and keeping animals without company authorization. Houses were for residential purposes only; although residents could not use company property to generate extra income, families could rent rooms to single workers as a way to supplement their incomes.[10]

Inaugurated almost three decades later, the company town of Paipote shows the continuity of the company towns as well as the emergence of a new model in this region: state-owned company towns. In 1952, President Gabriel González Videla inaugurated the National Smelter of Paipote to smelt the copper ore produced by small- and medium-scale mining. Paipote was part of a larger project of state-sponsored industrialization and a process of import-substitution industrialization that included the construction of a steel mill in the southern city of Huachipato and an oil refinery in the central coast (Con-Con). Paipote was conceived as a symbol of economic and social progress, representing the country's national industrialization effort. Located about five miles from the city of Copiapó, the capital of what at the time was the province of Atacama, Paipote became a symbol of modern architecture and construction. Its houses made of concrete and functional design were unique in a region that was still dominated by colonial and neoclassical architecture.[11]

Despite their efforts, company towns in Atacama were never isolated and had an important impact on the region. They dominated in the production of the region's most valuable natural resource and were an important local source of employment. Traditional region cities such as Copiapó and Chañaral and smaller towns such as Pueblo Hundido complemented Potrerillos, Paipote, and eventually El Salvador by informally providing housing, health-care services, schools, and recreational spaces to company workers, and supplied an available labor force to company management. In the late 1960s, for example, the Chilean Ministry of Public Housing reported that about seven hundred Andes Copper workers and their families lived in the town of Pueblo Hundido — located more than forty miles west of El Salvador.[12]

The impact of Andes Copper on the Atacama region is representative of the growth of a "mining region." The notion of "mining region" represents the idea of a "territory," active in terms of entrepreneurship, industrial plants, human settlements, and road and port infrastructure, so that all the elements are inter-dependent in order to operate as a large industrial space. The mining region, located outside the formal control of the company but closely dependent on it, was the result of the impacts and demands generated by company towns. The construction and activity of industrial facilities transformed the Atacama region, which became connected to the operation and success of the mining in-dustry. For example, the Ministry of Public Housing stated that in the Province of Chañaral — where Potrerillos and Salvador are located — the population was concentrated around "important mining activities" and depended on the "boom experienced by these mining activities," suggesting the ways in which company towns and company land interacted.[13] But company towns also cre-ated enormous social and economic tensions in the peripheries or company land, and towns and cities usually developed an oversized service sector, an economic dependence on company towns, an unstable job market and popula-tion, and acute social problems such as crime, alcoholism, and prostitution. The social tensions in Pueblo Hundido, a small town located forty miles from El Salvador, evidenced these tensions. For example, in the early twentieth century, local authorities and newspapers usually complained about how mine workers from Potrerillos engaged in heavy drinking, gambling, and fights in local bars in Pueblo Hundido.[14] In addition, the environmental degradation caused by mining activities is another evidence of the many links between company towns and their region.

The construction of El Salvador between 1956 and 1959 continued a long tradition of company towns in this region. As at Potrerillos, the company created an isolated and company-owned camp completely dependent on mining production. As at Paipote, it introduced newer planning and production ideas, reviving a blind confidence in industrialization and modernization. And as at most company towns, it had a profound impact on the region.

EL SALVADOR PROJECT AND THE MODERNIZATION
OF THE COPPER-MINING INDUSTRY

In the 1950s, Anaconda launched its largest construction project in Chile since the 1920s: the El Salvador Project. The two components of this project, production facilities and living space (camp), were closely interconnected not only geographically but also ideologically, showing the complex relationship between work and home that characterized company towns throughout the Americas. New production facilities included a mine (Indio Muerto, later renamed El Salvador), two crushing plants, a concentrator, a molybdenum plant, and several shops and auxiliary services. The new living spaces included a completely new camp with housing, services, and infrastructure. Overall, between 1956 and 1960, Anaconda spent more than $100 million on this project.[15]

Both international and local factors motivated Anaconda to pursue this project. The 1950s was a time of rapid transformation in the copper industry both in Chile and in the world. Growing competition from the aluminum industry and from mines located outside the control and monopoly of the largest U.S. mining corporations forced copper companies to modernize and increase productivity and efficiency. Growing nationalism in the Global South and the politics of the cold war also forced mining companies to reframe their labor and political discourse, shaping the organization of production and investment decisions. In 1952, Anaconda recognized these tendencies in a special report to its stockholders: "The company has embarked on a program of expansion, rehabilitation, and improvement which affects principal operating units of the business. . . . Completion of the program will bring about a marked increase in the production of copper and zinc from Company mines over present levels. Expanded treatment facilities will handle a large tonnage of crude material while improvements at the fabricating level will enable the Company to better process the flow of refined copper and zinc."[16]

In November 1958, a special issue of the *Engineering and Mining Journal* titled "Planning the Modern Mine" focused on the question of modernization in the mining industry, and it included a special article on Anaconda's project in El Salvador. In an article titled "How Modernization Benefits the Mine and the

Man," the journal argues that "from a businessman's point of view, [it] is obvious that the objectives of a good modernization program should be to increase productivity, cut costs and maintain a good profit margin."[17] Influenced by what the journal called a modern management philosophy and the incorporation of modern scientific management, the mining industry was paying closer attention to quality control, operations, maintenance, and plant layout. For example, an efficient and compact layout became a key issue to reduce the use of energy and the waste of ore in a time of rising fuel and labor costs.

According to the journal, mining engineers and designers were also concerned with improving working conditions, especially safety, in order to increase productivity and reduce costs of production. "One added aspect of modernization," explained the *Engineering and Mining Journal*, "became astonishingly clear as we interviewed prominent mine plant designers, equipment manufacturers, mining and metallurgical engineers, and industrial engineers, to obtain information and ideas for this issue. It's this, if we make mines and minerals processing plants better, safer, cleaner, and more comfortable, less arduous for the man, we automatically achieve the economic benefits mentioned above."[18]

Influenced by the latest ideas in industrial planning and management, Anaconda started a long process of modernization and expansion to increase productivity, reduce costs of production, and become more competitive. To meet these challenges Anaconda transformed its Engineering Department into a new subsidiary company, Anaconda-Jurden Associates, led by Wilbur Jurden. With more than two hundred engineers specialized in design, engineering, and construction of metallurgy facilities, Anaconda-Jurden undertook the task of building for the new era.[19] Jurden, who came to be known as "Anaconda's master builder," played a central role in this process. A mechanical engineer, Jurden started working for Anaconda in 1917 and had supervised many important Anaconda projects in the United States, Mexico, and Chile, including the Potrerillos and the Chuquicamata mines in the 1920s. In the 1950s, he designed the Sulphide Plant at Chuquicamata (1948–52), the Yerington mine in Nevada (1953), and the aluminum plant at Columbia Fall, Montana (1955).

Chile, the site of the largest foreign operation of Anaconda, became important in the company's modernization and expansion effort. A new favorable political conjuncture improved investment conditions for U.S. copper companies. In 1956, the approval of Nuevo Trato (or New Deal), Chile's official copper policy for the next six years, improved the investment environment for foreign companies and compelled Anaconda to modernize and invest in its Chilean properties. Specifically, the Nuevo Trato stated that if copper companies increased production above their average production between 1949 and 1953, they would receive a generous tax reduction.[20] As Clyde E. Weed, chairman of the board of Anaconda, clearly recognized, "The contribution of the Chilean Government is acknowledged in establishing a sound, long-range policy governing the development of natural resources, an investment climate conducive to making large risk investments possible and a true democracy working its way toward a stabilized economy."[21]

The design of the mine, the plants, and the camp in El Salvador provided Anaconda with new opportunities to modernize production, increase efficiency, and improve workers' living conditions. Anaconda advertised El Salvador as a modern and model mine based on the latest ideas and advances in mining production. The mine incorporated the block-caving system similar to the one recently implemented in the Greater Butte Project. From the adit, or entry passage, the electric railway transported the ore to the primary crushing plant, and the belt conveyors transported it to the secondary crushing plant and to the concentration plant or flotation section. The copper concentrate was pumped through a fourteen-mile gravity pipeline to Llanta and transported by railway to the smelter in Potrerillos.[22] The entire design guaranteed the efficient, economical, and fast transportation of ore from the mine to the smelter.

Descriptions of the plants at El Salvador highlighted their efficient layout, showing the adaption of new trends in mining design. As in Yerington and Columbia Falls, Jurden introduced in El Salvador the concept of a compact layout that could increase the plants' efficiency and reduce the company's waste and production costs. Descriptions of El Salvador evidence the novelty of this design: "the buildings are arranged symmetrically so that conveyor belts transporting the ore are parallel to or at right angles to each building and to each other. In the concentrator, the ore is processed through a series of parallel circuits, again designed at right angles to a main feeding bin. This rectangular motif accounts for the orderly plant layouts designed by Anaconda-Jurden engineers, and eliminates many costly and specialized structures which would be necessary if conveyors were permitted to juncture at odd angles."[23]

The success of this scheme, however, depended on regaining control over the labor force. In mid-twentieth-century Chile, Anaconda faced not only an active and strong union movement but also high rates of absenteeism, labor turnover, and local wildcat strikes. While the union movement successfully struggled for better living and working conditions, workers' traditional work habits jeopardized the project of an efficient mine. To shape the labor force, Anaconda attempted to revitalize and reform the traditional institution of the company town.

EL SALVADOR: THE MODERN COPPER COMPANY TOWN

In November 1959, Charles M. Brinckerhoff, president of Anaconda and former general manager of Andes Copper, traveled to Chile from New York City to attend the inauguration of the mine and labor camp of El Salvador. In the speech he gave for the occasion, he described the camp as a major improvement in workers' living conditions. "It has been our effort," explained Brinckerhoff, "to offer our employees all the means and elements needed to have a good quality of life, according to the environment and the possibilities of a mining center. In our towns, you can see that employees and their families enjoy living conditions, from both the economic and welfare point of view, superior to the ones that exist in any other mining camp in the country."[24] As Brinckerhoff's speech suggests, the inauguration of the camp of El Salvador evidenced the company efforts to build a modern company town that would improve labor, political and social relations.

El Salvador can be placed in the history of modern urbanism, with its curved layout, housing design, and urban philosophy. The camp was carefully designed by U.S. architect Raymond Olson and Anaconda-Jurden Associates staff and built by Chilean contractors. Little is known about Olson, but as a U.S. architect working at Anaconda's headquarters in New York City in the 1950s, he was probably influenced by the urban planning experiences and debates in the United States at the time, such as the garden city movement, the rise of suburbs, the Regional Planning Association of America, and the International Congress of Modern Architecture (CIAM).[25] In 1933, CIAM agreed to the Athens Charter, laying the basic ideas for what came to be known as the functional city. By addressing the four central questions of modern urbanism (living, working, recreation, and circulation), the Charter of Athens argued that modern cities had to satisfy the biological needs of their residents as well as guarantee their individual freedom and provide for their collective material and spiritual needs.[26] In Latin America, the planning and construction of Brasília in the 1950s better exemplified the extreme application of these ideas.[27]

Drawing on all these influences, Olson planned El Salvador as a modern camp and an attractive community, looking to avoid the traditional limitations and the look of previous experiences of industrial towns. "The aim of the architectural planning at El Salvador," explained Olson in an article published in 1960, "was to develop an attractive, modern town that would be a highly desirable place to work and live. The final plan, selected from a number of layouts, completely avoids the industrial look."[28] Along with providing good living, health, and recreational conditions, Olson established a clear physical separa-

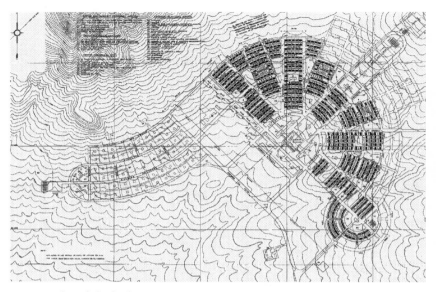

Figure 8.1 Plan of El Salvador, 1959. Eugenio Garcés Feliú et al., *Las ciudades del cobre*, 110.

tion between industrial and living areas, placing the town site about six miles from the mine. Overall, Olson believed that a model, rational, and professionally designed camp would reduce social tensions between employers and workers, create a social bond between the company and the workforce, and, above all, increase productivity.[29]

Unlike previous mining camps built in Chile, the El Salvador camp communicated with its natural setting. Olson perfectly situated the town within a natural amphitheater. To maintain a harmonic relationship between the environment and the built space, Olson used the La Cruz mount as a protection to limit the impact of the geographical vastness, providing the town with very well-defined and natural boundaries. While a high-altitude desert limited the possibilities of maintaining green areas, the camp did integrate the natural environment and the mountain became a space for recreation and worship. Olson designed a semicircular layout, consisting of a set of concentric rings composed of wide avenues, streets, and lanes, with additional diagonals, drawn with angles of 45 degrees and 22.5 degrees, which converge into the square, as the focus of the composition. The layout and the curved streets created closed views and limited the visual impact of the high-altitude desert, a common problem of square-grid towns where the linear streets are monotonous and end in the desert.

Figure 8.2 Family homes, El Salvador, 1999. Eugenio Garcés Feliú et al., *Las ciudades del cobre*, 114.

The town was organized in square city blocks (the so-called *manzanas*), and each *manzana* contained about forty duplex townhomes. Houses had a small front garden and a back patio accessible from the alley, resembling traditional U.S. neighborhoods. The houses, however, incorporated the Chilean tradition of a front fence, guaranteeing the privacy of family life. Throughout the town, the curved layout left small areas in the shape of a triangle, where the designer placed playgrounds and buildings for social space, creating some sense of neighborhood. Unlike the proposals of the garden city and the greenbelt movements, El Salvador maintained a traditional downtown area. Services were built around the central plaza, including the Catholic Church, the social club, the company store, the theater, public offices, a post office, a bank, restaurants, and private retail shops. Most community events and social life took place in the plaza and its adjacent buildings.

Houses clearly evidenced the general improvement in living conditions and the implementation of new building techniques and architectural concepts, with two or three bedrooms and a private bathroom, including all the comforts of a modern town, such as gas and electricity. Olson considered building about six hundred houses and a large number of office, store, and social service buildings. Blue-collar and white-collar employees lived in the Chilean camp, where

Olson had designed eight different floor plans of his two-story duplex family homes. Olson put special care in the colors, painting houses in ten different pastel color combinations to break the drabness of the natural landscape. As he explained in the *Engineering and Mining Journal*, "The combination of pastel-colored exteriors with gleaming white-chip marble roof tops (to reflect heat) is expected to give El Salvador eye appeal akin to that exhibited by Bermuda's white-roofed, pink and white cottages."[30]

In contrast, the American camp was designed as an exclusive neighborhood for staff members and their families. It was placed on the west side of the town and outside the semicircle, and it offered four different types of bungalows. Staff family homes, described Olson and Chavez, included "a living room, dining room, kitchen, utility room, three or four bedrooms, and two bathrooms, as well as a carport, service annex consisting of maid's room and bath, and a large storage room."[31] The American camp also enjoyed the shade of the few trees, natives and exotic species, that grew in the area. Foreign employees had their exclusive services including a small elementary school and a social club.

Olson proposed El Salvador as a pedestrian community, with neighborhoods that had their own recreational spaces. Trucks could not enter the town, and workers commuted to work in company buses, a fact that was consistent with his effort of avoiding the "industrial look" of previous camps. To guarantee the safety of children walking to and from school, Olson placed the Chilean school outside the traffic areas. In doing this, he solved the problem of the previous camp, La Mina, where the school was located at a dangerous intersection. While the company provided the building, the school was considered public and was funded by the state. By 1970, the elementary school had fifteen hundred Chilean students, and the American school — located within the boundaries of the American camp — had thirty students.[32] While there was no high school in town until the early 1970s, the company offered some vocational classes for young men and women.

The company maintained social services and organized recreational options for workers and their families, which complemented the good housing. By law the company was required to provide health care and maintain an elementary school for the children, but in addition to its legal obligations it also sponsored recreational activities, sports leagues, a Boy Scout troop, and a newspaper called *Andino*. By providing these services, the company looked to promote good family relationships and social peace. Building on the tradition already implemented in Potrerillos, Andes Copper maintained a busy welfare department and a team of social workers. As an *Andino* journalist explained in 1958, the welfare department had the following responsibilities: maintenance of *camarotes* or bunkhouses for single workers, carpentry work, control of families (registering of newborns and dependents) and residents, repair of houses, and the general maintenance and welfare of the camp.[33] By "welfare," it meant a wide range of events, social activities, and sport competitions. The company maintained a company store to supply families with the basic products and gave concessions to private retail store owners, which usually sold on credit.

Social services were not free of contradictions, and the community usually complained about the quality or availability of services. This was the case with health-care services, which were provided for free to company workers and their families under an agreement signed with the National Health Service (Servicio Nacional de Salud). The hospital was a modern building located near the residential areas, between the Chilean employees' camp and the American camp. While the services provided were considered good, workers usually complained that the resources were insufficient. In 1970, the hospital served a community of 7,500 people (including male workers, women, and children), but it had only forty-eight beds and its full-time personnel only included six medical doctors, three pharmacists, five lab technicians (including two X-ray technicians), twelve nurses, eight midwives, and two dietitians.[34]

El Salvador continued to expand in the following years. In 1963, Andes Copper announced the construction of 25 buildings. By December 1966, the population had almost doubled, and Andes Copper began planning the construction of high-density buildings that had little in common with the master plan. In 1967, it approved the construction of 200 family houses. A second plan (1970) added another 150 houses with 1,076 square feet. And a third plan (1975–76) included 180 houses with 968 square feet. In 1988, the company built one-story single-family homes. Construction of new homes partially solved the initial housing shortage. While in 1960, the average number of residents per house was 5.69, by 1992 there was an average of 3.41 residents per house.[35] Despite all the changes, architects in the 1990s still considered the camp a "valuable contribution to solve the problem of mining-industrial cities."[36]

SOCIAL AND LABOR CONFLICT IN A MODEL MINING CAMP

The inauguration of El Salvador in 1959 coincided with the beginning of the most radical decade in the history of Chile and the copper labor movement. Between 1960 and the nationalization of copper in 1971, Salvadoreños participated in six legal strikes (following failed contract negotiations in 1960, 1961, 1962, 1964, 1967, and 1971) and joined one solidarity strike with copper workers from El Teniente in 1965, one industry-wide strike against the new national copper policy of 1965, and one national strike to protest a failed military coup in 1969. They also took part in an unknown number of wildcat and local strikes.[37] The period also included one of the most violent confrontations during the democratic period, the brutal police repression of the March 1966 solidarity strike that left eight people dead (six men and two women) and thirty-five people injured during a police raid at the union's local office in El Salvador.[38]

These intense conflicts and confrontations suggest that this model town did not achieve the harmonic balance between capital and labor that its planners had in mind, but that it suffered from acute contradictions and tensions. Some of the contradictions that defined the history of El Salvador were already evident during the construction process. Andes Company hired Chilean private contractors to do most of the construction work, and in its peak of activity, between 1957 and 1958, there were twenty independent contractors employing about 4,150 workers. The contractors subcontracted their own labor force, hiring them also on a unit-price basis.[39] Workers lived in temporary facilities housing between 100 and 120 single men and located next to the construction site. There was no room for family members in the construction camp. Workers hung out in the cantinas or mess halls for food and went to Pueblo Hundido for entertainment. Working and living conditions were precarious, hard, unpleasant, and dangerous. On the roads, truck accidents were frequent.[40]

In December 1957, the national Communist newspaper, *El Siglo,* denounced the problems of contract workers in El Salvador. In an article titled "Low Salaries, Bad Food and Worst Treatment in the Mine of El Salvador," *El Siglo* argued that contract workers were a sort of "underclass" of workers who were not entitled to the benefits of the city they were building. There were about two thousand workers in El Salvador, who. according to *El Siglo,* "work like in a concentration company. They are not allowed to unionize, social laws are not enforced, food at the *cantinas* is terrible, they cannot complain and their basic daily wage is 600 daily plus a bonus for a laborer and 1,200 to professional."[41] Although construction workers left after the end of the project, Andes Copper continued hiring contract workers to work on additional construction and maintenance. As their numbers have increased in the following decades, their working and living conditions have remained precarious, and they still lack a formal space in the camp.

As a mining camp, El Salvador was still attached to the old tradition of company towns both in Chile and in the rest of the Americas. And despite its complete program of housing, public space, and social and recreational infrastructure, its design was not free of the contradictions and conflicts of traditional copper company towns. The intersections of the living and working spaces, the strong presence of the company in workers' daily lives, the company's efforts to shape and control the labor force, coercion, urban and social segregation between foreign management and a native workforce, and the camps' isolation continued to create enormous tensions in the Chilean copper industry. The existence of an American camp, for example, was an outrageous continuation of the segregation policies of the company, already enforced in its previous company towns and reinforced by the racial division of labor and a dual pay system (American employees were paid in dollars and Chilean employees were paid in pesos). On the other hand, despite its emphasis on good-quality housing, El Salvador suffered from a continuous housing shortage. For example, the Ministry of Public Housing calculated a housing deficit of about seven hundred units in El Salvador in the late 1960s.[42]

Similarly, Andes Copper maintained some of the elements that characterized enclaves. A clear example of its enclave condition was the checkpoints, a control of the industrial space that extended to the residential areas. In El Salvador, police officers maintained a strict control of vehicles entering the town. As an *Andino* writer explained, the checkpoints recorded the license plate, cargo, passengers, and origin of every vehicle.[43] Despite the existence of these control posts, the company's dependence on supplies, labor force, and capital that came from local, national, and international sources established multiple relations and eventually integrated the camp into the territory, creating and expanding mining company land.

Following the inauguration of the camp, Salvadoreños pointed out the limitations of the camp, and they struggled to improve conditions through strikes, collective bargaining, and community activism. While the main issue behind legal strikes was always wage negotiations, demands also included housing conditions and social benefits. Throughout the 1960s, labor petitions included demands such as the construction of union halls, expansion of health-care services, improvement in the service of the company-owned stores, expansion of educational alternatives, and building of new houses. In doing so, the unions forced the company to expand the number of available housing units and to provide new services that would guarantee a good standard of living for workers and their families.

The success in moving beyond the work environment and addressing the wide range of problems that affected daily life in the community was emblematic of a union movement that had gained strength and legitimacy through the intersection of the workplace and the community. Labor unions provided social and recreational spaces outside the direct control of the company and appropriated company resources to satisfy their members' leisure needs. For example, they organized summer camps for children, sponsored celebrations and parties, and tried to meet people's everyday needs. These unique responsibilities were recognized by the Ministry of Public Housing, which reported that El Salvador and Potrerillos did not have traditional neighborhood associations or community government (the so-called *junta de vecinos*), but the labor unions had assumed most of these responsibilities.[44]

U.S. copper companies arrived in Chile in the early twentieth century, transforming production and bringing with them new forms of social benefits and labor engineering. Mining camps such as Chuquicamata, Sewell, and Potrerillos became emblematic of the introduction of the company town model, which was a popular institution in the United States. In doing so, they built both on the U.S. tradition of the "new company town" and on Chile's previous experiments, especially in the nitrate industry. In the late 1950s, Anaconda's newest camp, El Salvador, represented an effort to modernize and transform company towns, utilizing the latest ideas being implemented in other places.

The history of the El Salvador Project raises larger questions about the characteristics, changes, and continuities of the model of company town in the post–World War II era throughout the Americas. El Salvador was a comprehensive project of modernization that included both production and living arrangements. The construction of the camp, the mine, and the plants incorporated the latest technical improvements of the time; it was a modern and progressive industrial complex. From the layout of the plants to the design of a semicircular pedestrian community, El Salvador evidenced the 1950s' trends in mining production, architecture, and urban planning. Despite its novelty, however, El Salvador did not completely break with the past, and as in many previous experiences of company towns, coercion, segregation, and isolation continued defining working people's everyday lives. Labor and social conflict has characterized the history of this community until the present day.

El Salvador is a complex and real city, with a large population, housing units, and infrastructure. It is a community that has developed its own identity and sense of place. It has also experienced important transformations since its foundation as a modern company town in the late 1950s. In 1971, the National Congress approved the nationalization of copper, transforming El Salvador into a state-owned company town. Improvements in transportation and communication have broken down the traditional isolation of the camp, and people travel more, visit their relatives in other parts of the country, and go shopping in larger regional cities such as Copiapó and La Serena. It is not unlikely that workers commute from other cities, where their wives and children have access to more diverse opportunities for employment, education, and recreation. While in the past community events attracted a large crowd, today the large auditorium located in front of the main plaza usually remains empty.

Despite these changes, El Salvador, like almost every company town, still is a settlement that is completely dependent on a single economic activity, copper production. Codelco's decision to close the town by 2011 has confirmed the functional condition of El Salvador and its dependency on the exploitation of natural resources. Given the urban characteristics of El Salvador, and its role in Atacama, it is necessary to analyze and design strategies to reuse El Salvador, giving it new functions and activities as a complement and alternative to copper mining.

NOTES

The authors would like to thank Juan O'Brien for his helpful comments on an earlier draft of this chapter.

1. On the history of El Teniente, see María Celia Baros, *El Teniente: los hombres del mineral, 1905–1945* (Rancagua: Codelco-Chile, Mineral El Teniente, 1995); Luis Hiriart, *Braden: historia de una mina* (Santiago: Editorial Andes, 1964); Thomas M. Klubock, *Contested Communities: Class, Gender, and Politics in El Teniente's Copper Mine, 1904–1951* (Durham, N.C.: Duke University Press, 1998). For a history of Chuquicamata, see Janet L. Finn, *Tracing the Veins: Of Copper, Culture, and Community from Butte to Chuquicamata* (Berkeley: University of California Press, 1998); Eulogio Gutiérrez and Marcial Figueroa, *Chuquicamata: su grandeza y sus dolores* (Santiago: Imprenta Cervantes, 1920); Ricardo Latcham, *Chuquicamata Estado Yankee* (Santiago: Editorial Nascimento, 1926). For a history of company towns in the Chilean copper industry, see Eugenio Garcés, Marcelo Cooper, and Mauricio Baros, *Las ciudades del cobre* (Santiago: Ediciones Universidad Católica, 2007).

2. Latcham, *Chuquicamata Estado Yankee.*

3. There is a very rich literature, both in English and Spanish, on the nitrate industry. See, for example, Sergio González, *Hombres y mujeres de la pampa: Tarapacá en el ciclo del salitre* (Santiago: LOM, 2002); Julio Pinto, *Trabajos y rebeldías en la pampa salitrera* (Santiago: Editorial de la Universidad de Santiago, 1998).

4. The company store and the token system produced some of the most important grievances of nitrate workers, usually included in strikers' demands. Oscar Bermúdez, "El Dr. Nicolás Palacios y la industria del salitre," *Revista Chilena de Historia y Geografía,* no. 136 (1968): 202–49.

5. Eugenio Garcés Feliú, *Las ciudades del salitre* (Santiago: Orígenes, 1999).

6. "Memoria anual de la inspección provincial del trabajo de Antofagasta," Intendencia de Antofagasta, vol. 103, Archivo Nacional (Santiago, Chile).

7. Margaret Crawford, "John Nolen, the Design of the Company Town," *Rassegna* 19, no. 70 (1997): 46–53.

8. Margaret Crawford, *The Workingman's Paradise: The Design of American Company Towns* (New York: Verso, 1995); and Margaret Crawford, "The 'New' Company Town," *Perspecta* 30 (1999): 48–57.

9. The "American camps" were segregated neighborhoods, with housing and facilities specially designed to meet the U.S. executives' standards, far above those of the "Chilean villages."

10. Andes Copper Mining Company, "Reglamento Interno de la Andes Copper Mining Co. y Potrerillos Railway Co.," c. 1933, Biblioteca Nacional de Chile.

11. Juan Carlos Cancino, "Fundición Paipote 1952" (master's thesis, Escuela de Arquitectura, Pontificia Universidad Católica de Chile, 2008); Juan O'Brien, ed., *Fundición y territorio: reflexiones históricas sobre los orígenes de la Fundición Paipote* (Santiago: Empresa Nacional de Minería, 1992).

12. Ministerio de Vivienda y Urbanismo, *Chañaral: estudio pre-inversional* (Santiago: Ministerio de Vivienda y Urbanismo, n.d.), 42.

13. Ibid.

14. Angela Vergara, "Company Towns and Peripheral Cities in the Chilean Copper Industry: Potrerillos and Pueblo Hundido, 1917–1940s," *Urban History* 30, no. 3 (2003): 381–400.

15. $100 million in 1956 would be worth about $800 million in 2008.

16. Anaconda Company, "Anaconda Is Building: A Special Report to the Stockholders on the Postwar Construction and Improvement Program" (1952).

17. "How Modernization Benefits the Mine and the Man," in "Planning the Modern Mine," special issue, *Engineering and Mining Journal*, no. 159 (November 1958).

18. Ibid.

19. In 1961, Anaconda-Jurden Associates was bought by a larger engineering and construction company, Ralph M. Parsons Co. Together they became Parsons-Jurden Co.

20. Mario Vera, *La política económica del cobre en Chile* (Santiago: Ediciones de la Universidad de Chile, 1961).

21. Clyde E. Weed, "El Salvador," *Mining Engineering*, April 1960, 340.

22. Julian L. Hayes, "Brief Description of El Salvador Mine Project of Andes Copper Mining Company," November 6, 1956, American Heritage Center, Anaconda Geology Department Collection, box 85709; Robbins, Dunstan, and Dudley, "Development of El Salvador Mine."

23. "How Anaconda-Jurden Associates Achieve Modern Industrial Planning," in "Planning the Modern Mine," special issue, *Engineering and Mining Journal*, no. 159 (1958).

24. "Inauguración de El Salvador inicia una nueva época en la historia de la minería chilena," *La Nación* (Santiago), November 13, 1959.

25. For a discussion of the impact of these ideas on the planning of the company town, see Christopher Post, "Modifying Sense of Place in a Federal Company Town: Sunflower Village, Kansas, 1942 to 1959," *Journal of Cultural Geography* 25, no. 2 (2008): 137–59.

26. The Athens Charter was published by José Luis Sert, with the title *Can Our Cities Survive? An ABC on Our Urban Problems, Their Analysis, Their Solutions* (Cambridge, Mass.: Harvard University Press, 1942).

27. On Brasília see James Holston, *The Modernist City: An Anthropological Critique of Brasília* (Chicago: University of Chicago Press, 1989).

28. Raymond Olson and Sergio Chavez, "Townsite, Housing, Transportation, and Welfare," *Mining Engineering*, April 1960, 379.

29. A report on the El Salvador Project was published by the *Engineering and Mining Association Journal*, no. 159 (1958), and by *Mining Engineering*, April 1960.

30. "How Anaconda-Jurden Associates Achieve."

31. Olson and Chavez, "Townsite, Housing, Transportation, and Welfare."

32. Pablo Huneeus, *Estructura y dinámica social en los trabajadores del cobre* (Santiago: Instituto de Sociología Universidad Católica de Chile, 1974).

33. *Andino*, 26 April 1958.

34. Huneeus, *Estructura y dinámica social*.

35. Instituto Nacional de Estadísticas, *Población de los centros poblados de Chile, 1875–1992* (Santiago: Instituto Nacional de Estadística, n.d.).

36. "El Salvador, ciudad minera proyectada como tal," *AUCA* 5 (1996).

37. For a larger discussion on the labor history of El Salvador, see Angela Vergara, *Copper Workers, International Business and Domestic Politics in Cold-War Chile* (University Park: Pennsylvania State University Press, 2008).

38. Brian Loveman and Elizabeth Lira, *Las ardientes cenizas del olvido: vía chilena de reconciliación política, 1932–1994* (Santiago: LOM, 2000), 266.

39. Stewart Carpenter, "Plant Construction and Procurement of Supplies," *Mining Engineering*, April 1960.

40. See, for instance, "Low Salaries, Bad Food and Worst Treatment in the Mine of El Salvador," *El Día* (Copiapó), December 11, 1957, and an untitled article, August 13, 1958. A similar situation has been described for the construction of Brasília; see Holston, *Modernist City*.

41. *El Siglo*, December 17, 1957.

42. Ministerio de Vivienda y Urbanismo, *Chañaral*, 41–47.

43. *Andino*, March 15, 1958.

44. Ministerio de Vivienda y Urbanismo, *Chañaral*, 33.

CHAPTER NINE

Labor and Community in Postwar Argentina

The Industry of Agricultural Machinery in Firmat, Santa Fe

SILVIA SIMONASSI

In 1949, Roque Vassalli, a self-made man and son of Italian immigrants, opened the first factory of agricultural machinery in Firmat, a small town of about eight thousand people located in the southern part of the Santa Fe province. This chapter explores the history of Vassalli Metallurgical Factory and its impact on social and urban relations in Firmat between the establishment of the factory in 1949 and the early 1970s. Although Roque Vassalli did not build a traditional company town in Firmat, he exerted a strong influence over the city and its residents. He was a successful industrial owner, one of the largest employers, president of a famous local sports club, and head of the municipal government for twenty years. Firmat's residents, workers, and local unions developed a complex relationship with Vassalli and his company. While they consented to and accepted his influence and many of the benefits he provided, they also resisted and made efforts to improve working conditions, joining national labor organizations such as the Unión Obrera Metalúrgica. The history of Firmat and Vassalli Metallurgical Factory illustrates how employers controlled social and political institutions and urban space, extending their influence and power beyond the factory and into the local community. Vassalli's experience and practices were also unique and different from those of other places in Argentina, as they were a direct response to the characteristics of the region and of the agricultural machinery industry.

The history of how Firmat became the "capital of agricultural machinery" in post–World War II Argentina is emblematic of the social and economic trans-formation of the humid Pampa since the nineteenth century. By the end of the nineteenth century, Firmat and other small towns in the humid Pampa sup-ported the growth of commercial agriculture and the production of wheat and maize. The concentration of land in a few hands and abusive working conditions in the countryside had inspired rural workers to organize in the early 1900s; and labor, political, and social institutions expanded throughout the province. The transformation and mechanization of agriculture that started in the 1920s accel-erated a process of migration from the countryside into these towns and cities. In the 1940s–1950s, propelled by changes in the national economy and President Juan Domingo Perón's economic policies, places like Firmat experienced a rapid process of industrialization. In the following years, the establishment of fac-tories and plants such as the Vassalli Metallurgical Factory completely trans-formed social and economic relations throughout the province, creating new forms of urbanization and labor relations. To be able to produce the agricultural machinery, Vassalli envisioned a factory town in which he would develop pater-nalistic practices to control labor and social relations.

THE TRANSFORMATION OF THE ARGENTINEAN COUNTRYSIDE

The history of Firmat and the Vassalli Metallurgical Factory was shaped by the transformation of the countryside and agricultural production that had started in the 1870s. In the last decades of the nineteenth century, commercial agri-culture, based on the production and export of agricultural products such as wheat and maize, consolidated in Argentina. The region known as the humid Pampa, located south of the province of Santa Fe, became the center of agricul-tural growth. Its rich soils, the good transportation networks, and the influence of the fluvial port of Rosario guaranteed the success of export agriculture. On the eve of this agricultural boom, the region still had very diverse forms of land ownership: a combination of small-, medium-, and large-sized proper-ties. However, the agricultural boom gave new value to the land and increased the concentration of land in a few hands. In the area near Firmat, by the end of the nineteenth century, 52 percent of the land was owned by only 3 percent of landowners, and large estates (called *latifundios*) controlled local economic and political power.[1]

The transformation of the countryside also increased tenant farming and reinforced many of its abuses. The independence of land owners contrasted with tenants' working arrangements. While owners of small- and medium-sized plots of land planned production and directly hired the labor force (permanent and seasonal workers), tenants were controlled by large landowners who made all the decisions regarding cultivation, harvesting, and maintenance. A large number of agricultural peons and seasonal workers worked the land, a population that usually increased during the planting and harvesting of maize, wheat, and flax.

In the 1910s, tenant farmers and peons started organizing and protesting against the unequal distribution of land and abusive labor conditions. The first strike, the "Grito de Alcorta," took place in 1912. The movement started among tenant farmers in Firmat and Alcorta, and it rapidly expanded to other rural areas. While the strike was sparked by a cycle of bad harvests in 1910 and 1911, it had deeper roots in the abusive working conditions, systems of hiring, and high cost of rent that characterized the agricultural boom. Two months after the beginning of the strike, tenant farmers successfully organized the Argentinean Agrarian Federation (Federación Agraria Argentina, FAA), an organization that has represented small- and medium-sized agricultural producers throughout Argentina until the present day.

Agrarian mobilization in Firmat relied on a rich fabric of social institutions. Founded in 1911, the Cosmopolitan Society of Agricultural Producers of Firmat (Sociedad Cosmopolita de Agricultores de Firmat) represented tenant farmers in their struggle to reduce the rent and improve their living and working conditions. Anarchist and socialist groups were also part of the city's political life. Social unrest continued in the following years, suggesting the permanence of problems such as limited access to credit, the rising price of agricultural supplies, and bad weather conditions.

In the following years, rural workers also started organizing, increasing the elites' fears and repression. Influenced by the anarchist movement, rural workers organized in the *gremios de la cosecha* (labor unions during harvest), which included agricultural workers employed in the cutting, reaping, and threshing of wheat and flax, and in the removal of the corn from the maize cob. They demanded better salaries and working conditions. Conditions were especially hard in the case of the cultivation of maize, which employed a large labor force, including women and children, working long days under unsafe working conditions.[2] Since the beginning of the twentieth century, employers kept salaries very low by bringing in large numbers of seasonal workers during the harvest season. In addition, chronic unemployment not only kept salaries low but also discouraged unionization despite union propaganda and organizing efforts. As a result of this cycle of strikes, rural workers became a regional and national social actor.[3]

Repression increased in the following years. Both police and employers' organizations such as the Sociedad Protectora del Trabajo Libre (an organization that supported strikebreakers) and the Patriotic League (Liga Patriótica) were active in repressing workers' political activism. In March 1917, the Firmat police and local political authorities forbade and eventually repressed an anarchist meeting, leaving a large number of victims — among them an important anarchist leader from Rosario.[4] In 1919, the movement led by *chacareros* (small- and medium-sized agricultural producers) expanded and became more violent as they eventually raised the very controversial question of agrarian reform. Their movement was also part of a larger wave of social unrest that swept Argentina after World War I. In Buenos Aires, social conflict reached its highest point in January 1919, during the so-called Tragic Week (Semana Trágica).

In Firmat, labor organizations were especially strong among railroad workers and included various resistance societies (*sociedades de resistencia*). By the 1920s, historian Eduardo Sartelli argues, longshoremen, cart drivers (drivers of small and precarious carts that transported cereals), and day laborers had created "extensive institutional networks that introduced a new culture and social practices far away from anything considered traditional."[5] Retail workers unionized in 1924, and a teachers union was formed in 1930.

Along with the increase in rural unionization, the urban middle class created new forms of organizations. Cities historically linked to rural colonization had experienced diverse and early forms of social institutionalization. In Firmat, the Socialist Party had an important influence on social organizations and institutions, Italian and Spanish immigrants, and the cooperative movement. Some of the most representative local organizations of the early twentieth century were the Club Social (1903), "Centro Socialista 1° de Mayo" (1904), Tiro Federal (1904), Firmat Foot Ball Club (1907), the newspaper *El Correo de Firmat* (1914), the Centro Recreativo, the "Nosotros" library (1916), ethnic organizations representing Italian immigrants (1907) and Spanish immigrants (1911), and the sport club Atlético Argentino (1922).[6]

In the 1920s and 1930s, the incorporation of new technology in the countryside transformed organization of agricultural production and work and local social relations. According to Argentine historian Adrián Ascolani, mechanization expanded rapidly throughout the countryside as a response to the demands of large-scale commercial agriculture at the end of the nineteenth century. The number of machines, most of them imported from Europe and the United States, increased from 1,352 in 1925 to 4,565 in 1926 and to 5,083 in 1927. Similarly, historian Eduardo Sartelli estimated that the number of harvesting machines increased from thirty thousand in 1930 to more than forty thousand in 1937.[7]

Figure 9.1 Group of agricultural workers during the harvest, province of Santa Fe, Argentina, early twentieth century. Banco de imágenes Florian Paucke, 2006.

Grain trucks started replacing wagons in the early 1920s, and the number of tractors was also increasing.

Harvesters, trucks, and grain elevators helped reduce both the size of the labor force and the costs of production. In 1929, 25 percent of the land cultivated with grains and flax used agricultural harvesting equipment, and the cost of harvesting had declined between 50 and 75 percent. The number of workers per harvesting machine also decreased, from six to three or four workers.[8] In 1930, about 180,000 people worked in the wheat harvest, but on the eve of World War II the harvest employed only 100,000 people.[9] The structural transformation of agricultural production also included improvements in the system of transportation. In contrast, the mechanization of the corn harvest was slower. The low cost of the labor force and the persistence of a family type of work delayed the introduction of harvesting machinery in the corn harvest until the mid-1940s.[10]

The mechanization of agriculture transformed the composition and characteristics of the labor force, creating a smaller, stable, and more homogeneous workforce. Migration from the cities to the countryside stopped (and reverted), and local workers started following the harvest around the region. In places like Firmat, where the cultivation of wheat complemented maize, workers were usually employed year round and developed a strong "tradition of rural unioniza-tion."[11] But the introduction of the harvesting machine also reduced the labor force and contributed to the loss of skills in the rural labor force and the decline in wages (from its highest level in 1921 to almost half in 1930). Because of these changes, the local unions that had led the strikes during the previous period (1918–21) lost influence and were forced to negotiate new contracts in a more restricted labor market.

A new cycle of social activism started in 1928 and this time included rural workers and militants of the Communist Party, who had helped organize rural workers and politicize their struggles. The influence of the Communist Party among rural workers in the province and Firmat had expanded in the 1920s, and Communists were influential among railroad workers, meat workers, printers, shoemakers, utility workers, cabinetmakers, and construction workers. Their influence on rural organizations remained small, however, and they did not hold leadership positions.[12]

When Roque Vassalli opened his factory in Firmat, the city had a complex and diverse network of social institutions and a history of labor activism. In the 1940s, Firmat had popular libraries, cooperatives, sport clubs, newspapers, eth-nic and cultural organizations, and organizations representing property own-ers, business people, and industrialists. For example, the Centro Comercial, Industrial y Rural was created in the mid-1940s by land owners and urban businesspeople. By 1957, it had 250 members. Labor unions were also strong among construction workers, stevedores, and teachers. The city had several banking institutions, a small hospital, and rural and urban entrepreneurs who were looking forward to modernizing the urban infrastructure and promoting industrialization.

Vassalli built a factory in a community with a strong labor tradition that included rural and urban organizations and anarchist and socialist gropus. To shape the labor force, impose an industrial discipline in the workplace, and re-duce labor conflicts, Vasalli implemented a wide range of paternalistic practices and programs.[13]

THE INDUSTRY AND THE COUNTRYSIDE UNDER PERÓN

Juan Domingo Perón assumed power in 1946, in the midst of deep economic, political, and social transformations.[14] For the first time in the history of Argentina, the manufacturing industry contributed more to the gross internal product than did agriculture, consolidating Argentina as an industrial nation. Between 1935 and 1946, industrial production and the number of industrial workers had almost doubled. The decline in imports during World War II had created favorable market conditions for national industrial products, and industrial production increased. This favorable economic environment came to an end in 1946. To support the national industry, Perón raised import tariffs, provided affordable credits to local entrepreneurs, and eliminated barriers to manufacturing supplies. Yet the most distinctive characteristic of his administration was the income redistribution policies both to benefit urban workers and to increase the internal consumption of industrial products. During the first years of his administration, the increases in salaries and wages and in housing and educational benefits for blue-collar workers expanded workers' purchasing power. The increase in the number of blue-collar workers also expanded the internal market for consumer products.

These policies worked until the economic crisis of 1949 that forced the government to choose between either enforcing unpopular economic policies and completely alienating its base of political support or protecting workers' recent economic gains. To solve this dilemma, the government turned to the countryside and encouraged agricultural production and the mechanization of agricultural activities, creating the conditions for the expansion of the agricultural machinery industry.[15]

Although urban workers were the main beneficiaries of Perón's economic policies, rural workers played an important role in the Peronist agenda. The government enforced important measures to satisfy the demands of rural workers. Beginning in 1943, the government had started regulating rent and contracts and suspended land evictions, improving conditions for land tenants. In 1944, the "Statute of the Rural Peon" regulated labor conditions for permanent rural workers, improved working conditions, increased salaries, and regulated safety, housing conditions, food rations, and rest time. In 1947, seasonal workers — most of them migrant workers — received the right to negotiate salaries and working conditions. Under the slogan "la tierra para el que la trabaja" (land for the people who work it) and with the support of the FAA, the government subdivided large properties and public lands and redistributed some land among chacareros. In the province of Santa Fe, the government distributed about 2 million acres of land.[16] This program of land redistribution contributed to decreased social tensions among chacareros. While Perón's agrarian agenda was initially motivated by the need to increase electoral support, soon it also became a tool to promote industrialization and control social unrest in the countryside.[17]

Despite these changes and transformations, working and living conditions for seasonal workers underwent little change in the Firmat area. On April 3, 1946,

El Correo de Firmat denounced employers who were, once again, bringing in an oversupply of workers for the corn harvest. Far from the advertised payment of 2.50 pesos per bag, salaries did not exceed 0.70 pesos per bag (other versions mentioned between 0.90 and 1.30 pesos). "Here we have a sufficient number of workers who are in need, outsiders must realize that this is not Jauja, and they will continue their pilgrimage." By the end of the following year, however, newspaper reports acknowledged that there were no unemployed "people wandering through the countryside," changes that were attributed to stable work and the unionization of rural workers. Despite these improvements, newspapers continued to denounce poor living conditions among rural workers. On May 19, 1948, *El Correo de Firmat* mentioned a letter from the labor union representing rural workers in the province of Santa Fe to President Perón in which the local union denounced the fact that "the rural population lives without clean or comfortable housing."

THE AGRICULTURAL MACHINERY INDUSTRY

The industry of agricultural tools and machinery started in the 1880s in cities such as Firmat located in the national leading grain-producing provinces of Santa Fe and Buenos Aires. The province of Santa Fe had a rich tradition of blacksmiths, mechanics, agricultural contractors, and *chacareros* who had experience making tools and adapting imported tools to the particularities of the agricultural work in the pampas. In the 1930s, the Great Depression, the decline in production and exports, and the devaluation of the national currency slowed down the national production of agricultural machines, which was heavily dependent on imported capital goods and machinery. Thus, until the mid-twentieth century, the Argentinean countryside continued to import agricultural machines. The beginning of World War II, however, and the new restrictions on international trade reduced imports of agricultural machinery, creating a favorable market for the local production of machinery that required little technology.[18] It was a response to the local needs of agricultural production and the growing use of harvesting machines in the Argentinean countryside. The new plants were strategically located near the farms, allowing them to respond promptly to any technical problems.

The economic crisis of 1949 evidenced the challenges faced by the industry of agricultural machinery in Argentina. On the eve of the crisis, the industry was outdated and obsolete and required the support of the national state. The production of harvesting machines was dependent on foreign-made spare parts. In 1949, the Industrial Bank (Banco de Crédito Industrial) started lending special credits to local industrial owners, and the government declared the agricultural tools and machinery industry a national priority.[19]

In the 1950s, this industry started growing. In 1950, the Cámara de Industriales Metalúrgicos de Rosario, an organization representing industrial owners in Rosario, created a new department representing agricultural machinery makers that attracted influential businesspeople. In the following years, the makers of agricultural machinery became a pressure group with significant power at the regional level.[20] The state policies of the 1950s were successful in supporting the efforts of expert and small-scale capital investors, and by the beginning of the 1960s there were more than four hundred agricultural machinery factories throughout the country.

In Firmat, local newspapers reported on the growth and consequences of the establishment of agricultural machinery factories. They encouraged the local bourgeoisie to join the process of economic diversification. On March 9, 1949, *El Correo de Firmat* wrote: "Since about two years ago, [the city] has experienced real promising change thanks to the decision and great vision of a group of working men. They, with their own means, have opened workshops and small factories, which are the basis of future industries. This example should be followed by those wealthier neighbors. . . . [These plants] would promote all other activities. Firmat, thus, would be the emporium of work, which should be, which we have always dreamed and for which prosperity we have not stopped asking."

ROQUE VASSALLI AND THE AGRICULTURAL MACHINERY INDUSTRY

The case of Roque Vassalli is representative of the establishment of agricultural machinery factories in Argentina. The son of Italian immigrants, Roque Vassalli was born near Firmat in 1915. His father had arrived in the province of Santa Fe in the 1910s, during the agricultural boom, and had worked as a land tenant. Like other provincial manufacturers, he only had an informal education and training, and his knowledge and success were based on the informal acquisition of work skills and work values. As a child, Vassalli mentioned in his memoirs, he had a great "fascination for the world of steel machines" and learned the importance of "work and sacrifice" and "discipline and duty."[21] Like many other "self-made men" who specialized in metallurgy, he learned his trade working in local blacksmith shops and repair shops for agricultural tools, trucks, and airplanes.

He opened Establecimiento Metalúrgico Vassalli in 1949 in Firmat because of its strategic location near transportation networks and with good urban services. In a floor space of nearly eleven thousand square feet, he started producing his famous integral corn-gathering equipment, an accessory that could be attached to any grain harvester. Initially, Vassalli recalled, the machine met strong resistance from skeptical farmers, unionized workers who feared losing their jobs, and grain gatherers who perceived that the new machines notably decreased their work.[22] Once resistance was overcome, its use expanded rapidly throughout the countryside.

Vassalli received the support of the Perón administration, which was emblematic of the government's effort to industrialize the countryside. The Peronist policy "return to the countryside" of the late 1940s and early 1950s was encouraging the establishment of factories such as Vassalli's, providing credits and protection. In 1953, for example, Vassalli received from the Ministry of Agriculture a proposal to build 250 machines for the maize harvest within the context of the Second Quinqueneal Plan. He received a loan of 7.5 million pesos from the Industrial Bank (Banco de Crédito Industrial), which allowed him to expand his plant and satisfy the new demand. The government decree that determined and standardized the size of the furrows facilitated and expanded the use of Vassalli's integral corn-gathering equipment.

The plant expanded in the following decades. In the mid-1950s, Vassalli started exporting machines to Uruguay and Brazil, where he also opened a new plant in the 1960s. In 1958, the company became Vassalli Fabril S.A., continuing a process of innovation, the adaptation of new machinery to the specificities of national agricultural production. He also brought to the market more than twenty new models of agricultural machines.[23] He expanded the repair parts distribution service from a system of small planes to the establishment of a large network of concessionaires and distribution centers. In the early 1960s, according to Rougier, Vassalli provided about 60 percent of all harvesting machines in the country. By the early 1970s, the plant occupied a space of nearly 325,000 square feet, employed about four hundred people, and had an annual production capacity of five hundred harvesting machines and about thirty corn-gathering machines.[24] Despite the economic instability of the 1970s and 1980s, the factory survived until it was sold in 1987, in the midst of a deep crisis that affected the entire industry. Recently, the heirs of Roque Vassalli bought Vassalli Fabril SA.[25]

Vassalli's factory had a strong impact on Firmat, a city that had been traditionally oriented to the countryside and agricultural production. The factory stimulated demographic growth, the creation of other commercial and industrial activities, the diversification of production, and the consolidation of an urban and local working class. Local newspapers reported the impact of this process, suggesting the ways in which the people at the time perceived these changes. The first references about Vassalli appeared in *El Correo de Firmat* on October 30, 1948, when Vassalli, at the time working as a mechanic, exhibited in the local train station the adaptation of a harvesting machine. The paper stated that this machine "will demonstrate with its work, the efficiency of the improvements introduced by the already prestigious industrialist" and announced the opening of his workshop.[26] After that the paper constantly referred to the impact and presence of Vassalli's factory in the life of the community and the region. In addition to the rapid acceptance of his products by local farmers, Vassalli received important distinctions in rural exhibitions in nearby cities.

In the 1950s, Vassalli promoted his new products under the slogan "a factory in the service of the Argentinean countryside." Advertisements highlighted his innovative character and explained that the new machine saved money and time: "It only needs fifteen minutes to transform a seed drill into a ridger or weeding hoe." The *Correo de Firmat* also argued that these innovations could bring relief to agricultural work, "elements that have revolutionized old and expensive systems and at the same time humanize backbreaking activities, as it is the case of the integral corn gathering equipment." According to the media, salaries and bonuses paid to local workers also had a positive impact on the community. During a good maize harvest, the positive remarks multiplied, and advertisements about a bright future were frequent. "The perspective for this year, given the superb conditions that the maize plantations show, can be predicted to be extraordinary. For this harvest, the production plan of corn gathering equipment will include 300 units." In 1956, Vassalli also announced a new and more economic harvesting machine "to reduce the costs of the next harvest" and the study of tractors. The existence of new markets for agricultural machinery, the newspaper argued, would stimulate production and increase job opportunities.

Newspapers were optimistic about these innovations and the positive impact of the factory on the city, a city that was already experiencing rapid demographic growth. Workers arrived in Firmat looking for a "stable job."[27] The local census of 1957 reported that of the 8,642 people who lived in Firmat, 7,088 lived in the city itself and 1,554 in the rural areas surrounding the city. The working population in the city included 130 people working as steelworkers, 90 mechanics, and 360 day laborers.[28] These changes also had an impact on the union movement. The Unión Obrera Metalúrgica (UOM; Union of Metallurgical Workers), a national workers' federation representing steel and metalworkers, was closely allied with the Peronist movement and maintained chapters throughout the nation. In 1951, UOM opened a local chapter in Firmat, and by 1963 it had 415 members.[29]

In 1959, according to a survey conducted by Dirección General de Industrias of the province of Santa Fe, there were eighty-three industrial shops in Firmat, including eighteen steel plants and metal shops, seventeen furniture factories, and twelve food-processing plants.[30] One of the most important plants was the recently inaugurated elaboration plant for milk products plant by Nestlé. Between 1960 and 1970, the local population increased from 9,887 to 12,148. While the urban population increased from 8,421 to 11,127, the rural population decreased from 1,466 to 1,021. During this period, Firmat was the second-fastest growing city in the southern department of General López in the province of Santa Fe.[31] In other words, Firmat was evolving according to the plans of its intellectuals, professionals, and business owners: an industrial city located in the middle of the fertile and humid Argentinean Pampa.

FACTORY AND COMMUNITY

Studies on company towns in the Americas have shown how benefits such as free housing, health care, and education have shaped the relationship between factory and community and between managers and workers.[32] In his famous study of Loma Negra, Argentinean anthropologist Federico Neiburg developed the concept of *sistema de fábrica con villa obrera* (a factory system with a workers' village) to explain the impact of the factory on workers' everyday life. In Loma Negra, a cement factory located in the district of Olavarría in the province of Buenos Aires, the company designed benefits such as free housing and social services to overcome its geographical isolation, recruit its workforce, limit workers' mobility, and discipline the labor force. As in other company towns throughout the Americas, Loma Negra's managers used these benefits to control workers both at the work place and outside the factory.[33] For Argentinean Patagonia, scholars have also demonstrated how the growth of the oil and coal industries had a strong impact on the formation of urban and working spaces.[34]

Company and industrial towns in Argentina were heterogeneous and diverse. Not all employers provided free housing or were able to have complete control over the reproduction of the labor force or restrict workers' mobility. Their practices changed according to the specific characteristics of each region, economic activity, labor market, and time period. Workers' responses also differed, from confrontation and conflict to consensus and adaptation.

Vassalli opened his factory during a time of structural economic transformations and massive migration from the countryside. Because large numbers of rural migrants arrived in cities such as Firmat looking for a well-paying and stable industrial job, Vassalli did not need to provide housing to attract and retain a labor force. Instead, he developed traditional paternalistic practices such as providing monetary assistance and prizes to "loyal workers." He also assisted workers in finding inexpensive housing, provided health care to workers and their families, and supported local schools. He directly and personally supervised the factory to guarantee workers' loyalty, expanding his influence and control to recreational time and space outside the factory. The plant was located in a small city, giving Vassalli considerable influence over the local community. He was not only an industrial owner and employer, but he was also president of a local sports club, Club Argentino (1955–83), and was elected head of the municipal government (1963–83).

Established in 1922, the Club Argentino was one of the most important local sports clubs. Vassalli loved this club, he wrote in his memoirs, because it "went along with my spirit." At the time, he recalled, it was only "a small club" for family leisure activities. While the Club Argentino was popular among workers from his own factory, its rival institution, the Firmat Football Club, included the more traditional social groups and, according to local accounts, initially had rejected Vassalli because of his social origin and Italian accent. Under Vassalli's presidency, the Club Argentino board included his closest friends and collaborators. As its president, Vassalli led the modernization and expansion of the club, supervised the purchase of land for the construction of new sport facilities, sponsored many social events, and formed a mutual aid society for its members. It was common that the annual raffles included pieces from his factory that he had personally donated, such as harvesting machines, corn-gathering equipment, and tractors. When Vassalli became club president, the company personnel could attend the club at no cost. In doing this, Vassalli transformed a previously important and popular social space into a place for the "families of Firmat," taking away its working-class character and using it as a mechanism of social control.[35]

Roque Vassalli was elected *intendente* of Firmat in 1963, representing the Unión Cívica Radical Intransigente (UCRI), a political party that had its origin in the 1957 division of the historical Radical Party. During his campaign, Vassalli promised to improve conditions in neighborhoods and support and expand industrial production.[36] In the local paper, he assumed the responsibility to "strive for the establishment of industries that have a concrete application and that do not exist in our region such as factories that produced working clothes, textiles or other ones." These new factories could take advantage of the new electrical plants that the national state was going to build in the area.[37] A strong supporter of his campaign, the local newspaper *El Correo de Firmat* published numerous references to him and his factory on the paper's front pages. In 1963, Vassalli's factory, among nineteen international agricultural machinery plants, had won a contract for $800,000 from Chile's Economic Development Agency (CORFO) to supply a thousand machines to the Chilean countryside. The local paper celebrated Vassalli's "entrepreneurial capacity" and highlighted how he promoted progress, created job opportunities, and brought foreign exchange to the country.[38] Vassalli used the Club Argentino to support his political ambitions. Similarly, during the electoral campaign, the Club Argentino announced the inauguration of a gym and the construction of a chapel, "San Roque," on land donated by Vassalli in his industrial neighborhood.[39]

His administration was characterized by a paternalistic tone and his efforts, as he noted, to satisfy the needs of "all the people" and not only those of his political party. He led the modernization of the city, improving communication with and transportation to other cities (telephone service, roads, and a bus station), sanitation (running water, sewage, electricity, and housing) and recreation (parks, theater, and movie theater). He was head of the municipal government for more than twenty years, until 1983, and survived national political upheavals through dictatorships and democracy.

As an employer, Vassalli enforced policies and practices that addressed both working and leisure time and the production and reproduction of the labor force. The company provided monetary assistance for building or furnishing a home, and many company workers built a house and settled in *Barrio Vassalli* (Vassalli's neighborhood). He complemented this program with a more complete and broader housing project sponsored by the municipal government. The first program of housing construction started in 1971, financed by a loan from the provincial government, the Dirección Provincial de la Vivienda. To carry out this program, the municipal government created the Instituto Municipal de la Vivienda. In addition, Vassalli used the Club Argentino, which also contributed money.[40]

Vassalli also intervened in the local schools, looking to create and train a loyal and skilled labor force for his factory. In Firmat, educational institutions trained students to work in traditional industries. For example, in 1949, the local school of Artes y Oficios (arts and trades) trained students in carpentry and mechanics. The following year the school was divided in two sections: a male factory school that trained boys to work in a machine, carpentry, and blacksmith shop and a professional school for girls. In the mid-1950s, the city opened a technical school specializing in the making and repairing of agricultural machinery. Although the majority of workers learned their trade informally, most workers at Vassalli had attended one of the local technical schools. Vassalli showed a strong interest in this school, its equipment, and its location, and he personally oversaw its finances and the negotiation of state loans.

The company provided many educational benefits to its workers and families. In 1969, the company opened a child-care center at no cost for the workers, providing free transportation, uniforms, school supplies, breakfast, and lunch for the children. The school was personally directed by Vassalli's wife, Españita Vassalli. This initiative, as many others, was celebrated by local newspapers, especially because the governor — the highest provincial authority — personally attended its inauguration. In addition, the company organized a craft school for older girls and boys between twelve and eighteen years old. The school offered a wide range of art and technical workshops including drawing, painting, sculpture, wood marquetry, wrought iron work, plumbing, electricity, interior decoration, synthetic resin, and copper, metal, and leather crafts. The company also sponsored a scholarship program for workers' children attending high school or college.[41]

Vassalli closely supervised the recruitment of his workers. The first group of workers had arrived at the factory because of established social and personal networks, and over time at least three generations of workers had been employed at the plant. However, in the 1960s the expansion of the factory and the increase in the size of the labor force led the company to start recruiting in other cities, organizing a system of daily commutes on company buses. To recruit workers, the company used a complex system of interviews and carefully checked previous work experiences to determine the reasons why employees had been fired from previous jobs and to define their salary scale. Although Vassalli recruited many of his workers from the local technical school, the company also posted ads for jobs in the newspaper.

The health of workers and their families was also an important aspect of the company's policy. The company health-care benefits included a dental plan, pediatric services, a discount on medications, and vaccination campaigns, among many others. The local newspapers regularly reported on how Vassalli's policies expanded beyond the company, helping to expand the local health-care services and the hospital.

The development of social and sports activities played an important role in the politics of the company. Every September 7, the national day of the metalworker, the factory and local unions organized popular soccer tournaments

Figure 9.2 Group of metalworkers in the province of Santa Fe in the 1960s. Photo courtesy of the author's family.

against other plants. Sports competitions among staff members and white-collar workers or among the different departments such as the technical office, finance office, personnel and purchasing, and spare parts, were also frequent.

The most important time of encounter between management, staff members, workers, and their families was during the parties and events organized by the company to celebrate festivities such as International Labor Day (May 1st), Christmas, and New Year's Eve. May 1st was a particularly important celebration because of its historically strong political and class character. By controlling this particular celebration, the company intended to take from workers the spaces and times that defined a working-class culture. Vassalli vividly remembered these celebrations in his memoirs: "That day, the blue-collar worker, the white-collar worker, the collaborators used to come to the plant. We showed a movie, and then we all gathered at the club. In a true atmosphere of communion, I returned all that affection and dedication that they expressed with presents. They came with their wives. . . . Many of them were the live history of the factory, they had started with me when this was only a dream."[42]

The company also gave presents to workers and their families at Christmas time, at the beginning of the school year, and during the vacations for school-children. In 1975, the company created a department for social services to "attend the special problems that affected employees."[43] In the annual report for 1974, the company explained that the main goal of the company's social policies was the construction of a "harmonically integrated community."

The benefits, however, were not distributed evenly to all workers. Many of the benefits were very selective and assigned according to workers' seniority, work capacity, attendance, loyalty, or punctuality, showing the disciplinary aspect of the paternalist practices, its hierarchical structure, and inequality.[44] The company's salary policy became a mechanism to neutralize social conflict. Vassalli personally announced the holiday bonus, wage increases, and seniority gifts. At the end of the year, the holiday celebrations were full of rituals and symbols. In 1956, during the annual toast, Vassalli announced a substantial wage increase. The announcement was received "with an explosion of applause and grateful voices."[45] During the party, workers, department supervisors, and representatives of the regional metalworkers union gave speeches. The crowd cheered the arrival of stockholders and a group of workers and their wives from a small plant owned by Vassalli and located very close to the big plant. The following year, he made a similar announcement; he also received "a very loud ovation," and workers "carried him on their shoulders into the large facilities of the factory."[46]

Although there were many conflicts and tensions between the company and the labor union (affiliated with UOM), Vassalli was able to control workers with a conciliatory policy and salary concessions. This was made clear during the national metalworkers strike of May and June 1954. Metalworkers throughout the nation were demanding a wage increase. Vassalli attempted to prevent the strike by offering a wage increase independently of the results of the national negotiation. Despite workers' support for Vassalli's offer, the strike continued because of the strong union discipline of metalworkers. In addition, Vassalli attempted to co-opt local union representatives by making them foremen of the company.

Once the strike was resolved, the company offered a wage increase of 25 percent, in addition to paying the strike days. On June 17, *El Correo de Firmat* announced that a union officer requested to publish a letter from the local Unión Obrera Metalúrgica to "deeply thank, the altruist and magnificent gesture to consider and pay the hours that they did not work because of the strike . . . and, in addition, to provide a wage increase higher than the one agreed by the Convenio Metalúrgico."[47] The paper also stated that "in fair acknowledgment" the white-collar and blue-collar workers would make a bigger effort to "increase the prestige of the company that they belong to." In printing this, the paper was in concordance with the larger national debate about the need to increase productivity by increasing the intensity of work instead of incorporating more technology.

Most of the personal memoirs and oral interviews highlighted the friendly atmosphere that existed in the plant. The relationship between workers and management was described as excellent, and the company was referred to as "a big family."[48] Vassalli's collaborators described his work as very "Italian" because of his effort to build a company "like it was a home."[49]

In contrast, conflicts and tensions are difficult to document. Bosses usually suspended or fired workers who arrived late or missed a day of work. While selective firing of "undisciplined" workers existed, they were also contested by the local union. Supervisors and foremen identified with these actions became common victims of attacks in public social places. While Vassalli was the one who announced "the good news" of wage increases, prizes, and public works in parties, in the media, and on the streets, supervisors were responsible for disciplining, suspending, and firing workers.[50] Working conditions were dangerous, and accidents and occupational diseases such as saturnism (or lead poisoning) were frequent. Most local accounts, however, point out that the company did provide safety gear, but that workers refused to use it. Workers also engaged in dangerous behavior such as smoking while painting. The role of the labor union needs to be studied, although it is possible that the co-optation and the concessions were powerful elements and neutralized organized protest.

The establishment of a plant to produce harvesting machinery in the small city of Firmat was a novel event. Its success was emblematic of the profound transformations that were taking place in Argentina at the time. The agricultural boom and the favorable conditions of the 1930s and 1940s had encouraged a process of industrialization. Until World War II, Firmat was characterized by the overwhelming presence of rural activities, the organization and conflicts produced by agricultural society, and the presence and militancy of political and labor movements. The Perón administration enforced state policies that promoted industrialization and a discourse that protected workers and encouraged class conciliation. These new economic and political forces under Perón encourage the establishment of new industrial plants in places like Firmat.

The personalization of labor relations became an emblematic characteristic of small- and medium-scale factories in Argentina. Employers such as Roque Vassalli attempted to neutralize social conflict by personalizing labor relations and enforcing welfare programs for workers and their families. While he did not need to build a company town, he provided health care, housing programs, education, and recreational spaces for his workers.

Vassalli was unique in his capacity to reinforce his work policies in other arenas. As head of the municipal government, he supported social and modernization programs that benefited the local population. As president of the local sports club, he restated the importance of daily life outside the walls of the factory to oversee workers and their families. It was a small community, and the local club was one of the favorite spaces of working-class sociability that was controlled and supervised by the company's owners. The three roles of Vassalli consolidated a community image that emphasized his attributes as an entrepreneurial, hard-working, and kind employer. This image allowed him to participate and succeed in local politics, in which he reinforced his paternalistic attitude toward his workers. From the halls of the municipal government and the fields of the sport club, he challenged traditional class identity, promoting a wider identity as member of an organized and integrated community.

The disciplinary aspect of the salary "concessions," such as on housing and health care, was evident in the selective way they were allocated as rewards to the "model worker," a dedicated and loyal worker.[51] Disregarding the company's regulations could lead to losing one's job, rewards, incentives, or benefits. Despite tensions and conflicts, the paternalistic model remained in place.

NOTES

Translated by Angela Vergara.

1. Marta Bonaudo and Cristina Godoy, "Una corporación y su inserción en el proyecto agro-exportador: la Federación Agraria Argentina, 1912–1933," *Anuario*, no. 11 (1985): 194–207; Marta Bonaudo and Elida Sonzogni, "Cuando disciplinar fue ocupar, Santa Fe, 1850–1890," *Mundo agrario: revista de estudios rurales*, no. 1 (2000), http://mundoagrarioold.fahce.unlp.edu.ar/nro1/bonaudo.htm (accessed August 20, 2009).

2. Adrián Ascolani, "Labores agrarias y sindicalismo en las villas y ciudades del interior santafesino (1900–1928)," in *Historia del sur santafesino: la sociedad transformada (1850–1930)* ed. Adrián Ascolani (Rosario: Ediciones Platino, 1993); Adrián Ascolani, "Las categorías proceso de tecnificación y proceso de civilización contrastadas en el estudio de la sociedad agraria de un país periférico: el caso de la región del cereal en Argentina (primera mitad del siglo XX)," *Revista gestão industrial* 1, no. 4 (2005), http://www.pg.cefetpr.br/ppgep/revista/revista2005/pdf4/RGIv01n04a01.pdf (accessed June 7, 2009).

3. Ascolani, "Labores agrarias."

4. *El Correo de Firmat* (hereafter *ECF*), March 15, 1917, 1–3; Alfredo Luis Cecchi, *Tras la huella socialista en Firmat* (Firmat: Luis Rubén Casaccia Impresos, 2004).

5. Eduardo Sartelli, "Ríos de oro y gigantes de acero: tecnología y clases sociales en la región pampeana (1870–1940)," *Razón y revolución*, no. 3 (1997): 1–32.

6. *Álbum biográfico del cincuentenario de Firmat* (Firmat: Italo y Laura C. Bassi Cortes Hnos, 1938); Gladys Seguí de la Vega and Oscar Ziraldo, *Firmat en imágenes y relatos (1888–1949)* (Firmat: Luis Casaccia Impresos, 1995); Cecchi, *Tras la huella.*

7. Ascolani, "Labores agrarias"; Sartelli, "Ríos de oro."

8. Sartelli, "Ríos de oro"; Ascolani, "Labores agrarias."

9. Sartelli, "Río de oro."

10. Ascolani, "Labores agrarias."

11. Sartelli, "Río de oro," 23.

12. Hernán Camarero, *A la conquista de la clase obrera: los comunistas y el mundo del trabajo en la Argentina, 1920–1935* (Buenos Aires: Siglo XXI, 2007), 101–2.

13. For a longer discussion on paternalism in this region, see Silvia Simonassi, "Conflictividad laboral y políticas disciplinarias en la industria metalúrgica de la ciudad de Rosario 1973–1976," *Anuario IEHS*, n° 22 (2007): 465–86.

14. Some of the policies he enforced were a continuation of the policies implemented by the military government between 1943 and 1946, which Perón had joined as vice president, minister of war, and secretariat of labor.

15. Pablo Gerchunoff and Damián Antúnez, "De la bonanza peronista a la crisis de desarrollo," in *Nueva historia Argentina*, vol. 8: *Los años peronistas (1943–1955)* (Buenos Aires: Sudamericana, 2002); Jorge Schvarzer, *La industria que supimos conseguir* (Buenos Aires: Planeta, 1996); Silvia Simonassi, "Perfil industrial y dinámica social en la provincia

de Santa Fe (1943–1976)," in *Nueva historia de Santa Fe*, vol. 11: *De los cordones industriales al eje de integración Mercosur (1940–2005)*, ed. Gabriela Aguila (Rosario: Protohistoria, La Capital, 2006).

16. In March 1949, the local newspaper announced the expropriation of a large estate located near the city. *ECF*, March 16, 1949.

17. Mario Lattuada, *La política agraria peronista (1943–1983)* (Buenos Aires: CEAL, 1986).

18. Claudio Belini, *La industria peronista* (Buenos Aires: Edhasa, 2009).

19. Graciela García, "El sector agropecuario pampeano como demandante de maquinaria agrícola: algunas reflexiones acerca de su comportamiento," *Estudios Sociales*, no. 5 (1993): 109–32; Noemí Girbal-Blacha, *Mitos, paradojas y realidades en la Argentina peronista (1946–1955)* (Buenos Aires: Universidad Nacional de Quilmes Editorial, 2003); Marcelo Rougier, "Encadenamientos productivos entre el agro y la industria: la fábrica de cosechadoras Vassalli en el sur de Santa Fe, Argentina," *XIV International Economic History Congress* (Helsinki, Finland, 2006).

20. Silvia Simonassi, "Historias de metal: industria e industriales metalúrgicos de Rosario, 1973–1983" (MA thesis, Rosario 2004); Silvia Simonassi, "Industria y dinámica asociativa: la Asociación de Industriales Metalúrgicos de Rosario como expresión de la conformación de un área industrial regional (1943–1976)," in *Las escalas de la Historia Comparada*, vol. 2, ed. Susana Bandieri, Graciela Blanco, and Mónica Blanco (Buenos Aires: Miño y Dávila Editores, 2008), 107–30.

21. Silvia Simonassi, "De cómo los patrones parecían padres: una mirada histórica a los menores aprendices de las fábricas metalúrgicas del Gran Rosario," *Revista de la Escuela de Antropología* 5 (November 2000): 33–34.

22. Roque Vassalli, *Casi memorias: pasajes de la vida de un gran industrial* (Rosario: Ediciones Grandes Industriales, 1990).

23. Ibid.; also see the factory's website, http://www.vassallifabril.com.ar.

24. Rougier, "Encadenamientos."

25. Marcelo Rougier has conducted the most important studies about Vassalli. See Rougier, "Encadenamientos," and "La fábrica de cosechadoras Vassalli frente a la inestabilidad macroeconómica de la segunda mitad del siglo XX," in *Políticas de promoción y estrategias empresariales en la industria argentina, 1950–1980*, ed. Marcelo Rougier (Buenos Aires: Ediciones cooperativas, 2007).

26. *ECF*, October 30, 1948.

27. *El Orden* (Firmat), from September 27, 1958, to October 5, 1958.

28. *ECF*, April 11, 1957.

29. *La Capital* (Rosario), August 30, 1963.

30. Ministerio de Hacienda, Economía e Industrias Provincia de Santa Fe — Instituto de fomento industrial — Dirección General de Industrias, *Mapa industrial de la provincia de Santa Fe* (Santa Fe: Instituto de Fomento Industrial, 1959).

31. Provincia de Santa Fe, Consejo Provincial de Desarrollo (COPRODE), *Cuaderno*

N°6, *Evolución intercensal 1960/1970 de la población de la provincia de Santa Fe* (Santa Fe: COPRODE, 1972).

32. For the perspective of social anthropology, see Federico Neiburg, *Fábrica y villa obrera: historia social y antropología de los obreros del cemento* (Buenos Aires: CEAL, 1988). For the perspective of labor history, see Mirta Z. Lobato, *La vida en las fábricas: trabajo, protesta y política en una comunidad obrera, Berisso (1904–1970)* (Buenos Aires: Prometeo Libros-Entrepasados, 2001). For the perspective of business and immigration history, see María Inés Barbero and Mariela Ceva, "La vida obrera en una empresa paternalista," in *Historia de la vida privada en la Argentina*, vol. 3, ed. Fernando Devoto and Marta Madero (Buenos Aires: Taurus, 2000).

33. José Sérgio Leite Lopes, "Fábrica e vila operária: considerações sobre uma forma de servidão burguesa," in *Mudança social no nordeste: a reprodução da subordinação*, ed. Leite Lopes et al. (Rio de Janeiro: Paz e Terra, 1979).

34. Daniel Márquez, "Conflicto e intervención estatal en los orígenes de la actividad petrolera: Comodoro Rivadavia (1915–1930)," in *Distinguir y comprender: aportes para pensar la sociedad y la cultura en Patagonia*, ed. Daniel Cabral Márquez and Mario Palma Godoy (Comodoro Rivadavia: Ediciones Proyección Patagónica, 1995); Daniel Cabral Márquez and Edda Lía Crespo, "Entre el petróleo y el carbón: empresas estatales, trabajadores e identidades sociolaborales en la Patagonia Austral, 1907–1976," in *Hecho en Patagonia: la historia en perspectiva regional*, ed. Susana Bandieri, Graciela Blanco, and Gladys Varela (Neuquén: CEHIR-Facultad de Humanidades Universidad Nacional del Comahue, 2006).

35. Vassalli, *Casi memorias*, 144; personal interview with J. M., employee at Vassalli's plant and personnel supervisor between 1954 and 1987, and conversation with N. R., both conducted in 2008. *Publicación conmemorativa del 75 aniversario del Club Atlético Argentino* (Firmat, 1997).

36. *La Capital* (Rosario), August 30, 1963.

37. *ECF*, June 19, 1963.

38. Ibid., June 27, 1963.

39. Saint Roque is the saint of agricultural laborers; it is also interesting that many local institutions were named after him.

40. *ECF*, August 19, 1971.

41. Vassalli, *Casi memorias*; *ECF*, March 27, 1969.

42. Vassalli, *Casi memorias*, 81.

43. Roque Vassalli SA, *Memoria y Balance*, 1974, 1975.

44. Vassalli, *Casi memorias*; and personal interview with J. M. For the case of Rosario, see Silvia Simonassi, "Relaciones laborales en las fábricas metalúrgicas del Gran Rosario en los años '70," *Actas de las Jornadas de Antropología de la Cuenca del Plata y II Jornadas de etnolingüística* (Rosario, October 1997), and Simonassi, "Historias de metal."

45. El Correo de Firmat, December 27, 1956

46. *ECF*, December 26, 1957.

47. *ECF*, June 17, 1954.

48. Vassalli, *Casi memorias*.

49. Personal interview with J. M.

50. Ibid.

51. José Sierra Álvarez, *El obrero soñado: ensayo sobre el paternalismo industrial (Asturias, 1860–1917)* (Madrid: Siglo XXI, 1990).

SELECTED BIBLIOGRAPHY ON COMPANY TOWNS IN THE AMERICAS

BIBLIOGRAPHIES

Knight, Rolf. *Work Camps and Company Towns in Canada and the U.S.: An Annotated Bibliography*. Vancouver: New Star Books, 1975.

Levenson, Rosaline. *Company Towns: A Bibliography of American and Foreign Sources*. Monticello, Ill.: Council of Planning Librarians, 1977.

Maguire, Robert K. *Socio-economic Factors Pertaining to Single-Industry Resource Towns in Canada: A Bibliography with Selected Annotations*. Chicago: CPL Bibliographies, 1980.

McDonald, JoAnn, and Melissa Clark-Jones. *Globalization and the Single-Industry Town: An Annotated Bibliography*. Lennoxville, Qué.: Eastern Townships Research Centre, Bishops University, 2004.

Porteous, J. Douglas. *The Single-Enterprise Community in North America*. Monticello, Ill.: Council of Planning Librarians, 1971.

Robson, Robert S. *Canadian Single-Industry Communities: A Literature Review and Annotated Bibliography*. Sackville: Mount Allison University, 1986.

GENERAL AND COMPARATIVE

Bucci, Federico, ed. "Company Towns." *Rassegna*, no. 70 (1997).

Davis, Horace B. "Company Towns." In *Encyclopedia of the Social Sciences*, vol. 4, 119–23. New York: Macmillan, 1931.

Detomasi, Don D., and John W. Gartrell, eds. *Resource Communities: A Decade of Disruption*. Boulder: Westview Press, 1984.

Garner, John S. *The Company Town: Architecture and Society in the Early Industrial Age*. New York: Oxford University Press, 1992.

Neil, Cecily, Markku Tykkläinen, and John Bradbury, eds. *Coping with Closure: An International Comparison of Mine Town Experiences*. London: Routledge, 1992.

Porteous, J. Douglas. "The Nature of the Company Town." *Transactions of the Institute of British Geographers*, no. 51 (November 1970): 127–42.

CANADA

Bowles, Roy T., ed. *Little Communities and Big Industries: Studies in the Social Impact of Canadian Resource Extraction.* Toronto: Butterworths, 1982.

Bradbury, John H. "Declining Single-Industry Towns in Québec-Labrador, 1979–1983." *Journal of Canadian Studies* 19, no. 3 (1984): 125–39.

Bradbury, John H., and Isabelle St. Martin. "Winding Down in a Québec Mining Town: A Case Study of Schefferville." *Canadian Geographer* 27, no. 2 (1983): 128–44.

Bray, Matt, and Ashley Thomson, eds. *At the End of the Shift: Mines and Single-Industry Towns in Northern Ontario.* Toronto: Dundurn Press, 1992.

Clark-Jones, Melissa. *The Logic and Survival of Single-Industry Towns.* Lennoxville, Qué.: Eastern Townships Research Center, 1997.

Clover, T. R. *A Corner of Empire.* Cambridge: Cambridge University Press, 1937.

Derbyshire, Edward. "Notes on the Social Structure of a Canadian Pioneer Town." *Sociological Review* 8, no. 1 (July 1960): 63–75.

Dignard, Louise. "Reconsidering Staple Insights: Canadian Forestry and Mining Towns." PhD diss., Carleton University, 2004.

Fortier, Robert, ed. *Villes industrielles planifiées.* Montreal: Boréal, Centre Canadien d'Architecture, 1996.

Frank, David. "Company Town/Labour Town: Local Government in Cape Breton Coal Towns, 1917–1926." *Social History* 14, no. 27 (1981): 177–96.

Glenday, Daniel. "Le Domain Colonial: Class Formation in a Natural Resource Enclave." *Canadian Journal of Sociology* 9, no. 2 (Spring 1984): 159–77.

Goltz, Eileen. "Espanola: The History of a Pulp and Paper Town." *Laurentian University Review* no. 6 (1974): 73–103.

Graham, Humphrys. "Schefferville, Quebec: A New Pioneering Town." *Geographical Review* 48, no. 2 (April 1958): 151–66.

Innis, Harold. "Settlement and the Mining Frontier." In *Settlement and the Forest Frontier in Eastern Canada*, edited by Arthur R. M. Lower, 170–407. Toronto: Macmillan, 1936, 170–407.

Institute of Local Government, Queen's University. *Single-Enterprise Communities in Canada: A Report to the Central Mortgage Commission.* Kingston, Ont.: Queen's Printer, 1953.

Johnson, Walter. "Striking in a Québec Paper Town." *Our Generation* 10, no. 4 (1975): 32–43.

Krahn, Harvey, and John W. Gartrell. "Labour Market Segmentation and Social Mobility in a Canadian Single-Industry Community." *Canadian Review of Sociology and Anthropology* 20, no. 3 (1985): 322–45.

Lash, S. D. "Recent New Towns in Canada." *Engineering Journal* 41, no. 3 (1958): 43–58.

Lucas, Rex A. *Minetown, Milltown, Railtown: Life in Canadian Communities of Single Industry.* Toronto: University of Toronto Press, 1971. Anniversary ed., with introduction by Lorne Tepperman, Don Mills, Ont.: Oxford University Press, 2008.

Mawhiney, Anne-Marie, and Jane Pitblado. *Boom Town Blues: Elliot Lake: Collapse and Revival in a Single-Industry Community*. Toronto: Dundurn Press, 1999.

McCann, L. D. "The Changing Internal Structure of Canadian Resource Towns." *Plan Canada* 18, no. 1 (1978): 46–59.

Mochoruk, James D. "Oral History in a Company Town: Flin Flon, 1926–1946." *Canadian Oral History Association Journal*, no. 7 (1984): 5–17.

Parr, Joy. *The Gender of Breadwinners: Women, Men and Change in Two Industrial Towns 1880–1950*. Toronto: University of Toronto Press, 1990.

"Planning and Building New Towns in Canada: Kipawa." *Conservation for Life* (Commission of Conservation, Canada) 5, no. 1 (January 1919): 10–16.

"Planning and Building a Modern Industrial Town in Northern Québec." *Journal of the Town Planning Institute* 7, no. 1 (1928): 10–12 and 14–15.

Riffel, J. A. *Quality of Life in Resource Towns*. Ottawa: Ministry of State, Urban Affairs Canada, 1975.

Robinson, Ira. *New Industrial Towns on Canada's Resource Frontier*. Chicago: University of Chicago Press, 1962.

Robson, Robert Stewart. "Flin Flon: A Study of Company-Community Relations in a Single-Enterprise Community." *Urban History Review* 12, no. 3 (February 1984): 29–43.

———. *Forest Dependent Communities in Canada: An Interpretive Overview and Annotated Bibliography*. Brandon: Rural Development Institute, Brandon University, 1995.

———. "The Politics of Resource Town Development: Ontario's Resource Communities, 1883–1970." PhD diss., University of Guelph, 1986.

———. "Strike in the Single Enterprise Community: Flin Flon, Manitoba, 1934." *Labour* no. 12 (Fall 1983): 63–86.

Stelter, Gilbert, and Alan F. J. Artibise. "Canadian Resource Towns in Historical Perspective," *Plan Canada* 18, no. 1 (1978): 7–16.

Wichern, Philip Howard. *Two Studies in Political Development on Canada's Resource Frontier*. Winnipeg: University of Manitoba, Center for Settlement Studies, 1972.

UNITED STATES

Allen, James B. *The Company Town in the American West*. Norman: University of Oklahoma Press, 1966.

Amundsen, Michael A. *Yellowcake Towns: Uranium Mining Communities in the American West*. Boulder: University Press of Colorado, 2002.

Andreas, Carol. *Meatpackers and Beef Barons: Company Town in a Global Economy*. Niwot, Colo: University Press of Colorado, 1994.

Andrews, Gregg. *City of Dust: A Cement Company in the Land of Tom Sawyer*. Columbia: University of Missouri Press, 1996.

———. *Insane Sisters, or, the Price Paid for Challenging a Company Town*. Columbia: University of Missouri Press, 1999

Bensman, David. *Rusted Dreams: Hard Times in a Steel Community*. New York: McGraw-Hill, 1987.

Berry, Brian J. L. *America's Utopian Experiments: Communal Havens from Long-Wave Crises*. Hanover, N.H.: University Press of New England, 1992.

Buder, Stanley. *Pullman: An Experiment in Industrial Order and Community Planning, 1880–1930*. New York: Oxford University Press, 1967.

Carlson, Linda. *Company Towns of the Pacific Northwest*. Seattle: University of Washington Press, 2003.

Clark, Norman. *Mill Town: A Social History of Everett, Washington — Beginning to the Present*. Seattle: University of Washington Press, 1970.

Clyne, Richard J. *Coal People: Life in Southern Colorado's Company Towns, 1890–1930*. Denver: Colorado Historical Society, 1999.

Coman, Edwin T., and Helen M. Gibbs. *Time, Tide, and Timber: A Century of Pope and Talbot*. Stanford: Stanford University Press, 1949.

Crawford, Margaret. *Building the Workingman's Paradise: The Design of American Company Towns*. New York: Verso, 1995.

———. "John Nolen, the Design of the Company Town." *Rassegna*, no. 70 (1997): 46–53.

———. "The "New" Company Town." *Perspecta*, no. 30 (1999): 48–57.

Drobney, Jeffrey A. "Company Towns and Social Transformation in the North Florida Timber Industry, 1880–1930." *Florida Historical Quarterly* 75, no. 2 (Fall 1996): 121–45.

Emmons, David M. *The Butte Irish: Class and Ethnicity in an American Mining Town, 1875–1925*. Urbana: University of Illinois Press, 1989.

Esch, Elizabeth Durham. "Fordtown: Managing Race and Nation in the American Empire, 1925–1945." PhD diss., New York University, 2003.

Ficken, Robert E., and William R. Sherrard. "The Port Blakely Mill Company, 1888–1903." *Journal of Forest History* 21, no. 4 (October 1977): 202–17.

Garner, John S. "Leclaire, Illinois: A Model Company Town (1890–1934)." *Journal of the Society of Architectural Historians* 30, no. 3 (October 1971): 219–27.

———. *The Model Company Town: Urban Design through Private Enterprise in Nineteenth Century New England*. Amherst: University of Massachusetts Press, 1984.

Gaventa, John. *Power and Powerlessness: Quiescence and Rebellion in an Appalachian Valley*. Oxford: Clarendon Press, 1980.

Greene, Julie. *The Canal Builders: Making America's Empire at the Panama Canal*. New York: Penguin Press, 2009.

Hall, Jacquelyn Dowd, et al. *Like a Family: The Making of a Southern Cotton Mill World*. Chapel Hill: University of North Carolina Press, 2000.

Herring, Harriet Laura. *Passing of the Mill Village: Revolution in a Southern Institution.* Westport, Conn.: Greenwood Press, 1977.

———. *Welfare Work in Mill Villages.* New York: Arno Press, 1971.

Johnson, Ole S. *The Industrial Store: Its History, Operations, and Significance.* Atlanta: School of Business Administration, University of Georgia, 1952.

Magnusson, Leifur. "A Modern Copper Mining Town." *Monthly Labor Review* (U.S. Bureau of Labor Statistics) 7, no. 3 (September 1918): 754–60.

Mercier, Laurie. *Anaconda: Labor, Community, and Culture in Montana's Smelter City.* Urbana: University of Illinois Press, 2001.

Mosher, Anne. *Capital's Utopia: Vandergrift, Pennsylvania, 1855–1916.* Baltimore: Johns Hopkins University Press, 2004.

Mulrooney, Margaret M. "A Legacy of Coal: The Coal Company Towns of Southwestern Pennsylvania." *Perspectives in Vernacular Architecture,* no. 4 (1991): 130–37.

Murphy, Mary. *Mining Cultures: Men, Women, and Leisure in Butte, 1914–41.* Urbana: University of Illinois Press, 1997.

Olien, Roger M. *Oil Booms: Social Change in Five Texas Towns.* Lincoln: University of Nebraska Press, 1982.

Perales, Monica. *Smeltertown: Making and Remembering a Southwest Border Community.* Chapel Hill: University of North Carolina Press, 2010.

Post, Christopher. "Modifying Sense of Place in a Federal Company Town: Sunflower Village, Kansas, 1942 to 1959." *Journal of Cultural Geography* 25, no. 2 (June 2008): 137–59.

Potwin, Marjorie Adella. *Cotton Mill People of the Piedmont: A Study in Social Change.* New York: AMS Press, 1968.

Shifflett, Crandall A. *Coal Towns: Life, Work, and Culture in Company Towns of Southern Appalachia, 1880–1960.* Knoxville: University of Tennessee Press, 1991.

Smith, Carl S. *Urban Disorder and the Shape of Belief: The Great Chicago Fire, the Haymarket Bomb, and the Model Town of Pullman.* Chicago: University of Chicago Press, 2007.

Spann, Edward K. *Hopedale: From Commune to Company Town, 1840–1920.* Columbus: Ohio State University Press, 1992.

Stein, Clarence S. *Toward New Towns for America.* New York: Reinhold, 1957.

U.S. Bureau of Labor Statistics. "Welfare Work in Company Towns." *Monthly Labor Review* 25 (August 1927): 314–20.

Walker, Charles R. *Steeltown, an Industrial Case History of the Conflict between Progress and Security.* New York: Harper and Bros., 1950.

Walkowitz, Daniel J. *Worker City, Company Town: Iron and Cotton-Worker Protest in Troy and Cohoes, New York, 1855–84.* Urbana: University of Illinois Press, 1978.

Wright, Gwendolyn. *Building the Dream: A Social History of Housing in America.* Cambridge, Mass.: MIT Press, 1998.

Zukin, Sharon. *Landscapes of Power: From Detroit to Disney World.* Berkeley: University of California Press, 1991.

LATIN AMERICA

Aranda Dioses, Edith. *Del proyecto urbano moderno a la imagen trizada: Talara, 1950–1990.* Lima: Pontificia Universidad Católica del Perú, Fondo Editorial, 1998.

Barbero, María Inés, and Mariela Ceva. "La vida obrera en una empresa paternalista." In *Historia de la vida privada en la Argentina, Tomo 3,* edited by Fernando Devoto and Marta Madero, 141–67. Buenos Aires: Taurus, 1999.

Barrera, Manuel. *El conflicto obrero en el enclave cuprífero.* Santiago: Instituto de Economía y Planificación, Universidad de Chile, Facultad de Economía Política, 1973.

Blay, Eva Alterman. *Eu não tenho onde morar: vilas operárias na cidade de São Paulo.* São Paulo: Nobel, 1985.

Cárdenas García, Nicolás. *Empresas y trabajadores en la gran minería mexicana, 1900–1929: la revolución y el nuevo sistema de relaciones laborales.* Mexico: Instituto Nacional de Estudios Históricos de la Revolución Mexicana, 1998.

Chomsky, Aviva. *West Indian Workers and the United Fruit Company in Costa Rica, 1870–1940.* Baton Rouge: Louisiana State University Press, 1996.

Chomsky, Aviva, Garry M. Leech, and Steve Striffler. *Bajo el manto del carbón: pueblos y multinacionales en las minas de El Cerrejón, Colombia.* Bogotá: Casa Editorial Pisando Callos, 2007.

Correia, Telma de Barros. *Pedra: plano e cotidiano operário no sertão.* São Paulo: Papirus Editora, 1998.

DeWind, Josh. *Peasants Become Miners: The Evolution of Industrial Mining Systems in Peru, 1902–1974.* New York: Garland, 1987.

Di Tella, Torcuato S. *Sindicato y comunidad: dos tipos de estructura sindical latinoamericana.* Buenos Aires: Editorial del Instituto, 1967.

Dinius, Oliver Jürgen. *Brazil's Steel City: Developmentalism, Strategic Power, and Industrial Relations in Volta Redonda, 1941–1964.* Stanford: Stanford University Press, 2010.

Eakin, Marshall C. *British Enterprise in Brazil: The St. John D'el Rey Mining Company and the Morro Velho Gold Mine, 1830–1960.* Durham, N.C.: Duke University Press, 1989.

Farnsworth-Alvear, Ann. *Dulcinea in the Factory: Myths, Morals, Men and Women in Colombia's Industrial Experiment, 1905–1960.* Durham, N.C.: Duke University Press, 2000.

Finn, Janet L. *Tracing the Veins: Of Copper, Culture, and Community from Butte to Chuquicamata.* Berkeley: University of California Press, 1998.

Flores Galindo, Alberto. *Los mineros de la Cerro de Pasco, 1900–1930: un intento de caracterización social.* Lima: Pontificia Universidad Católica del Perú, 1974.

Galindo Díaz, Jorge. *Arquitectura, industria y ciudad en el valle del Cauca: tipos y técnicas (1917–1945)*. Cali, Colombia: Centro de Investigaciones CITCE, Universidad del Valle, 2003.

Garcés Feliú, Eugenio. "Las ciudades del cobre: del campamento de montaña al hotel minero como variaciones de la company town." *EURE* 29, no. 88 (2003): 131–48.

———. *Las ciudades del salitre: un estudio de las oficinas salitreras.* Santiago: Editorial Universitaria, 1999.

Garcés Feliú, Eugenio, Marcelo Cooper, and Mauricio Baros. *Las ciudades del cobre.* Santiago: Ediciones Universidad Católica, 2007.

García Díaz, Bernardo. *Un pueblo fabril del porfiriato: Santa Rosa, Veracruz.* Mexico: Fondo de Cultura Económica, 1981.

Godfrey, Brian J. "Boom Towns of the Amazon." *Geographical Review* 80, no. 2 (April 1990): 103–17.

González M., Sergio. *Hombres y mujeres de la pampa: Tarapacá en el ciclo del salitre.* Santiago: LOM, 2002.

Grandin, Greg. *Fordlandia: The Rise and Fall of Henry's Ford Forgotten Jungle City.* New York: Metropolitan Books, 2009

Klubock, Thomas Miller. *Contested Communities: Class, Gender, and Politics in Chile's El Teniente Copper Mine, 1904–1951.* Durham, N.C.: Duke University Press, 1998.

Kruijt, Dirk. *Labor Relations and Multinational Corporations: The Cerro de Pasco Corporation in Peru (1902–1974).* Assen, Netherlands: Van Gorcum, 1979.

Lobato, Mirta Zaida. *La vida en las fábricas: trabajo, protesta y política en una comunidad obrera, Berisso (1904–1970).* Buenos Aires: Prometeo Libros, 2001.

Leite Lopes, José Sérgio. *A tecelagem dos conflitos de classe na "cidade das chaminés".* São Paulo: Editora Marco Zero, 1988.

———. "Fábrica e Vila Operária: Considerações sobre uma forma de servidão burguesa." In *Mudança social no nordeste: a reprodução da subordinação*, edited by José Sérgio, Leite Lopes, et al. Rio de Janeiro: Paz e Terra, 1979.

Márquez, Daniel, and Edda Lía Crespo. "Entre el petróleo y el carbón: empresas estatales, trabajadores e identidades sociolaborales en la Patagonia Austral, 1907–1976." In *Hecho en Patagonia: la historia en perspectiva regional*, edited by Susana Bandieri, Graciela Blanco, and Gladys Varela. Neuquén, Argentina: CEHIR-Facultad de Humanidades Universidad Nacional del Comahue, 2006.

Márquez Terrazas, Zacarías. *Pueblos mineros de Chihuahua.* Chihuahua, Mexico: Universidad Autónoma de Chihuahua, 2007.

Nash, June C. *We Eat the Mines and the Mines Eat Us: Dependency and Exploitation in Bolivian Tin Mines.* New York: Columbia University Press, 1979.

Neiburg, Federico B. *Fábrica y villa obrera: historia social y antropología de los obreros del cemento.* Buenos Aires: Centro Editor de América Latina, 1988.

Novelo, Victoria, and Augusto Arteaga. *La industria en los Magueyales: trabajo y sindicato en Ciudad Sahagún.* Mexico: Editorial Nueva Imagen, 1979.

O'Brien, Thomas F. *The Revolutionary Mission: American Enterprise in Latin America, 1900–1945*. New York: Cambridge University Press, 1996.

Olivares, Jaime Ramon. "The Creation of a Labor Aristocracy: The History of the Oil Workers in Maracaibo, Venezuela, 1925–1948." PhD diss., University of Houston, 2003.

Pavilack, Joann Clements. "Black Gold in the Red Zone: Repression and Contention in Chilean Coal Mining Communities from the Popular Front to the Advent of the Cold War." PhD diss., Duke University, 2003.

Piquet, Rosélia. *Cidade-empresa: presença na paisagem urbana brasileira*. Rio de Janeiro: Jorge Zahar Editor, 1998.

Porteous, J. Douglas. "The Company State: A Chilean Case-Study." *Canadian Geographer*, no. 2 (1973): 113–26.

———. "Social Class in Atacama Company Towns." *Annals of the Association of American Geographers* 64, no. 3 (September 1974): 409–17.

Préstamo, Felipe. "The Architecture of American Sugar Mills: The United Fruit Company." *Journal of Decorative and Propaganda Arts*, no. 22 (1996): 63–80.

Ramalho, Jose Ricardo. *Estado-patrão e luta operária: o caso FNM*. São Paulo: Paz e Terra, 1989.

Ryder, Roy, and Lawrence A. Brown. "Urban-System Evolution on the Frontier of the Ecuadorian Amazon." *Geographical Review* 90, no. 4 (October 2000): 511–35.

Santamarina, Juan C. "The Cuba Company and the Expansion of American Business in Cuba, 1898–1915." *Business History Review* 74, no. 1 (Spring 2000): 41–83.

Santiago, Myrna I. *The Ecology of Oil: Environment, Labor, and the Mexican Revolution, 1900–1938*. Cambridge: Cambridge University Press, 2006.

Sariego Rodríguez, Juan Luis. *Enclaves y minerales en el norte de México: historia social de los mineros de Cananea y Nueva Rosita, 1900–1970*. Mexico: Centro de Investigaciones y Estudios Superiores en Antropología Social, 1988.

Tinker-Salas, Miguel. *The Enduring Legacy: Oil, Culture, and Society in Venezuela*. Durham, N.C.: Duke University Press, 2009.

Vergara, Angela. "Company Towns and Peripheral Cities in the Chilean Copper Industry: Potrerillos and Pueblo Hundido, 1917–1940s." *Urban History* 30, no. 3 (2003): 381–400.

———. *Copper Workers, International Business, and Domestic Politics in Cold War Chile*. University Park: Pennsylvania State University Press, 2008.

Zapata, Francisco. *Los mineros de Chuquicamata: ¿productores o proletarios?* Mexico: Centro de Estudios Sociológicos, Colegio de México, 1975.

CONTRIBUTORS

OLIVER J. DINIUS is Croft Associate Professor of History and International Studies at the University of Mississippi. His research focuses on the social and economic history of twentieth-century Brazil. Stanford University Press is publishing his book entitled *Brazil's Steel City: Developmentalism, Strategic Power, and Industrial Relations in Volta Redonda, 1941–1964* (Winter 2010). He is currently working on two projects: a book on twentieth-century Brazil as industrial society and a history of the beer industry in the Americas.

MARSHALL C. EAKIN is Professor of History at Vanderbilt University and Executive Director of the Brazilian Studies Association (BRASA). A specialist in twentieth-century Brazilian history, he is the author of *British Enterprise in Brazil: The St. John d'el Rey Mining Company and the Morro Velho Gold Mine, 1830–1960* (Duke, 1989), *Brazil: The Once and Future Country* (St. Martin's, 1997), *Tropical Capitalism: The Industrialization of Belo Horizonte, Brazil* (Palgrave, 2001), and *The History of Latin America: Collision of Cultures* (Palgrave, 2007). He has been awarded grants from Fulbright-Hays, the Tinker Foundation, the American Historical Association, the Corporation for National Service, and the National Endowment for the Humanities.

ELIZABETH ESCH is Assistant Professor of History at Barnard College–Columbia University, where she teaches courses in U.S. imperialism and the history of race. Her work has appeared in *Souls: A Critical Journal of Black Politics, Culture and Society*; *Cabinet: A Quarterly Journal of Art and Culture*; and *Historical Materialism*. Her book *One Symptom of Originality: Race and the Management of Labor in the United States*, coauthored with David R. Roediger, is forthcoming from Oxford University Press in 2012.

EUGENIO GARCÉS FELIÚ is Professor of Architecture at the Facultad de Arquitectura, Diseño y Estudios Urbanos at the Catholic University in Santiago, Chile. He has researched and published on the historical and architectonical aspects of mining towns in Chile. His most important publication is *Ciudades del salitre* (Editorial Universitaria, 1999). He is currently researching company towns in Tierra del Fuego.

AURORA GÓMEZ-GALVARRIATO is a professor and researcher at the Department of Economics in the Centro de Investigación y Docencia Económicas (CIDE) in Mexico City. She currently also serves as the director of the Archivo General de la Nación. Her most important publications include *El Porfiriato*, coauthored with Mauricio Tenorio, and *México y España ¿Historias Económicas Paralelas?* coedited with Rafael Dobado and Graciela Márquez. She has published numerous articles on the economic and social history of the textile industry in Mexico. Her monograph *Industry and Revolution: Social and Economic Changes in the Orizaba Valley, 1890–1930* is forthcoming with Harvard University Press. Her current research focuses on the evolution of prices and wages in Mexico from the eighteenth to the early twentieth centuries.

ANDREW HEROD is Professor of Geography at the University of Georgia in Athens. He is also an elected official — a member of the government of Athens-Clarke County, Georgia. He has published widely on the questions of work, space, and globalization. His most important publications include *Handbook of Employment and Society: Working Space* (Edward Elgar, 2010), coedited with Susan McGrath-Champ and Al Rainnie, *Geographies of Globalization: A Critical Introduction* (Wiley-Blackwell, 2009), *Labor Geographies: Workers and the Landscapes of Capitalism* (Guilford, 2001), and *Organizing the Landscape: Geographical Perspectives on Labor Unionism* (University of Minnesota Press, 1998). His next book will be *Scale*, for the series "Key Ideas in Geography" (Routledge, 2010).

LAURIE MERCIER is Professor of History at Washington State University, Vancouver. She specializes on U.S. history with a focus on gender and the history of mining. She is the author of *Anaconda: Labor, Community and Culture in Montana's Smelter City* (University of Illinois Press, 2001), the coeditor of *Mining Women: Gender in the Development of a Global Industry* (Palgrave Macmillan, 2006), and the coeditor of *Speaking History: Oral Histories of the American Past, 1865–Present* (Palgrave Macmillan, 2009).

CHRISTOPHER W. POST is Assistant Professor of Geography at Kent State University at Stark in North Canton, Ohio. He has published articles on company towns, exurbanization in the American West, and memorialization of American Civil War–era guerilla violence in journals such as the *Journal of Cultural Geography*, *Geographical Review*, *Professional Geographer*, and *Historical Geography*. He is currently finishing a book-length manuscript on *The Memorialization of*

Guerilla Warfare: Tales of Preservation on the Trans-Mississippi Frontier (forthcoming, Center for American Places). His ongoing research focuses on the impact of exurbanization on rural family cemeteries in the American West.

SILVIA SIMONASSI is Professor of History at Universidad Nacional de Rosario in Argentina and a researcher at the Centro de Estudios Sociales Regionales — Universidad Nacional de Rosario — Argentina. She has published extensively on the history of labor and industry in Rosario. She is presently researching working conditions and labor relations in the province of Santa Fe throughout the second half of the twentieth century.

FERNANDO TEIXEIRA DA SILVA is Professor of History at the Universidade Estadual de Campinas (UNICAMP). He also directs the Edgard Leuenroth Archives, Brazil's foremost collection of historical documents on the labor movement. He is the author of *Operários sem patrões: os trabalhadores da cidade de Santos no entreguerras* (Campinas: Ed. da Unicamp, 2003) and of *A carga e a culpa: os operários das docas de Santos, 1937–1968* (São Paulo: Hucitec, 1995). His current research focuses on the history of Brazil's labor justice system.

ANGELA VERGARA is Associate Professor of History at California State University, Los Angeles. She is the author of *Copper Workers, International Business, and Domestic Politics in Cold-War Chile* (Penn State University Press, 2008). Her work has also appeared in *Revista Historia, Urban History*, and the *Bulletin of the History of Medicine*. She is currently working on a history of cooperative wineries and small wine producers in twentieth-century Chile.

INDEX

Amazon: population of, in racial theories, 95–96; rubber plantations in, x, 28, 92, 94, 97, 105

Americas, the, 1, 93; company towns in, 11, 15–16, 111, 179, 184, 192, 194, 209; historiography of, x–xi, 6–8, 10–11; history of, 1, 3–5; scholarship on company towns in, 7–10

Anaconda, Mont.: local community in, 166, 169; Mine Mill local at, 165–68; women's auxiliary in, 165; women workers in, 168–69

Anaconda Copper Company, x, 3, 14, 176n29; in Chile, 178–80, 184–86, 187; company towns of, 180, 187–93; and modernization of production, 184–86; in Montana, 160, 167–68

anarchism: in Argentina, 200–203; in Santos, Brazil, 68, 81

Andes Copper Company, 178, 180, 183; company town model of, 178, 180–83; and El Salvador, 179, 187–93; nationalization of, 194; Potrerillos mine of, 178, 180–84, 186; social assistance programs of, 190–91

anticommunism: in Canada, 14, 161, 165; at Fordlândia, 103; and Orlich scandal, 163; targeting Mine Mill, 161–64, 172; in United States, 14, 161, 165; in Volta Redonda, 139, 140, 144, 149

architecture, ix, 26–27, 30–32, 34, 125, 182–83, 187, 194

Arizona: copper mining strike, 170–71;

Magna Copper in, 3; women, 169; Women's Auxiliary Convention, 164

Atacama (Chile): company towns in, 179–95; desert, 4, 181; mining in, x, 181, 183; nitrate fields in, 179–80; province of, 182

Belterra: as civilizing project, 94, 104–6; and Fordism, 104; labor recruitment at, 103; modeled on midwestern town, 105; move to, 103–4; and rubber cultivation, 105; schools at, 104–5

Boulder City, Nev., 3, 116, 122–24, 129

Brasília, 187

Brazilian Labor Party (Partido Trabalhista Brasileiro; PTB), 148–49

caboclo, 99

capitalism, industrial: in Americas, x, 16; and company towns, 2, 6, 12, 29–30; cycles of, 152–53; frontier of, 4–5; geography of, ix, 22–23, 26, 28–29, 102; global, 12, 15–16, 26, 152; national, x, 62, 138, 150; as shaping landscapes, 24; and social welfare, 3; spatial structure of, 23–26, 28–29; spread of, 2–3

Catholic Church, in Brazil: and labor laws, 138, 140; and lay movement, 139–40, 146–47, 150; and Liberation Theology, 152; and military coup (1964), 150–51; relations of, with Vargas government, 138–39; social doctrine of, 138–39, 149–52; and workers' circles, 140–42, 151

GEOGRAPHIES OF JUSTICE AND SOCIAL TRANSFORMATION

Made in the USA
Middletown, DE
20 May 2020